MONEY, SEX AND SERVITUDE

SERVITUDE

ADVENTURES IN THE WONDERLAND OF SCIENTOLOGY

Peter Bonyai

*To my wife who stood by me
through thick and thin*

CONTENTS

FOREWORD

I was a Scientologist for more than 10 years, spending the majority of this time as a church staff member. I started out as a lowly bookseller and personality test evaluator (of the infamous "free" tests) in one of the small Scientology organizations (called missions) in Hungary. I then joined the so-called elite of the movement, the Sea Organization and rose through the ranks, eventually becoming the second-in-command of the Central European branch of the Church (located in Budapest, Hungary).

I also spent a few months at the "Continental Liaison Office Europe," located in Copenhagen, Denmark and one month in Clearwater, Florida at the church's "international spiritual headquarters" (the Flag Service Organization). I have seen many faces of Scientology and have written this book with the intention of presenting a relatively accurate picture of the movement.

I had two goals in mind. First, I wanted to show how my personality changed as I progressed in Scientology, if one can call that progress. I also wanted to describe in detail how the middle management of the Church operates, as it was a fascinatingly bizarre experience.

I sincerely hope I have been able to provide some unique insight into the inner workings of the Church and the minds of its followers.

Peter Bonyai
September, 2014

CHAPTER ONE

The Little Brown Church in the Vale[1]

A BOOK THAT CHANGED EVERYTHING

On an otherwise uneventful day in the summer of 1994, our beloved and slightly eccentric Hungarian grammar and literature teacher presented the class a book that he was clearly excited about. The word "Dianetika" in shining gold letters was emblazoned on its cover, which was dominated by a volcano – probably with the purpose of dominating its reader from the outset.

He loved to cover unusual topics (which were often completely unrelated to the beautiful Hungarian language), so this presentation was not an uncommon occurrence. In essence, he told us that the author of the book, L. Ron Hubbard, was either a genius or a madman and that he had never read so many bold claims about the nature of man compressed into a single book.

Well, let's check this out, I said to myself. At that time (second year in high school) I was pretty heavily involved in a great invention called role-playing (that had just appeared in Hungary). As a result, my interest was sparked in the magical and the unknown. I was also reading a huge amount of sci-fi and fantasy books, and was particularly impressed with the *Foundation* series by Isaac Asimov, as well as by the works of some fantasy authors. Interestingly, I did read some short stories from Hubbard too, but at that time I rated him "mediocre" on my official sci-fi author scoreboard. This hobby provided an interesting diversion from mathematics and computer technology, my main areas of interest.

So, I checked out *Dianetics* from the local library and read it. At first reading, the book seemed to be a lengthy essay on a shaky theory written by an overly confident and arrogant person who wanted to sound truly authentic and legitimate. I definitely had a good idea of what "overly confident and arrogant" is, being such a person myself – an excellent student attending one of the best high schools in my hometown, Pécs.

Hubbard wrote the following right on the first page: "*You are beginning an adventure. Treat it as an adventure. And may you never be the same again.*"

---

[1] A reference to an L. Ron Hubbard writing of 23 March 1985, where he condemns the kind of image where a Scientology Church is portrayed as a place "where people can get together, sing and are not too unhappy."

Let's just simply say that I did not suspect at the time that his wish would be so thoroughly fulfilled.

Apparently he had discovered the reason for all human misery and claimed to have a solution for that. In a nutshell, his great discovery was the following: all human suffering and illness is caused by a portion of the mind called "the reactive mind" (the subconscious one). This part takes control when one is affected by pain and/or unconsciousness, stores everything related to these experiences (all events as they happen with sight, sound etc), and takes each sentence uttered during such a period of pain and/or unconsciousness literally, which function later as hypnotic commands. Hubbard coined a name for these stored subconscious experiences; he called them "engrams."

An example: a person is hit by a car and passes out. Someone from the crowd that has gathered around the scene says, "Look at his leg! He will never be able to walk again!" According to Hubbard, this would be registered by the reactive mind as a hypnotic command and the unfortunate fellow would probably live out his remaining days in a wheelchair.

Hubbard stated even wilder assumptions in his book. According to *Dianetics*, the recording of external stimuli begins in the womb, and the sentences uttered during marital fights are recorded in a similar manner. For example, if a man hits his pregnant wife in a way that his unborn son becomes unconscious, and then says that he is out of luck with women, then his son, once born, would have serious problems finding a suitable female partner.

Luckily for mankind, Hubbard offered a solution for these problems, which unsurprisingly was also his invention, a therapy called "auditing." Despite his claims to the contrary, the method is rather similar to psychoanalysis: the therapist ("auditor") gets the patient to find these engrams and tell about them in detail over and over again, until their effect on the present is eradicated. Therapy sessions also address the engrams created before birth. When someone gets rid of all engrams, he becomes a "Clear." According to Hubbard, Clears are completely rational, free of any and all "aberrations," which he defined as "any deviation or departure from normal thought or behavior." The whole thing sounded very unrealistic at that time. Frankly, I found it hard to believe that a discovery of such magnitude would have gone unnoticed and was unknown to the general public. A week or so later I had already forgotten about Hubbard and his self-proclaimed science of the mind.

A year later, my best friend filled out a Scientology personality test and received an evaluation at the local Dianetics Center. After that, he was invited to a Dianetics workshop. I was not particularly happy about it and told him to avoid that place, stating that he should not become "a brainwashed Dianetics moron."

Despite my warnings, my friend attended the workshop. He was not too convinced by what he saw and experienced there, so he could not recommend it to me. Overhearing our conversation, another friend urged me to take another look at the movement, as he was involved in similar self-help groups (José Silva's Mind Control and "The Forum" of Werner Erhard fame). He had also visited the Dianetics Center, but upon seeing the rather overweight local leader, he thought that it was definitely not a recipe for success.

I was not doing well at that time, so I was much more receptive to such suggestions. I was very disillusioned with the materialistic society around me and I was very concerned about the future of humanity. I felt something was very wrong with the world and no one seemed to care about the real issues. Even worse, pursuing spiritual fulfillment as opposed to amassing material wealth and living a "normal" life was considered ridiculous by most of the people I interacted with. At that time, my future looked pretty bleak. I could not really picture myself living a completely "normal" life – completing my education, working for 40-50 years, followed by retirement and death. This was something I was trying to avoid, but I had no idea how. Also, it seemed there was no real alternative to that kind of lifestyle that appealed to me. All in all, I was often depressed and unhappy.

Due to this bleak outlook, I gave it some more thought and decided to have a look at Dianetics. I asked for a personality test and filled it out. At that time I had a really high opinion of myself and expected a rather good result. So, I made an appointment and went in to hear their evaluation of my test.

A red-haired woman in her thirties greeted me. She introduced herself as a priestess of the Church of Scientology, trained to deliver personality test evaluations. I thought, "Wow, apparently this bunch got even more bizarre since that book was written." I took a seat and looked across at her with a condescending smile.

I was told that I was an irresponsible, nervous, unstable and pathetic individual in urgent need of attention. She made sure that each statement hit home, and repeated them over and over when I expressed my doubts. She was adamant about the evaluation and gave me an unquestioning gaze each time I wanted to contradict her and explain myself. And she mentioned several times that Dianetics could help me to improve that condition. I was completely overwhelmed at the end of it and felt totally devastated. My overconfidence was gone as if it never existed. I walked around in the town almost completely devoid of life. All my problems seemed to fall on me. Thinking it cannot get any worse and I could definitely use some help to address my deep-lying unhappiness, I decided to give Dianetics a chance.

A week later I found myself in the Dianetics workshop.

AN INTERNATIONAL CONSPIRACY…
AND A LOCAL BREAKDOWN

After walking around the block of the Dianetics Center two times, I gathered my courage and entered the building.

The Center (which was officially called a "Church of Scientology Mission of Pécs") was located in a small flat on a street near the central square of the city. Oddly enough, the street itself was almost always peaceful and completely deserted. Not much "body traffic" as Scientologists say, referring to unsuspecting people passing by on foot.

The lecturer was a tall, burly and very confident man. First, he showed us a short film about the basic teachings of Dianetics. I learned nothing new – it was basically a recap of the key concepts described in the book. The obvious question came to mind again: "If this is so workable and so good, then why is this method not used in psychotherapy?"

I asked this question to the lecturer. He gave it a long and hard laugh (in true Hubbard-style, as I later learned), then told me that this would go against the vested interests of people involved in the mental health business. After the lecture was over, we were told to put the theory into practice – we were supposed to "co-audit" each other, which meant that we had to form pairs, and apply Hubbard's method to address painful memories of the past. The whole thing had a kind of a "psychoanalysis for dummies" feeling – the patient (called "preclear" – someone who was not yet Clear) had to close his eyes and choose an incident from his past which involved spiritual or physical pain. We were warned not to select a tough incident for the first attempt. The "auditor" had the preclear recount what happened – you were supposed to be halfway between remembering and "reliving" in your mind. This had to be done over and over again, until the preclear was visibly relieved and became cheerful.

I had to choose an incident of minor emotional discomfort as a "preclear." I selected a minor altercation that happened during a school trip. To be honest, after describing the incident several times and how and why we fought verbally about a trivial matter, I started to feel better and I felt a genuine relief. I re-evaluated the situation and my viewpoint about the conflict and my role in it had changed.

It was a very important moment for me – I experienced for the first time in my life that it was possible to improve spiritually and felt I had discovered a way to combat bad choices made in the past. This effectively sold the subject to me and made me decide to become involved.

Then we continued with the next incident, but that one went awry. I got a bit lost in the maze of my mind and started to see strange things. The mission auditor had to intervene so I could be freed from its effect. After that he told me I need auditing done on an E-meter to "crack my case[2]" so I could continue auditing to Clear.

He showed me this E-meter. It looked very much like the instruments my father used in his work as an electrician. He explained that its full name was "electropsychometer," and it was a precise machine which could assist the auditor in finding the real reasons for spiritual distress. The instrument would give a signal if a problem is found and its needle would be "floating" (i.e. slowly and evenly moving back and forth, as if floating in the air) if the issue had been addressed. He even demonstrated its use – I had to hold two cans (which were electrodes) while he pinched my arm. Then he had me recall the incident and the needle indeed moved on the dial when I remembered the pinch.

The relief I felt earlier, the sight of a precision instrument and the possibility to improve spiritually provided sufficient incentive to carry on.

When the workshop was over, the Executive Director of the Mission explained to me how Scientology worked: man, according to Hubbard, consists of three parts – body, mind and spirit. We ARE the spirit, immortal spiritual beings entrapped in bodies. The mind (which is not the brain) is a collection of memories, closely resembling a collection of photos, and floats around you and is completely invisible. The body is our tangible, flesh-and-blood part. Dianetics handles the mind; Scientology develops your spiritual power and allows you to unleash it.

He told me that though Hubbard "left his body" in 1986, he had managed to chart the exact route to the highest states of spiritual consciousness, calling it the "The Bridge to Total Freedom." The road leading to that state was partitioned into steps, each promising exact abilities to be gained.

On the right side of the Bridge, the auditing steps leading to these super powers were listed, and one was supposed to do these as a patient. The left side showed the auditor training courses corresponding to these levels of ability; the completion of these courses was also a requirement to delivering the corresponding levels of auditing.

Dianetics auditing and the state of Clear was situated in the middle of the chart, as according to Hubbard, certain steps had to be taken to prepare someone to face his or her engrams. Then an updated version of Dianetics called "New Era Dianetics" was used to make someone Clear. After achieving this, one could move on to the so-called OT levels. "OT" is short for "Operating Thetan," a spiritual being who can properly operate on a higher spiritual level

---

[2] case: the totality of issues, psychological problems, aberrations (used to denote any deviation from rational thought or behavior in Scientology) etc. plaguing someone

and has abilities considered supernatural on this planet. There were 15 OT levels listed on the chart, and by progressing up to OT XV, one could achieve "total spiritual freedom." The exact nature of this state was not defined.

The materials of these OT levels were "confidential," so the Executive Director was not able to tell me anything more about them. He did tell me though that OT VIII was the highest level available, as the levels above it "have not been released as yet."

I asked him about the cost. He told me that the first step, the Purification Rundown (apparently, it was a detoxification program) would cost 100,000 HUF (500 USD), it would then cost 4-7 million HUF (20,000 – 35,000 USD) more to achieve the state of Clear (if most of the auditing was done in Hungary). The OT levels would cost 30-40 million HUF (150,000 – 200,000 USD) up to OT VII, and OT VII would cost an additional few hundred thousand dollars. The amounts did not include the training courses on the other side of the Bridge, the various management training courses Scientology offered, nor the various donations asked by certain other organizations in the Scientology movement.

Despite the shocking price tags, I was still interested, as I was always looking for a way out of the mundane world and wanted to gain all these cool super abilities. Scientology promised this and more. As a first step, the man suggested that I do the "How to Overcome Ups & Downs in Life Course," a Scientology Life Improvement Course, so I could have so-called "stable gains" from Scientology and thus realize a steady growth in spiritual abilities.

MY FIRST COURSE AND LAST COURSE AS A "PUBLIC"[3]

I had some money set aside, so I paid for the course and started it. I finished in two days. Usually I was the only student in the course room, but the maximum number of people studying was three.

I had to progress through the course alone using a "checksheet," which listed the theory and practical steps necessary to complete the course. Studying in Scientology consisted of reading a specific part, then writing essays and/or "demonstrating" the material studied using a "demo kit" consisting of small everyday items (rubber bands, corks, plastic toys etc.). If I had a question, I had to notify the course supervisor, who just asked which word I had not understood. It was a bit frustrating to study like that – the official reason was that

---

[3] public: someone who is not a staff member, just a regular member of the Church of Scientology, a "parishioner." It is used as a singular noun in Scientology.

only in that way could I have a real personal understanding. But on the other hand, I had to accept that the text was good, understandable and true, and that if something was not clear, then the problem was with me.

The course pack was a collection of low-quality photocopied pages in a cheap paper binder and it looked like a pirated version of the real deal. The course itself was about so-called "Suppressive Persons" or "SPs" and their victims, the "Potential Trouble Sources" or "PTSes." According to Hubbard, all illnesses and accidents, without exception, are a result of a "PTS situation" – a present or past connection to an evil, antisocial person, a "Suppressive Person." It was not particularly earth-shattering and sounded a bit forced and unrealistic.

One thing somehow found its way into my thinking. Hubbard was analyzing the behavior of these Suppressive Persons and stated that they have 12 characteristics that you can use to identify them. If someone had the majority of these 12 characteristics, then he or she was a suppressive person. One of the characteristics was that the person is very much against beneficial treatments and psychoanalysis. Two similar attributes were also included: 1) he wildly attacks beneficial organizations and 2) rails against helping others. The message was clear: attackers of Scientology, an organization that helps people and provides an effective therapy, can be strongly suspected to be SPs. One looks at family members and relatives a bit differently after such indoctrination – you are prepared to be attacked because of your choice, and their disagreement could indicate they are suppressive persons in disguise! This puts a mental defense there against being dissuaded from your choice to be involved and the usual "it's a brainwashing cult"-type arguments.

While spending some time in the mission, the main thing that caught my attention was the sheer amount of materials available in Scientology. I took the opportunity to check what else was there to study. I was impressed by the huge number of lectures and volume of writing this man had left to the world. And apparently all was organized, dated and the whole thing looked like a real science – something that I thought was impossible to accomplish in the subject of the human mind. On the top of it, Hubbard claimed to have figured out everything about the human mind and how it works, in addition to handling drug use, the subject of administration and a lot more.

So I was definitely interested to find out more. After completing the course, I was interviewed by one of the mission staff members, a really attractive young lady. She asked, "What do you think about joining staff on a part-time basis?" She explained that it would mean working 20 hours a week. There would be no pay, but I wouldn't have to pay for future courses.

As I was on summer vacation, I was curious about Scientology and I had nothing better to do, I agreed. So I signed a staff contract on 15 July 1995, at the age of 17. I was technically a minor, but it did not seem to be an issue.

HOW TO INSTANTLY BECOME AN EXECUTIVE

When I joined, the mission had about 10 staff and a few were training in the nearest "org," located in Munich. The word "org" is often used in Scientology. It is an abbreviation for "organization" and refers to local churches, where Scientologists could go up to the state of Clear on the aforementioned Bridge. OT levels were offered by "Advanced Orgs," which were one level higher in the byzantine network of Scientology.

After joining staff, I had to do two short courses (what else?) called Staff Status Zero and Staff Status One, abbreviated as "SS 0" and "SS I." In SS 0, I had to learn the names of the divisions, and do a tour in the mission (wasn't that hard, as it had 3 offices in total). SS I was about some simple organizational basics, like the communication system used in the Church, how to write internal memos called "despatches" and the advantages of doing jobs right now instead of trying to do them later, plus the infamous KSW (Keeping Scientology Working) policy letter.

When I first read it, I was really confused. Hubbard made this remark at the beginning: *"Note: Neglect of this PL [policy letter] has caused great hardship on staffs, has cost countless millions and made it necessary in 1970 to engage in an all-out international effort to restore basic Scientology over the world."* Apparently, he was talking about a period in the history of the church when violating his policies resulted in an internal catastrophe, which almost wiped out the movement. That was the first small crack in my newfound "faith" – if that happened once, what's the guarantee that it won't happen again?

Then he went on describing Scientology as the only path to salvation, deeming all other methods evil: *"... man has never before evolved workable mental technology and emphasizing it is the vicious technology he did evolve – psychiatry, psychology, surgery, shock treatment, whips, duress, punishment, etc., ad infinitum."*

He really turned on the heat at the end of the policy letter:

"When somebody enrolls, consider he or she has joined up for the duration of the universe – never permit an 'open-minded' approach. If they're going to quit let them quit fast. If they enrolled, they're aboard, and if they're aboard, they're here on the same terms as the rest of us – win or die in the attempt. Never let them be half-minded about being Scientologists. The finest organizations in history have

16

been tough, dedicated organizations. Not one namby-pamby bunch of pantywaist dilettantes have ever made anything. It's a tough universe. The social veneer makes it seem mild. But only the tigers survive – and even they have a hard time. We'll survive because we are tough and are dedicated. When we do instruct somebody properly he becomes more and more tiger. When we instruct half-mindedly and are afraid to offend, scared to enforce, we don't make students into good Scientologists and that lets everybody down. When Mrs. Pattycake comes to us to be taught, turn that wandering doubt in her eye into a fixed, dedicated glare and she'll win and we'll all win. Humor her and we all die a little. The proper instruction attitude is, 'You're here so you're a Scientologist. Now we're going to make you into an expert auditor no matter what happens. We'd rather have you dead than incapable.'

...

"We're not playing some minor game in Scientology. It isn't cute or something to do for lack of something better.

"The whole agonized future of this planet, every man, woman and child on it, and your own destiny for the next endless trillions of years depend on what you do here and now with and in Scientology.

"This is a deadly serious activity. And if we miss getting out of the trap now, we may never again have another chance."

Frankly, I did not believe it at that time. I was still interested in becoming a real-life Jedi knight, so I chose to ignore that part of Scientology, which sounded like the teachings of a fanatical fundamentalist sect.

Shaking off the after-effects of the KSW policy letter, I went on studying Hubbard's writings on administration and management. I learned from the course that no matter how big the organization, it has to adhere to an elaborate 9 division organizational chart called an "org board" (which was changed to a 7-division one for missions). So, in the mission, most of the people were theoretically "division heads" or "executive secretaries" – even when there was no one in their divisions! So, I became "Field Control Director," supposedly an executive, and it was my responsibility to control the "Field Staff Members" or "FSMs" of the mission. They were not regular staff, but public who were involved in bringing people for services (for all intents and purposes, they were sales agents), and they received 10-15% percent commission for all payments made by their selectees for Scientology services.

I was quite proud of myself, achieving a status like that at such a young age. I told my parents (who were suspicious about the whole affair), and they had a good laugh about me being an executive.

I started to do whatever was expected – I organized a meeting for the Field Staff Members, gave them references to study, administered their so-called "selection slips" and commissions, and helped out wherever it was needed.

After all, Scientology was still in the pioneer phase in Hungary. There was only one Clear in the entire country, one trained auditor in Budapest Mission and no OTs (spiritual state above Clear) whatsoever. Most people had some Dianetics auditing, read the book or had done the "Purification Rundown," an intense program involving exercise, megadoses of vitamins and hours sitting in a sauna "to sweat out all the poisons" – the first step on Scientology's Bridge. Almost nothing was translated into Hungarian – and almost anything translated was unofficial and unauthorized. Therefore my lack of experience and knowledge was not really an issue.

We had absolutely no awareness of the dark side of Scientology – we never heard about Operation Snow White[4], the Sea Org was not present at this part of the globe yet. Overall, the whole movement seemed to be an association of genuinely well-intentioned people seeking spiritual betterment. The people working there were sincerely dedicated to helping others and were utterly convinced that they were doing the right thing. Nothing, not even the next-to-nothing wage, would make them quit. No one had any experience with the higher-level sci-fi type things or the abusive behavior displayed by senior management that I would come to learn about later. All we had access to was an unauthorized translation of one of the books written by Hubbard, called "History of Man," circulated among the Hungarian Scientologists as a peek into higher level OT stuff.

I had to do two more courses as part of my training. One of them was called "Success Through Communication." It was a dumbed-down version of Hubbard's communication drills, tailored to businessmen and salesmen. The course gradually took you through the various phases of communication. According to Hubbard, the first phase was *being there* in a spiritual sense. The basic idea was to establish the elements of communication: being there, speaking to someone, ability to receive an answer, then answer that, repeat the unanswered question if needed, or steer the conversation back to its original topic (if needed), and to conclude the conversation. These elements had to be practiced individually. "Being there" was practiced by sitting in a chair, not thinking about anything, just being there. It was quite difficult for me to get through this step (the Course Supervisor kept talking about huge potential spiritual gains to encourage me and that kept me going. It took quite a while to struggle through it. "Bullbaiting" was much more interesting though – one

---

[4] Operation Snow White: a project during the 1970s to purge unfavorable records about Scientology and its founder L. Ron Hubbard. This project included infiltration and thefts from 136 government agencies, foreign embassies and consulates, as well as private organizations critical of Scientology, in more than 30 countries. This program included the single largest infiltration of the United States government in history.

had to sit in a chair with a straight face, while his study partner tried to elicit some reaction with jokes, yelling or whatever it took to make the other one react. You were supposed to "confront" these insults and attempts to make you laugh – which meant to face them without flinching or avoiding, showing no reaction.

In retrospect, this ability was a blessing and a curse. It was undoubtedly useful to have greater tolerance to provocation, but it also blocked proper emotional reactions. It also had a hidden side-effect (at least on me): I had a better tolerance of the crazy things going on in the Church. I was not disturbed too much by them, and I was able to put up with much more than I should have. This contributed to my prolonged stay in the Church by making me more susceptible to its indoctrination. Somehow it was a part of Hubbard's ideal scene – in his world, emotions do not exist, just unconditional compliance to his tenets and organization.

I did experience some improvement in my ability to communicate after completing the course, but it was not very dramatic, and it did not last long.

The other one was the "FSM Specialist Hat" ("hat" is a term in Scientology denoting a specific organizational position, the accompanying training and the materials needed for it). This was much more interesting, as it tried to teach sales techniques to field staff working for commission, so they could sell the subject to others. I did not have much experience with selling Scientology (it had not worked out well with my family so far) and I was not involved in selling anything really before that, so I had difficulty relating the theory to practice.

I did learn some things, though. The sales techniques were imported by Hubbard from Les Dane, a used car salesman, who later became a sales guru. His book, "Surefire Sales Closing Techniques" was the Bible of Scientology salesmen. (They were called "Registrars," as Hubbard envisioned the general public so desperately wanting Scientology that you would only have to register the masses of applicants). There was even a technology for getting new recruits (it was called "dissemination" in the Church). It had four steps: 1) contact 2) handle any reservations the person had about Scientology (it was much easier before Internet access became more prevalent) 3) finding his "ruin"; this was a thing the person considered his greatest problem, that ruins and destroys him eventually. For example: marital difficulties, study problems, alcohol addiction, trouble at home (mother-in-law, children etc.), financial issues, troubles at work, etc. Then you were supposed to push him into the problem really hard, making him believe that it will only get worse, and he is not capable of solving it, as he has not solved it so far. Finally, you get him to understand that

19

he needs help on a right-now basis – from Scientology of course. And then you had to sign him up for the appropriate service.

The free personality test was all about "finding a ruin"; its purpose was to push you into your greatest problem, so you would want a solution, and then offer Scientology as the way out.

So, that's what I taught to my men and tried to apply on new people coming in.

LOVE IS A BURNING & CHILLING THING

My first taste of Scientology's incredibly oppressive justice system was brought about by a love affair. I fell in love with one of the key executives, the HCO Executive Secretary[5], and she felt the same. The only problem was she already had a boyfriend, who was away in Munich org for full-time training. The story was the usual – she helped me a lot in my early days on staff, we became good friends, and the friendship turned into love. We had to hide this fact, as it was a "high crime" to disturb someone's "progress on the Bridge" with such unethical behavior.

Nevertheless, I felt really happy and attributed it to Scientology. Apparently all those courses and knowledge started to produce results. This kind of thinking is part of the Scientology mentality, which is implanted from the very beginning. The direct cause-effect relationship becomes blurred somehow. This arises from the basic Scientology tenet that we are spiritual beings, and things going on in the "spiritual universe" determine what happens in the "material universe." This logic dictates that any spiritual progress (by studying Scientology or getting auditing) influences our fate in the material world – like experiencing something unexpectedly good or a lucky turn of events –, and it assumes we would do better in life in general. It does have some truth to it, but this viewpoint is given enormous importance, and you get the feeling that all you have to do to become lucky and successful in life is to think positively, improve your spiritually and to be enthusiastic about the subject. Hard work and actually doing things become less important. Another consequence is that you attribute anything good and lucky in your life to Scientology and anything bad is the result of lack of progress in Scientology, or not spending enough time in the Church. The net result of this (you can observe this with the majority of

---

[5] the executive over Divisions 1 (personnel, communications, ethics & justice matters) and 2 (sales and marketing of books, lectures and courses to existing public). "HCO" stands for "Hubbard Communications Office," the name of Division 1 in Scientology Churches.

the Scientologists) is a partial loss of the sense of reality, or a specific kind of financial irresponsibility where you can spend any amount of money on your own spiritual progress, as by doing so you believe you will achieve a better spiritual state, and money will thereafter mysteriously find you as a result. The evolution of this attitude is very much needed by the Church, as it serves to make members more eager to fulfill its demands. Thus, Scientologists tend to want to solve their problems almost exclusively in the "spiritual universe," i.e. in their heads as opposed to real-world problem solving. Interestingly it is reversed again in the higher echelons of the Church (exclusively among the upper-level staff though), and the real solutions to problems become all-important again. The average Scientologist is ridiculed behind his back (one of the top executives called these people "airheads"), or their attitude is knowingly abused to rake in more cash from them.

To sum it up, I was quickly thinking in this way – I was not particularly successful with girls before Scientology, and now I had a meaningful relationship. Scientology works and it helps people – just as they say. Our relationship was dominated by Scientology, and even selecting which movies we would see together was done with this in mind: "Natural Born Killers" (due to Juliette Lewis, and unfavorable portrayal of psychology), "Pulp Fiction" (Travolta was in it) and finally, "Braveheart" (as it was so "theta"[6] and about freedom).

I was pretty happy with the whole thing, but the relationship with my family became really strained. My parents were initially happy about me having a girlfriend and working somewhere, but at Christmas dinner the entire thing took a bad turn. I got into a heated conversation with my first cousin, whom I always had great respect for, just as my family did. He was a true genius, a computer programmer who had Internet access and looked up Scientology on the net. Needless to say, he was not impressed and dismissed the whole subject as an oddball cult started by a mediocre sci-fi writer, and a scam to boot. I bitterly defended the Church and the subject but I was worried about the direction my relationship with the family was taking. Specifically, I was worried about the fact that I might have to disconnect from them if this continued down the path it was heading. The indoctrination from the Ups & Downs course caused me to consider some of my family members as potential Suppressive Persons, intent on trying to stop me from achieving spiritual freedom.

After a few months, in January 1996, our secret relationship with my Scientology girlfriend soured. She was increasingly concerned about her official

---

[6] theta: as an adjective, it means something aesthetic, causing good feelings or spiritual joy; cute and charming in case of a person. As a noun, it means "life force" in Scientology.

boyfriend and what our relationship would cause, and he was supposed to return any day.

Additionally, the mission was not doing well. The "stats" (statistics measuring production that had to be evaluated and acted upon on a weekly basis) were down. The mission had also "pulled in" (as they say in Scientology: it means "got it as a deserved action") a serious problem – one of the staff members on training in Munich called Noemi lost her sanity. In Scientology, this is called "going Type III PTS." It means that the person thinks everyone is an SP, a Suppressive Person, and even imagines that ghosts, etc. are hunting him or her and "everyone" is against them. Hubbard supposedly had a solution for this, so the girl was secretly brought back to Hungary and our Ethics Section (e.g. my girlfriend) had to take care of her. I was a relative newcomer, so most of the data about it was carefully hidden from me. Hubbard's tech ("technology" the term used in Scientology to describe the application of Hubbard's methods) for handling this called for complete isolation and specific steps taken so that the person regains his or her sanity. I was never informed about the handling or the outcome, but I saw daily/weekly faxes coming from Munich giving detailed instructions on what to do, and daily or weekly reports were sent as well. Noemi was taken to a country house and was placed under the "Type III Watch" which meant someone was always with her so she did not harm herself.

I found out later that the attempt was unsuccessful. Noemi was escorted to the home of her family, and was left there. She ended up in a psychiatric institution.

Due to these troubles, the Executive Director asked for help, which came from another Hungarian mission in Szeged.

A self-appointed "ethics specialist" arrived. It meant that he studied the entirety of the Introduction to Scientology Ethics book, which was no small feat as it was not available in Hungarian, and only a few Scientologists knew enough English or German to study Hubbard's writings.

So, naturally my girlfriend confessed our entire affair. As a result, she was deemed unfit to be the executive over the Ethics section and was demoted to Treasury Secretary. I also got a briefing from the "ethics specialist" on how dangerous this was to the mission. He told his story ("I used to be the Don Juan of the mission in Szeged" he said) and how he changed after he realized the error of his ways. He got me to read some of Hubbard's writing about the danger of unethical behavior on the second dynamic[7], or 2D, and what I did

---

[7] Hubbard claimed that the command "Survive!" was the lowest common denominator of all existence, and the primary purpose of all life forms. He divided this urge into 8 subdivisions (self,

was considered "out-2D" in Scientologese. He went a bit overboard, describing the horrors of such behavior eventually leading to the total destruction of the group.

The girl did a "Doubt" condition formula – which meant that she had to compare me with her other boyfriend through a set series of steps and decide which one of us would mean the "greatest good for the greatest number of dynamics." It was about as unromantic as could be.

She chose to reunite with the other guy. The Executive Director and the old-timers of the mission wanted to see blood though. Especially mine. I was a relative newcomer and was a great target to blame for the downstats[8] (which were totally unrelated to my area). So, a Committee of Evidence was called. This is a kind of a Scientology trial by jury, which is supposed to be impartial, establish all the facts and come up with a ruling. Its chairman was the Executive Director of the mission, so there went any impartiality. The "fact-finding" turned into a lengthy interrogation (recorded on tape of course) and detailed questioning of what exactly we were doing together. I was very frightened about losing the possibility of progressing on the Bridge, so I told everything. It was a relatively harmless relationship (all we did was some kissing, no sex or any serious petting), but I still felt at the end that I had committed a heinous crime.

The Committee found me guilty and put me in a condition of Liability, and I had to do amends to make up for the "damage" I caused. So I ended up distributing 30,000 fliers inviting people to come in for a free personality test to mailboxes all around Pécs. Winter was particularly harsh at that time and I had to fight through snow, sometimes a meter high, and had to flee from dogs some homeowners set on me.

My father burst out laughing when I explained to him what was going on. As an outsider, he found the entire story quite bizarre.

Anyway, I completed my "Liability condition" and apparently it satisfied the leaders of the mission, and all was well.

The boyfriend of the girl, Tamás, handled the whole thing surprisingly well. I was even invited to their wedding, along with all other staff members from the mission. Naturally, quite a number of them got drunk at the party (not me, though), and I ended up in the Trabant (a "car" produced by East Germany) of my senior, together with the Executive Director and another staff member from the Public Division, singing "Kicsiny falum" (My Little Town,

---

sex&family, group, mankind, all life, the physical universe, spiritual beings, and God or Infinity). The second dynamic covers all sexual activity and anything related to raising children and having a family.

[8] Having downward trending production statistics and/or performing badly.

a popular Hungarian pseudo-folk song) at the top of our lungs. You probably have to be a Hungarian to fully appreciate this, though…

PURIFYING MY LIFE

I was about to complete the last year of high school. Despite largely ignoring school due to Scientology commitments, I still had very good grades. My parents strongly urged me to go to a university but I had other plans. I wanted to go for full-time Scientology training. I wanted to go up the Bridge, to become a better person, and to improve spiritually. I was not attracted by the traditional career paths, the promises of Hubbard sounded so much better.

The Executive Director was not really happy about it, as the aforementioned incident was still fresh in his mind. I tried to do my best on post – I spent more time in the mission and did a lot of "body routing" (escorting people into the mission from the street to do personality tests). After a while we agreed that I would go to Munich for auditor training after completing high school (which was only a few weeks away). His decision was positively influenced by the landmark event in the history of Scientology – the announcement of the "Golden Age of Tech," where David Miscavige, the leader of the Church, released a revised version of all the levels of auditor training, promising a fast and easy route upwards. I was really excited to hear this news and so was the Executive Director.

I also had to sign an undated 5-year staff contract, which would go into effect upon completion of my training. I signed it without hesitation.

I even got a sponsor, which was almost a miracle. A fellow Scientologist told me about an international mailing list called TNX (Theta News Exchange). Only Scientologists in good standing with the Church were allowed to join, and you had to have a recommendation from a current member. I got a response to my introduction letter from an American Scientologist. He noticed that I wanted to go on training and asked if I had a sponsor – he had an amends program to do and he would gladly finance my basic costs due to the nature of the overt (sin or harmful act in Scientologese) he had committed. This would allow me to concentrate on my studies and give him a sense of "making amends" for whatever it was that he had done. This provided a further incentive to the mission to send me for training.

I had one more thing to do before leaving to Munich - the first step on the Bridge – the Purification Rundown. As I mentioned earlier, this is a program taking up 5 hours a day, for 2-3 weeks. The daily regimen is the same: you take a huge dose of vitamins (a package consisting of several different types) and a lot of niacin (max. 5000 mg per day, starting at a low dose, increasing gradually each day). It is followed by half an hour jogging, and then you spend several hours in a sauna with breaks. According to Hubbard's theory, the niacin removes toxins, chemicals, or drug residues from the fatty tissues. Taking it causes rashes, which is just the way for the body to relive effects of radiation, direct heat, sunburns etc.

Naturally, I had a job to do as well – some important people (for Scientology and the mission) were doing the program with me, so I had to keep an eye on them. They included the wife of the owner of one of the biggest book publishers in Hungary, the brother of a prominent Hungarian psychiatrist, the mother-in-law of one of the richest Scientologists and a renowned hunter, who has reached the state of Clear according to the mission (he died in an accident shortly after completing the Purification Rundown – he was cleaning his shotgun and accidentally fired it). The program was supervised by one of the most dedicated staff members of the mission, who had been disinherited by his parents due to Scientology and his decision to leave the university he was attending. He also disconnected from them.

I did the program for about 2 weeks, but no real changes occurred, though I reached the maximum level of niacin allowed. I thought that probably I did not have many toxins in my body to begin with, and completed the program.

CHAPTER TWO

Munich

ORIENTATION

When I arrived at the Munich train station, I took a taxi. Confident in the worldwide recognition of the movement, I asked the driver to take me to the local Scientology Church. He did not know what that was. I told him the address. He did not know where that street was, and had to look it up on a map.

I was rather surprised, as I was told in back in the mission that Munich Org was a major organization in Scientology and had a strong presence in the city. In reality, the org occupied a smaller four-story building on a side street (truth be told, it was close to one of the major avenues of the city).

A team of 15 Hungarian trainees greeted me. Several Hungarian missions sent their staff for training There. The schedule was rather tight; one was supposed to do courses or work each day between 9:00 and 22:30 (with 1 hour meal breaks two times a day, plus a 15-minute break around 15:00), including weekends. Trainees were allowed to have one morning off a week for washing their clothes and cleaning their apartment.

All trainees (except for me, as I had a sponsor) had to moonlight to earn money for basic necessities. Local Scientologist provided these jobs, and employed the trainees off the books. The pay wasn't exactly high, and they also received no support from their missions, so a visit to a local fast food restaurant was considered a luxury. Fortunately for us, one of the Hungarian students worked for a butchers' shop, so we were able to get some meat, eating the sausage and fried chicken remains he received as additional compensation.

I was placed in a nearby block of flats, owned by a local Scientologist. That's where I experienced the first major shock concerning the workability of Scientology.

The four-story building had 5-6 bedsits, one shared kitchen and a bathroom on each floor. I got one-half of a room, sharing it with a middle-aged Scientologist man. He told me his story. He got a huge amount of auditing, almost achieved the state of Clear, but ran out of money. He spent his entire inheritance on Scientology, even sold his house and now lived in a small room. He used to be a Scientology staff member, but he was fired when the Church found out that he served in the German Army and had to go through a national security check as a part of his assignment. This was forbidden in one of the internal regulations written by Hubbard.

I made acquaintance with the rest of the tenants. I found two more Scientology ex-staff with similar fates (something had been discovered about their past and they were dismissed). Four of the Hungarian trainees also lived there.

The rest of our group was living with a local Scientologist named Leila, who was OT III. She had a huge house, but was forced to let most of the rooms as she spent a large portion of her money on Scientology and her husband was re-doing the Bridge from the Purification Rundown to Clear for the third time now.

I soon got to know the staff members of Munich Org. They were well-intentioned and very determined, with a few odd ones (one of their auditors had a serious speech impediment, for example). I learned more about them over the next few weeks, and it became evident that staff pay was ridiculously low, thus most of them were supported by their families or their spouses. Around 30-40% of the income of the local Church was sent to the international and continental headquarters, and the balance was used to cover utilities and salaries. Staff pay had the lowest priority, so there were weeks (all statistics were calculated and monitored on a weekly basis, therefore the staff was paid weekly) when the staff were not paid at all. The "management fees" had to be sent to international management no matter what though.

Munich Org was the first Scientology entity where I encountered the phenomenon called "stat push." The performance monitoring and enforcement system of Scientology is built on statistical weeks which begin and end on Thursdays at 14:00. There was a huge push from the continental and international management organization of the Church to "get the stats up" each week, threatening the staff members with severe disciplinary actions if they failed to meet their quotas.

Pécs and the rest of the Hungarian missions were largely ignored by the stat pushers in Copenhagen. We rarely got any feedback on the statistics which had to be reported weekly, on Thursday afternoon. If there was a big change in one of the statistics, we got a phone call to check whether it was a typo or not.

But it was very different in Munich Org. Statistics were calculated and monitored on a daily basis. Staff members were mercilessly hounded if their statistics were not in the proper range to achieve a higher value than the previous Thursday.

Two major methods were used to increase productivity: there was some minor internal PR (pep talks, emphasizing the greatness of the purpose of Scientology, small rewards etc), but threats, yelling and enforced overtime was the favored method.

Most of the executives of Munich Org had completed advanced Scientology management courses. There was one thing in common, one skill they all mastered: they were experts at swearing. Interestingly, while they were questioning their staff in German, the threats and expletives were uttered in English. So, at the very least, my English vocabulary was expanded by a lot of four-letter words and profanities.

STUDYING AND COMING TO A HALT

I started on my training lineup. The first was a course called "The Student Hat," which contained Hubbard's study technology in its entirety. I managed to complete it in three weeks. I was still very enthusiastic about becoming a superman, so I quickly adapted to studying 12-14 hours per day, and I was not bothered by the lack of leisure time.

Hubbard stated that a student has to achieve full conceptual understanding of the materials. He identified four barriers to that. The first obstacle was the belief that one knows all about the subject already. The second was missing how something looks in real life (he called it "lack of mass"). The third was the missed gradient or step, and the fourth – and most important – was the misunderstood word. The Student Hat was all about identifying the symptoms caused by these barriers and handling them.

According to Hubbard, lack of mass was to be handled either by the obvious solution (e.g. if one studies automobiles, he might want to have a look at one), or by making a clay model of it. The use of clay to put concepts into a physical form "reality" was widespread in Scientology; executive training courses frequently included doing clay demonstrations of workflows or business policies. Hubbard said that it greatly aids understanding.

At the beginning of my studies in Munich, it was even more evident that studying in Scientology comes with a borderline obsessive urge for fully understanding words and hunting for misunderstood words. According to Hubbard, the vast majority of learning problems are caused by misunderstood words, phrases or idioms. He stated that the only way to fully understand a sentence or a text was to achieve full conceptual understanding of all the words in it.

The majority of this course revolved around finding and handling misunderstood words; how to identify them (they even had types) and how to achieve conceptual understanding of a word. Hubbard called this process "word clearing" – it involved using all the definitions of a word in sentences, until it was fully understood and then looking up its etymology. If, by chance, one stumbled into another misunderstood word in any of the definitions, then the same procedure applied.

Examinations were also handled differently than in the non-Scientology world. The course consisted of various Hubbard texts, mostly 2-3 page policy letters or internal bulletins, and one had to receive a "checkout" on each after studying them. The examiner (who could have been any other student from the course room who had studied that particular text previously) asked the meaning of a few randomly selected words from the text, and then asked a few questions about the practical application of the material. Wrong answers, any slight uncertainty or hesitation resulted in a "flunk," and a restudy of the text was in order.

There was also a written examination at the end of the course, accompanied by a "meter check" – whereby a Scientology staff member asked whether you completed the course and achieved the result promised by it, while hooked to an E-meter, which was plainly used as a lie detector at that time.

The next course included auditing on my studies. I had to make a list of all subjects I have ever studied. This was then "assessed" on an E-meter, hunting for and clearing any words that I had not understood while studying these subjects. The end result of this procedure, called "Method One Word Clearing," was supposedly the restoration of one's education, but I have never met anyone in Scientology who achieved that. After "clearing" a hundred words, all I could produce was a list of subjects that did not produce any reaction on the E-meter. This was apparently enough to complete this step. I was glad to finish it as I was not too interested in the subjects I had to study in high school, so I did not make a fuss about the omitted restoration of my education.

Then I had to do two courses, containing the hard and tough versions of the communication exercises invented by Hubbard, called "training routines" or "TRs." For example, the exercise for "being there" meant that I had to sit in a chair for two hours, facing ("confronting") another student without the slightest movement, twitching or looking away.

The experience I had in Pécs with these communication drills became even more intense: on one hand, I became more forthcoming and brave during communication, but life also became a bit surreal. External stimuli had even less effect on me, which dulled my emotions and caused me to experience a strange feeling: I often felt like an outsider, detached from reality, having "stepped out" of real life. My communication skill did improve though and these two courses had some real and lasting positive effects on my life.

The second part of these communication drills was all about control and giving orders and getting others to comply with them. The emphasis was on learning how to properly balance your sheer intention (as a purely spiritual thing) with physical force. This ability was supposedly needed by auditors so they could properly direct the attention of their patients and get their questions answered. There were drills to infuse your orders with such intention, such that the target would comply without thinking or hesitation.

This was another recurring theme in Hubbard's writings – the idea of getting others to do things whether they wanted to or not. In his marketing texts, he was looking for "command phrases" to manipulate the masses into buying products. He encouraged Scientology salesmen to use the mechanics of the reactive (subconscious) mind and to "push the buttons" of prospects to achieve what they want.

When I was done with both courses, I had to attest to achieving a new ability: being able to solve any situation by communication alone, no matter how hard, now and any time in the future. The wording is clever though: the student has to declare whether or not he FEELS that he had achieved this.

Note that it is not the Church which declares that the student has completed the course and now is a master of communication, it is *the student* who attests to the achievement of the ability in writing. It is not hard to guess why it is not the other way around.

Between the courses, I wanted to go back to Hungary, as my birthday was approaching and I was a bit homesick, too. I submitted a formal request to the training director. I was called into her office, where she explained to me that I was very much needed for the statistics and I was such a star student etc. She was an expert at mixing flattering remarks with veiled threats, and it worked. I reconsidered my position and stayed.

The next course was the Professional Metering (E-meter operator) course. After the initial successes, my progress was completely halted by one of the drills. I had to get another student hooked up to the E-meter, have him or her think about an exact date (year, month, day, hour, minutes, seconds), and then I had to use targeted question to find that date. It was supposed to go like this: "Is this date before 1950? Later than 1950? Is it in 1950?" The other student had to sit silently, and I had to watch the e-meter to find the correct answers, down to the second.

I simply could not complete this drill. Others seemed to have the same problem, but a few managed to get through (though mostly by using certain students as subjects). The course supervisors tried a lot to get me going (clearing words over and over again, redoing earlier theory and practical steps), but nothing worked. Finally, I was sent back to the communication (TRs) course to redo it, but I got stuck on the exercises as well.

I was truly disheartened by the constant failures and I did not think I could progress any further. The course supervisors got fed up with me and I was sent to the Ethics Officer for handling. Hubbard stated that if someone is "out-ethics"' (i.e. commits harmful acts, withholds some important detail about his life or is connected to a suppressive person etc.), then he would not progress in his studies.

The Ethics Officer, a rather unfriendly and rude person, propped up the E-meter and started to interrogate me about my family, asking if I had any family member who was antagonistic to Scientology. I was completely honest; I told him all about the situation in the family.

The Ethics Officer went ballistic and gave me an ultimatum: I had to return to Hungary, and either handle my family (meaning get them to be fully in accord with my involvement in Scientology) or disconnect from them. At that point, I was rather fed up with the whole thing, and was wondering whether I needed this in my life. Suddenly, going to a university did not seem to be such a bad option. I sort of got what I wanted anyway: I had lived in another country for a while, my communication skills had improved and I was more optimistic about my future. So, I was kind of happy to leave, but I did not really know what to do exactly. I was still attracted by the lofty promises Hubbard made, but my failure did cause me to consider other options.

BACK TO PÉCS

I went home and stayed there for a few days, taking a bit of a rest. Scientology did not give up on me, though. I had several lengthy conversations on the phone with staff members from Munich and Pécs, and I finally agreed to visit the mission. I knew that I faced a huge bill if I defaulted on my employment contract with the mission, as the prices for the courses done in Germany were rather high. I told the Executive Director what happened in Munich, in detail. He was not exactly happy to hear the news. In the end we agreed that I had to handle my relatives and we would take it from there. Nevertheless, the five-year contract that I signed before going on training was now in full force, so I had to work in the mission on a full-time basis. After spending a few days in the mission I was again under the influence of Hubbard and his philosophy and banished my doubts.

I was assigned to the so-called procurement line. I had to get people to fill out the free, 200-question personality test (which was my own first step in Scientology) and I had to study how to evaluate the results. Naturally, there was a separate course where I could learn all that. I quickly completed the course.

This course had a special significance in my life. This is where my transformation started. I was originally a shy, idealistic and good natured teenager, and

I started to change into a charming, silver-tongued and unscrupulous clone of L. Ron Hubbard, who embodies the phrase: "the end justifies the means."

Fortunately, the transformation was not complete, but I got more and more into this new personality as I progressed in the Church.

I found out on the course that the test is to be called "Oxford Capacity Analysis" in Europe and "American Personality Analysis" in the US, for purely marketing purposes. After thoroughly analyzing the questions, I realized that one has to think like Hubbard to achieve a good score on the test. It supposedly measures 10 personality traits (i.e. all traits are measured by the answer given to the 20 corresponding questions), namely stability, happiness, concentration/composure, self-confidence, activity, initiative, responsibility, judgment, empathy and communication. There was a key attached, which was used to calculate the values for each trait, the final results being somewhere between -100 (very bad) and +100 (perfect).

Tests could only be evaluated personally. The pattern was very strictly regulated. There were four written evaluation cards for each trait, depending on the calculated values. For non-Scientologists, usually the two bad ones were used. The evaluator had to take the card and read its text aloud in a very determined and suggestive tone, which sounded something like this for a run-of-the-mill person: "You are unstable and others can manipulate you easily. You find it very difficult to control things. You definitely have to do something about that if you want to achieve anything at all in life." If the person protested or disagreed about it, then it had to be paraphrased like "you are easily dissuaded by the arguments of others" etc., until he or she agreed with the wording. Then the evaluator had to look the person in the eye and state *"Scientology can handle that."* He had to find the vulnerabilities of the person and throw a lot of salt on these wounds and make it clear that this/these is/are a serious personality defect, which MUST be addressed, and of course, Scientology can do that. From time to time, the evaluation had to state that these are all scientific facts, not just personal opinions, as they are based on a scientific test. In the end, when the subject was visibly broken, his self-confidence in tatters and convinced that he really had to do something about himself, the evaluator had to tell him in confidence that he was just a simple test evaluator, does not know much about the courses offered here and he has to look for the Registrar to find out more.

My new boss, who held a position called "Public Services Executive Secretary," had added another element to it. A gray folder. Before entering the evaluation booth, I was supposed to place the printed evaluation in that folder, and upon entering the booth, I had to carefully open the folder and place the evaluation on the table. This was all part of the smoke and mirrors, to make our activity look more credible.

Meanwhile, I tried to handle the views of my family about Scientology. They refused to change their stance, but they were willing to let me do whatever I wanted with my life. This was enough for me and I reported that to the Executive Director, who sent it to the Ethics Officer in Munich.

I also made a mistake which did not help. I caught a cold and had a minor fever. As a result of the mental conditioning I received in Scientology (I must have done something bad to "pull this in"), I started to look for spiritual causes and used one of Hubbard's tools, the so-called "overt/withhold write-up." It was a kind of a do-it-yourself confession of sins; one had to write down any harmful acts committed, any omissions and provide the exact details (what happened where, when and how). The completed write-up had to be turned over to the local Ethics Officer, who "verified its completeness," then filed it in one's "Ethics Folder." The idea was to experience relief by getting rid of the guilty conscience and to avoid pulling in a punishment, improving one's personal karma.

In this case, it did not help. The fever got higher and I almost lost consciousness. Finally my parents brought me to a doctor, who administered an injection to bring down the fever. Then I grudgingly resorted to the traditional treatment.

Meanwhile, one of the trainees of the mission came back from Munich, as he completed his full training. He took over the Executive Director position as had originally been planned. He was very enthusiastic about implementing the entirety of the so-called administrative technology of Scientology, and started working on this in earnest. The first target of his sweeping reforms was my boss, Csaba. Csaba had a rather insouciant and bohemian personality and therefore did not consider it so important to strictly adhere to Hubbard's writings. One of the disagreements he had with the new Executive Director was the handling of his incoming memos. According to the relevant policy letters, Csaba had a "standard" in-basket set up for him. Instead of handling each memo in a standard fashion, he just glanced through the new ones each morning, dealt with the important messages (usually by answering them verbally), then threw them back on top of the heap. His basket was always overflowing with papers. After unsuccessfully trying to convince Csaba to handle his basket as Hubbard prescribed, the new boss ordered him in writing to redo the first and most basic staff training course, Staff Status I, which contained the policy letters about the handling of internal memos. I was very excited to see how this conflict would develop, as I was sure Csaba would not just obey, accept such humiliation and do whatever was asked of him. Therefore, it was a real surprise to see next morning that the in-basket of Csaba was completely empty.

The new boss couldn't have been happier. At the upcoming staff meeting, he was talking about this fantastic change at length, attributing it to the supreme workability of Hubbard's admin tech, which had now resolved a real-life problem in the mission. Then he went to the cupboard to get something for the next item on the agenda. When he opened the door, a huge pile of papers spilled out in front of him. As it turned out, Csaba simply took all the papers from his in-basket and placed them in the cupboard. The staff meeting had to be suspended, as everyone burst into laughter. The Executive Director was laughing along for a while, and then he had us stop laughing and announced that the appropriate measures would be taken to address this situation. Csaba never got around to doing the assignment and after a series of similar clashes over the interpretation of Hubbard policies, our brand new boss had it and left the mission and Scientology along with it. Csaba demoted himself to the lowest possible position (it was called "expeditor" in Scientologese, normally assigned to handle backlogged tasks). He was still doing what he had been doing before, but he refused to have any job title inside the organization.

As the person responsible for gross income, Csaba did put a lot of effort into training the staff and making them good salesmen. That kind of training had the highest priority in the mission, which was consistent with the real nature of the Church. Csaba held regular lectures on selling and sales, and we had to drill the methods devised by Hubbard and the ones contained in Les Dane's book, *Surefire Sales Closing Techniques.*

I learned two techniques, which I used extensively later. One of them was the "DEI Scale." "DEI" is an abbreviation for *Desire, Enforce, Inhibit.* According to Hubbard, if one starts to present a product or service to someone, at first he does not know anything about it (obviously). Then, as he hears more about it, he would try to inhibit the salesperson from selling him the product or service. If the person gets through this phase, then he would feel that was forced into something he would not want. Then, if the salesperson gets on with his sales pitch, the person would then feel a bit of desire to obtain it, and at the very end, he would be interested. Hubbard presented this as an unconscious mechanism to be exploited, and one was supposed to follow this pattern to sell Scientology: keep enlightening the prospect about the advantages of it and sooner or later he would reach for it.

The other one was changing the subject. Hubbard advised changing the subject to something that was close to the heart of the potential buyer, if the sales process got stuck or the conversation about the product or services became awkward. One would then talk about the new subject, gaining the confidence and sympathy of the other person, and then one would change back to the original topic and proceed with the sales pitch.

I had moderate success after all this training as a salesperson for Scientology. Seeing my dedication, the executives of the mission thought that I should continue my training in Munich. The Course Supervisor of the mission helped me grasp the concepts of auditor training better. Finally, I was declared fit for further training and sent back to Munich to finish what I had started.

MUNICH, ROUND TWO

I went back to Munich in the spring of 1997. My first stop was the Ethics Officer, where we reviewed the handling of my family. I had to do two courses before I could continue the metering course. The first was *"PTS/SP*[9] – *How to Confront and Shatter Suppression,"* and the second was the *Ministerial Course* (yes, one had to do *one course* to become a minister of Scientology), to avoid conscription.

The PTS/SP Course was basically a greatly expanded version of my first course in the Church, *How to Overcome Ups & Downs in Life*. Unsurprisingly, Hubbard devoted a lot of time to the topic of suppression, so I had lot to digest. (Note: this course was made sort of mandatory for all Scientologists in 2001.)

I already covered quite a lot about Hubbard's theories concerning suppression, stress, illnesses etc. but this course added quite some new ideas to it. According to Hubbard, if someone is against Scientology, then he is either a suppressive person or someone who is under the influence of a suppressive person (i.e. a potential trouble source).

Hubbard also stated that if someone attacks the Church, he then must have crimes – specifically such crimes that could land him in prison. He argued that Scientology uncovers the truth, therefore criminals will attack it violently so their crimes will not be discovered. This made me wonder about my relatives and their possible crimes, trying to imagine what they had done. I think this theory of Hubbard definitely influences the thinking processes of most Scientologists, pushing them farther away from their non-Scientology relatives and the non-Scientology world.

His exact words were the following (this is just one excerpt of a number of similar writings, but it encapsulates the worldview that Hubbard expected all Scientologists to adhere to – all presented as scientific "fact"):

---

[9] SP – suppressive (antisocial) person; PTS – potential trouble source, someone who is/was connected to a suppressive person

"If a group of 'scientists' were knowingly raising the number of insane to get more appropriation and 'treatment' fees and somebody came along with the real answer, that group would move heaven and earth to protect its billions of rake-off."

"And so individuals, governments and 'scientists' attack Scientology."

"It's as simple as that. We do not treat the sick or the insane. We break no laws. We do more good in any ten minutes of this planet's time than the combined efforts of all social ministries on Earth to better mankind."

"Stated that way, however, it looks pretty hopeless and even dangerous to be a Scientologist."

"Except it is totally hopeless and fatal not to be a Scientologist."

"Those who are not Scientologists are left in complete ignorance of the motives of the dishonest. And they have no chance of personal immortality. It is as simple as that. It is better to be endangered but with a chance than to be condemned utterly and without one."

"Those who criticize one for being a Scientologist or make snide remarks cannot stand a personal survey of past actions or motive. This happens to be a fortunate fact for us. The criminal abhors daylight. And we are the daylight."

He continues in this same vein, taking things even further in his condemnation of anyone who dares criticize Scientology and asserting that every such person has horrible "crimes" they are hiding.

"Now, get this as a technical fact, not a hopeful idea. Every time we have investigated the background of a critic of Scientology, we have found crimes for which that person or group could be imprisoned under existing law. We do not find critics of Scientology who do not have criminal pasts. Over and over we prove this."

"Politician A stands up on his hind legs in a parliament and brays for a condemnation of Scientology. When we look him over we find crimes – embezzled funds, moral lapses, a thirst for young boys – sordid stuff."

"Wife B howls at her husband for attending a Scientology group. We look her up and find she had a baby he didn't know about."

"Two things operate here. Criminals hate anything that helps anyone, instinctively. And just as instinctively a criminal fights anything that may disclose his past."

"Now, as criminals only compose about 20 percent of the race, we are on the side of the majority. This is quite true. In one country we have almost exactly 100 Scientologists for every member and supporter of psychiatry. They make the noise because they are afraid. But we have more general influence and more votes."

"The way we handle the situation now is simplicity itself and we are winning."

"We are slowly and carefully teaching the unholy a lesson. It is as follows: 'We are not a law enforcement agency. BUT we will become interested in the crimes of people who seek to stop us. If you oppose Scientology we promptly look up – and will find and expose – your crimes. If you leave us alone we will leave you alone.'"

"It's very simple. Even a fool can grasp that."

"And don't underrate our ability to carry it out."

"Our business is helping people to lead better lives. We even help those who have committed crimes, for we are not here to punish. But those who try to make life hard for us are at once at risk."

"We are only interested in doing our job. And we are only interested in the crimes of those who try to prevent us from doing our work. There is no good reason to oppose Scientology. In our game everybody wins."

Further assertions follow of "technical fact" that Scientologists have the moral high ground and can deal with anyone who is not in full agreement with Scientology by accusing them of "crimes."

"And we have this technical fact – those who oppose us have crimes to hide. It's perhaps merely lucky that this is true. But it is true. And we handle opposition well only when we use it."
"Try it on your next critic. Like everything else in Scientology, it works.
Sample dialogue:
  GEORGE: Gwen. if you don't drop Scientology I'm going to leave you.
  GWEN: (savagely) George! What have you been doing?
  GEORGE: What do you mean?

GWEN: *Out with it. Women? Theft? Murder? What crime have you committed?*
GEORGE: *(weakly) Oh. Nothing like that.*
GWEN: *What then?*
GEORGE: *I've been holding back on my pay..."*

"*If you, the criticized, are savage enough and insistent enough in your demand for the crime, you'll get the text, meter or no meter."*

"*Never discuss Scientology with the critic. Just discuss his or her crimes, known and unknown. And act completely confident that those crimes exist. Because they do."*

"*Life will suddenly become much more interesting – and you'll become much less suppressed!"*

Another novelty was a series of ferocious attacks against psychiatrists, psychologists and analysts, whom he collectively called "psychs." One of his more notorious writing was also included in the course. It was entitled "Pain and Sex" and stated that these psychs are reincarnated intergalactic criminals, who have been suppressing and wrecking spiritual beings for billions of years.

He put it this way:

"*Destructive creatures who do not want people big or reaching – since they are terrified of punishment due to their crimes – invented pain and sex to shrink people and cut their alertness, knowingness, power and reach. Thus, you see people who are 'experiencing' either pain or sex introverting and not producing much."*

"*Pain and sex were the INVENTED tools of degradation. Believe it or not, a being can be so overwhelmed by either that he or she becomes an addict of it. Priests become flagellants and cut themselves to pieces with self-whipping. Torturers drool over pain. Lovers are very seldom happy. People do the most irrational things when overcharged with sex, and prostitutes use it as a knowing stock-in-trade. Combined, pain and sex make up the insane Jack-the-Rippers (who killed only prostitutes) and the whole strange body of sex-murder freaks, including Hinckley, and the devotees of late-night horror movies. Under the false data of the psychs (who have been on the track a long time and are the sole cause of decline in this universe) both pain and sex are gaining ground in this society and, coupled with robbery which is a hooded companion of both, may very soon make the land a true jungle of crime."*

"Go into an asylum or a prison and look at the increasing institutional pop-ulation and know what you are looking at. In the main, these are pain and sex addicts, decadent and degraded and no longer capable. They were sent on that route down through the ages by the psychs and here they are still in the psychs' hands! And do they get well or go straight? Oh no. Whether in prisons or insane asylums they just get worse. And the psychs in both places rub their bloodied hands as they turn their products loose again upon the remaining population! It's no accident. And the stocks-in-trade of psychs are PAIN and SEX. They will even tell you it is 'natural' to steal! To compound their felony – if that is possible – they tell you it's the body doing it. Another crashing big false datum on top of all their other lies."

"These are data which emerged from recent thorough research of the whole track[10]. This is not theory or some strange opinion. It is provable electronic fact. The waves are just synthesized."

"They are the most-used tools in the campaign against beings in furthering the general goal of those creatures whose sole ambition is destruction. The universe does not happen to be either destructive or chaotic except as such obsessed creeps make it. Statements it is otherwise are just more false data from the same suspect 'author-ities.' It fits their purposes to make seem natural what they make artificially. The universe only seems that way to a being because such loathsome psychotics make it seem so. They destroyed every great civilization to date and are hard at work on this one. The one thing they can't stand is the light of truth, so despite their objections, one must turn it on them. Only in its glare do their lies wither. It is the potent weapon they can't fend off."

That was definitely a lot to digest. I did not really understand what he was talking about, but it definitely made it clear why the Church is attacking psy-chiatry so wildly. This was the ideological foundation. That's why the Church went to great lengths to hunt for evidence of the misdeeds and horrific acts of "the psychs." Hubbard said they are criminals and have been enslaving spiritual beings for billions of years. Since Hubbard said it, it must be 100% true (at least that's how Scientologists think), so the Church has a simple task: prove this to the rest of the population.

I learned new information on the exact method of "clearing the planet," which is one of the main stated goals of Scientology. As a part of the course, I had to read the first half of one of Hubbard's books, *Science of Survival*. In the

---

[10] whole track: also referred to as time track, and refers to the duration of the entire physical universe

book, he describes his invention, the Tone Scale and explains its mechanics. In short, this scale mirrors the general emotional state of human beings, the highest point being enthusiasm (has a numerical value of 4.0 assigned to it), and the lowest above death is apathy (0.5). According to Hubbard, the turning point of the scale is the chronic emotional (tone) level of antagonism (2.0). If someone is chronically under 2.0 on the tone scale, he or she is generally in apathy, covertly hostile, in constant fear or anger, and thus is a liability to society. He wrote the following about it:

"The reasonable man quite ordinarily overlooks the fact that people from 2.0 down have no traffic with reason and cannot be reasoned with as one would reason with a 3.0."

"There are only two answers for the handling of people from 2.0 down on the tone scale, neither one of which has anything to do with reasoning with them or listening to their justification of their acts."

"The first is to raise them on the tone scale... by any one of the three valid processes. The other is to dispose of them quietly and without sorrow."

"Adders are safe bedmates compared to people on the lower bands of the tone scale. Not all the beauty nor the handsomeness nor artificial social value nor property can atone for the vicious damage such people do to sane men and women."

"The sudden and abrupt deletion of all individuals occupying the lower bands of the tone scale from the social order would result in an almost instant rise in the cultural tone and would interrupt the dwindling spiral into which any society may have entered."

"It is not necessary to produce a world of clears in order to have a reasonable and worthwhile social order; it is only necessary to delete those individuals who range from 2.0 down, either by processing them enough to get their tone level above the 2.0 line – a task which, indeed, is not very great, since the amount of processing in many cases might be under fifty hours, although it might also in others be in excess of two hundred – or simply quarantining them from the society. A Venezuelan dictator once decided to stop leprosy. He saw that most lepers in his country were also beggars. By the simple expedient of collecting and destroying all the beggars in Venezuela an end was put to leprosy in that country."

I completed this course on March 13th, 1997, 13:58, which was also a Thursday, the closest thing Scientology has to a holy day. This was a great deed on more than one count. First of all, March 13th is the birthday of Church founder L. Ron Hubbard and all Scientologists are expected to give some sort of gift to the man. All Hubbard reportedly wanted for his birthday was the expansion of Scientology, so the gift should be something that forwards the aims of the Church. A sizeable donation for a Church campaign or project would be appropriate or personal advancement on the Bridge to Total Freedom, e.g. completing a course or an auditing level. Also, I managed to complete the course just before 14:00, so it could be added to the weekly production statistic.

I was immediately started on the Ministerial Course, which I completed in two weeks. I had to read a 100-page book about the major religions of Earth (*Floyd H. Ross – Tynette Hill: The Great Religions By Which Men Live*), and then I had to learn and practice how to minister the wedding, naming and funeral ceremonies of Scientology.

Several types of wedding ceremonies were written by Hubbard. There was even a version which did not contain any Scientology terms, presumably for marriages where there were no Scientologists among the relatives. He designed a very short ceremony, too, where the minister could wed the young couple in his study like Friar Laurence from Shakespeare's *Romeo and Juliet*. (The seriousness of the course was aptly illustrated by the method the would-be minister had to practice ministering the various ceremonies. Basically, I had to use stuffed toy dolls as my "audience.")

I became an ordained minister of the Church by completing this course and later on, the draft board of the Hungarian Army accepted the certificate I received.

After this short detour, I had to redo the communications course. The Course Supervisors paid more attention to me and I almost managed to complete it again. While doing the exercises over and over again, I had a very interesting experience. I realized that the best way to communicate was just to communicate naturally and not to constantly have attention on myself, whether I was doing the exercises as Hubbard specified them or not. After one particularly successful day I felt that I reached a new level of spiritual awareness. For that day, my eyesight and hearing was much improved. I was so awake and aware of my surroundings that I had difficulty falling asleep. I genuinely felt that I had risen above the material universe.

Later on, I found out that many people achieved a similar, temporary state of elevated consciousness in Scientology and in other spiritual movements. It is called "ascension experience." Usually it does not last long – it is just a brief glimpse into the unknown.

Next day, I was back again in the mundane of everyday existence. I found myself stuck on the course again and was unable to consistently produce what was expected of me. I could not even do what I had managed to do earlier. As a good Scientologist, I tried to address the situation by applying more Scientology to it. I started to look for additional Hubbard writings on the subject to expand my understanding and get through this rough patch. I located a few more writings, but I did not find them particularly useful. While studying these bulletins, I noticed that one of them was not signed by Hubbard, but by David Mayo, who was supposed to be the "Senior Case Supervisor International" – an executive in international Scientology management who was supposed to be the ultimate international authority on all matters related to the technology (the entirety of the theory and practice) of Scientology. I had been in Scientology for over a year by this time and had attended several local events where video footage of international Scientology gatherings were shown. These events consisted of a series of speeches, given by the international executives of Scientology. As I remembered, the current Senior Case Supervisor International was named Ray Mithoff.

I asked one of the Course Supervisors about David Mayo. I just wanted to know who he was and why I had not heard of him before. The Supervisor gave me an icy stare and asked why I was interested. I showed him the bulletin I had found. He told me that there is nothing more to be known about him, I should just accept that he was no longer holding that post.

This story was not over, though. The next day I was sent straight to the Ethics Officer. I was not progressing and on top of it, I was asking strange questions. At that point, I was really mad at myself. I was sure that I had done something wrong, as I was convinced that Hubbard's technology was 100% workable. I had felt ashamed and guilty for not progressing properly and asking strange questions about this David Mayo. The Ethics Officer tried to find out why was I so interested in him, but I could not really come up with any sensible answer. I was sitting in his office, completely introverted, when I had a very strange notion. I recalled the section of the PTS/SP Course where Hubbard was talking about the "psychs" – what if these intergalactic criminals had implanted a hypnotic command into me in a last lifetime to investigate Scientology? I explained my thoughts to the Ethics Officer, who turned positively white and then red. The Church was reportedly under surveillance by the German national security agency, which made the staff extremely paranoid about any security breach. Anyone who was suspected of being a spy was instantly put on an e-meter for security checks. One of the telling indicators was asking too many or suspicious questions.

So, to put it mildly, this was not the answer the Ethics Officer was looking for. I was immediately assigned to menial labor (I had to clean the restrooms of the org, as part of that assignment) and I was presented with a number of official Church issues about David Mayo, depicting him as a hardened criminal.

My entire world view was in tatters. One of the key executives of Scientology was a suppressive person? Why was he not caught earlier? It had happened once so what was the guarantee that it would not happen again? For all we knew then, there could be more SPs in International Management. And to make matters worse, it turned out that Mayo was the personal auditor of L. Ron Hubbard and one of his most trusted aides.

I could not understand how an SP could achieve such a high rank in Scientology, doing the entire training part of the Bridge (he was a "Class XII" auditor after all, which is the highest possible classification in Scientology). Hubbard repeatedly stated that suppressive persons are incapable of changing for the better and therapy (including Scientology) does not have any effect on them. I asked the Ethics Officer about this and he told me that Mayo pretended to achieve those abilities and gains, as he had been sent by the secret societies (the puppet masters of the "psychs") which control the world to destroy the Church. This official story had quite holes in it, but having no other choice if I wanted to continue in Scientology, I accepted it at that time.

In addition to the cleaning detail, I had to study five hours a day. My assignment was to listen to the tapes of one of the congresses held by Hubbard, called "The State of Man Congress." To sum it up, it was about one's own fate and responsibility and how someone is 100% responsible for everything that is happening to him. It did not exactly made me feel better, I felt even more at fault for the situation I found myself in.

After a week of cleaning and listening to Hubbard's lectures (I also read a few more Church writings about Mayo), I had a terrible realization. What if my progress is blocked because the staff members of Munich Org are not applying the technology correctly? There might be an SP here, too. I recalled one of the Hungarian trainees telling me that there must be an SP in the org, as it was not doing well.

After I gave that some thought, I decided to leave this den of suppressive persons. I wrote a bunch of reports on the org and its staff, sent it to the international management of Scientology and left Munich Org that night for good. I travelled back to my hometown, Pécs.

CHAPTER THREE

Between Two Lives

CLUELESSNESS

After arriving back home, I reported for duty at Pécs Mission and had a talk with the Executive Director. He did not really know what to do with this situation and nor did I.

I was still convinced that I should continue my Scientology career. Due to what had transpired in Munich Org, I thought maybe it would be better to work at a higher level organization, so I could make sure that Scientology operated exactly as Hubbard intended. Hubbard kept on repeating in his writings that his methods are fully workable, and their correct and full application would inevitably lead to huge expansion. I believed in him, so I thought that contributing to the enforcement of "standard tech" (as he called it) would be the best course of action.

In fact, there was an organization dedicated to upholding Hubbard's standards. It was called the Sea Organization or Sea Org, which was officially operating as a fraternal religious order, but it was rather an umbrella organization for all upper management staff. Additionally, membership in the Sea Organization was a requirement for working in the higher level service organizations of Scientology.

The Sea Org was founded in 1967 by Hubbard himself and was at that time operating on a small fleet of ships (hence its name). He appointed himself its Commodore. Only the most dedicated Scientologists were invited to join the organization and they had to sign a symbolic billion year contract and dedicate their lives to the Church.

The Sea Org has moved to land bases since then, but retained most of its tradition. Pay was still minimal, somewhere around 0-50 USD/week, depending on the income of the organization. Free time is minimal – you are almost always working for the Church when you are awake. Food and berthing are provided by the Church. You can have a day off every second week if your statistics are up, and theoretically, you can have a three-week vacation each year, but it was very rare that somebody was allowed to leave for such a long time. You know, the planet will not clear itself, so...

Anyway, I thought that joining the Sea Org would be the most optimum solution for my situation, but I had to face the music in the mission first.

Understandably, they were not really happy about my dismal failure, so I received another amends project to complete. I had to distribute a huge stack of fliers again, outside working hours, but at least it was summer. In my working hours, I was evaluating personality tests and selling Dianetics books to new public.

One day, unexpected guests arrived to the mission – a visit from the Commanding Officer of the newly formed Sea Org unit in Hungary, who also brought his deputy along. Apparently, it was prompted by one of the "unorthodox" measures taken by Csaba. They informed us that they are doing a so-called observation mission, so we should just get on with our work as if they were not here.

That was the first time I met with "Lt. Commander" Miklós Fekete, the highest ranking Scientologist in Hungary, the charismatic Commanding Officer of OTL (Operations & Transport Liaison) Hungary, which was the management unit responsible for all Scientology activities in the region, manned exclusively by Sea Org members.

They largely ignored the rank-and-file staff and concentrated their efforts on Csaba, who seemed to enjoy the attention. He kept saying that he had no real position – he was officially just an expeditor, assigned to handle backlogged tasks. Miklós then asked him why was he giving orders and why was he acting as an executive. He replied with his trademark mischievous grin that he was expediting things in the Executive Division as that's where most of the backlogs were.

Miklós then tried to get the Executive Director to assign Csaba a real position. He explained that Csaba is the "heart and soul" of the mission. Miklós then tried to get him to show the "heart and soul" post title on the org board (organizational chart) of the mission, but gave up after a while.

Meanwhile, Csaba was busily studying the license agreement and incorporation documents of the mission, which were supplied by international church management. He found out that no Sea Org member can enter a mission in an official capacity without a prior written authorization from Scientology Missions International, an entity within the Sea Org. They had quite an argument with Miklós about this (who showed him the writings of Hubbard about the unlimited ethics powers of Sea Org missions and other relevant references), and shortly after that the "observation mission" departed. Despite that rather poor showing, I still wanted to join the Sea Org, but I crossed off OTL Hungary from the list of Sea Org units to consider.

I did some research on the current structure of the Sea Org, and it seemed to be the best choice to try my luck in the US, namely at the "Mecca of Scientology," called "Flag Service Org" or "Flag" inside Scientology. It was the largest Scientology organization on the planet, manned exclusively by Sea Org members. As an added bonus, it was located in Clearwater, Florida.

They had a recruitment office in Budapest, so I went to the capital and met the two recruiters there. They were rather surprised to see someone wanting to join the Sea Org on his own volition. They were used to lengthy conversations and tough recruitment interviews, and usually it took a lot of convincing to get anyone to join. They voiced their concerns; namely, people who voluntarily want to join the Sea Org are usually either not qualified in the first place or have "other fish to fry" (gaining entry to the US through the Church). But, I managed to ease their concerns and László, the senior recruiter, promised that he would travel to Pécs and handle the mission and my parents.

He came down two weeks later and managed to arrange my release from my contract. He then told me that joining the Sea Org at Flag would take a bit more time, as I had to get a US visa and a security clearance from the Church. László wanted me to move to their apartment/office in Budapest while we handled these matters. I agreed and moved to Budapest.

ON THE WAY TO THE SEA ORG

As part of the application process, I had to fill out several questionnaires. Among them was the "Life History Form," which had a very long list of questions, covering virtually every aspect of one's life. I had to provide a lot of sensitive and private data about myself – I had to provide an itemized list of a) all the debts I had (if any) b) any and all (!) sexual encounters of any kind (including one-night stands and providing the names of all partners) and any perversions I was involved in (if any). I had to divulge if I ever had any homosexual urges or actual intercourse (again, the form asked for the name of the partner, too), as well as declaring whether I ever had suicidal thoughts and if any of them resulted in a suicide attempt. I had to declare if I ever committed any actionable criminal acts and list them if so.

When this form was completed, I had to get an e-meter check on it. The auditor asked in ten different ways whether I left something out (Did you fail to give any information on the form? Was there something omitted? Are you hiding anything? etc.). I passed the test (I did, in actual fact, answer all questions truthfully), and all these materials were faxed (!) to Clearwater.

I signed the employment contract for the next billion years and I was sworn in to serve the Sea Organization. There was even a ceremony for that – László and his assistant conducted it in full dress uniform. I had to read aloud the Code of a Sea Org Member and swear to uphold it under any and all circumstances. I pledged my unquestioned loyalty to Scientology and L. Ron Hubbard. It was quite a solemn ceremony and had a profound effect on me.

After all the paperwork was done, I submitted my application for an US visa, namely the R-1 visa for religious workers. According to László, its creation by U.S. Citizenship and Immigration Services was a direct result of successful lobbying conducted by the Church. In order to qualify for that visa, the applicant had to be a member of the Church for at least 2 years and only religious workers or ministers were eligible.

I could not help but notice that recruitment personnel had no problem lying or being liberal with facts and reality, when it came to presenting documents to "wog" (a derogatory term for non-Scientologists) authorities. There was enormous pressure on László (and apparently, on all other recruiters scattered across the globe) to send a lot of Sea Org recruits to Flag. They got at least 3-5 phone calls per day, and sometimes they were so loud that even I could hear the yelling and threats. They also received various faxed orders from time to time. The minimum expectation was to send at least one new recruit each week.

So, in short, the recruitment tour had to locate Scientologists who met the following criteria:

1. were fully qualified to join the Sea Org. For example, taking any LSD ever made one unqualified and no petitions were allowed; other qualification points were any visits to a psychiatrist or even a psychologist, having sizeable debts or children who were legally minors, having any relationship to national security agencies or having a family member who was antagonistic to Scientology;
2. had to speak at least some rudimentary English;
3. and then they had to be convinced to sign a billion year contact and burn all bridges behind them
4. had to get a US visa and meet the requirements thereof;
5. had to pay for an airplane ticket to Tampa, Florida (as the Church did not cover the airfare).

It was not an easy task to find suitable candidates, so if László managed to get someone to sign the Sea Org contract, he did not stop at anything (except willful forgery) to get a visa for that person, and his bosses in Clearwater assisted him willingly in providing whatever documents he requested. A good portion of the prospects did not meet the 2-year membership requirement, which was circumvented by locating any evidence of contacting that person, for example the first Scientology personality test they ever filled out (these were always dated), even if the person did not become a member at that time. As far as I know, they never resorted to forging documents, knowing full well the consequences of visa fraud. In order to prove that the applicants were in fact religious workers, the recruitment office in Clearwater sent invitation letters, detailing their future jobs. They were pretty inventive, e.g. if someone barely spoke any English, then he was invited to "cater to the spiritual needs" of the (nonexistent) community of Hungarian Scientologists in Clearwater.

If a visa application was rejected, then he was sent back over and over again and new documents were sent if requested; for example, if the consul was unsure what the applicant would do in the US exactly. The Scientologists visiting the US Embassy had to write detailed reports about their visa interview and they were extensively drilled by László on how to answer the questions asked by the consul.

At that time, there was a "situation." The consul responsible for immigration and visa matters was regularly rejecting Scientology-related applications, or at least that's what László and other recruitment personnel believed. He was regularly asking for additional documents, clarifications and according to László, always tried to find a way to reject the visa applications. Only Scientologists with a good command of English and had an overwhelming amount of proper documentation got R-1 visas easily. Therefore he was an "enemy," and recruiters in Clearwater had pushed the legal department of the Church (the infamous Office of Special Affairs) to investigate him. László told me that he was informed by his Clearwater bosses that the consul was in fact a *homosexual*. Then he referred me to Hubbard's book, *Science of Survival*. According to Hubbard, homosexual people were at the chronic tone level of covert hostility (1.1 was the numerical value assigned to it) on the Tone Scale, so they were incapable of real emotions, and secretly destroyed the lives of decent people around them. So the consul was a 1.1, backstabbing suppressive person. László also told me that the Clearwater office of OSA[11] had complained to the U.S. State Department and played the religious discrimination card, so we should not worry, sooner or later a new consul would arrive.

I had a relatively easy time with the visa application. I was officially a minister, had a nice certificate proving it and I spoke very good English. László even sent me to an ecclesiastical shop to get a black clerical shirt with a white collar, just to make it sure I conveyed the right image. I got an R-1 visa at the first attempt.

---

[11] OSA or Office of Special Affairs: the legal, intelligence and PR arm of the Church. It is a separate network inside Scientology. Its functions included monitoring the enemies of Scientology as well as suspicious members of the Church. They work with the attorneys and sometimes employ Private Investigators for certain operations. They also supervise the Citizens' Commission on Human Rights, an anti-psychiatry organization founded by the Church.

While I was waiting for my visa to arrive, I helped others get theirs, and acted as an interpreter to help those who did not speak English well enough to speak with the consul.

While working there, I gained some insight into the everyday workings of the recruitment office. László had a rather lengthy list which contained all Scientologists in Hungary, with remarks and descriptions added to almost all entries. The list had a section called the "DB Section." DB was an abbreviation for "Degraded Being." According to Hubbard, DBs were under suppression for a lengthy period and were wrecked by it in this or in an earlier lifetime, and thus were unable to function normally. They always felt an internal compulsion to disobey any orders given and were unrepentant "alterers" – incapable of doing exactly what was asked of them and if they were to pass information along, they would surely alter it. Additionally, they had an inherent hatred of "big beings" like L. Ron Hubbard (and presumably, the better Scientologists).

László added those Scientologists to the DB section whom he considered to be a waste of time for recruitment purposes. This section even had a special part, reserved for the so-called "five star DBs," who had to be avoided at all costs, since any communication with them was considered to be a waste of precious time and resources.

László, in one of his honest moments, told me about his experiences as a Sea Org recruiter in Clearwater. He recounted how hard it was sometimes to speak with OTs about the Sea Org. He had met Scientologists who had completed OT III and even OT V, but according to him, were still DBs and gave him ridiculous excuses for not joining the Sea Org. This was a minor shock for me, as Hubbard said that OT III cures that condition.

Meanwhile, Flag security personnel reviewed my application, and were not too happy about the whole Munich affair and especially the part about me being an implanted spy investigating Scientology. The Security Chief of Flag was apparently very strict regarding Sea Org qualifications and asked further question about anything he considered even remotely suspicious, sometimes bordering on paranoia. I remember one night when the phone rang at 2:00 AM (László was under strict orders to be available at any time). A security staff member was calling from Clearwater, asking for help in translating an answer to a Life History question. Under "government relations and contacts," one of the Hungarians wrote that he was working for a state-owned pig farm, spelling its name in Hungarian (he probably did not know the English word for it). They wanted László to tell them what sort of government agency that was...

I got the visa from the US Embassy a few days later, but I still did not receive approval from Flag to arrive there. László convinced me to go anyway, so I could answer any remaining questions on the ground. He then sold the whole idea to my parents and even got them to pay for the airplane ticket. So it was, in August 1997, I went to Clearwater to start a career, which was supposed to last for the next billion years.

THE MECCA OF SCIENTOLOGY

To be honest, when I disembarked at Atlanta airport (I had to change to a domestic flight there to get to Tampa), I had the feeling that I had arrived in the land of freedom. The US was somehow *different*. Not necessarily on the material plane, but rather on the spiritual level. This made me even more enthusiastic about the whole adventure.

It was late night when I finally arrived in Clearwater. I was taken straight to the recruitment office. The first thing I noticed was the diverse ethnicity of the staff. The division head was English, her deputy was French, the head of the personnel department was German, the recruitment officer was Italian and an American girl was doing all the paperwork.

When I first entered the office, a French Sea Org officer greeted me in full dress uniform. We had a small chat about my plans. He introduced himself as Alain Kartuzinski. I turned out that he was a Class XII auditor, which is the highest training level obtainable in the Church. He was practically halfway through the Bridge to Total Freedom. It was a bit strange to see such a highly trained person in the recruitment section. Class XII auditors were delivering the most expensive auditing at Flag and as far as I know, there were only a dozen or so of them. But, I learned my lesson not to ask questions like this.

(Note: I found out the truth 10 years later. Alain was involved in the series of events that had led to the unfortunate death of Lisa McPherson, a Scientologist at Flag. I think that's why he was assigned to the recruitment office. While in the Church, I had never even heard about Lisa.)

Half an hour later, Kathrin, the head of the personnel department came to see me. She explained that security was still undecided about my qualifications and overall eligibility due to the incidents in Munich. Until my application was approved by them, I could not move into staff berthing and I had to find a place to sleep. I had to pay for a few nights in one of the hotels of the Church. I did warn Kathrin that I did not have much money and I could only pay for a few days. She told me that they will ask one of the local Scientologists to provide a spare room for me.

The next morning I was told that a decision had been made and I needed to get a special metered auditing to clarify what went down in Munich. It was called PDH (Pain, Drug, Hypnosis) Check. As I understood, it was an often-used counterespionage tool to weed out infiltrators. Priest-penitent privilege did not apply to that sort of auditing, so they could use anything I said against me. It was basically an interrogation, using the e-meter as a lie detector. Some of the questions were quite laughable, like "Have you come here to kill L. Ron Hubbard?" Hubbard mandated that his standard tech was unalterable, so all auditing question remained the same after his death, including this.

Kathrin told me that it would take a while until they found an auditor to deliver the check. And I had to start doing some sort of work for the Church – if I wanted to eat at the Church dining room, that is. As a temporary measure, I was sent to the in-house print & copy shop to help sort publications and issues. The head of the shop was an Australian teenager, so I became familiar with a new type of English accent.

While working, I could not resist the temptation and read some the issues printed there. There was an "orders of the day" or OOD, printed each morning, issued by the Commanding Officer and other executives to the crew. I found out that around 1400 Sea Org members were working for the Church in Clearwater and it owned 23 buildings (of various sizes). These were referred to by two- or three letter abbreviations (Hubbard and his followers seem to LOVE abbreviations for some reason). The main building, named Fort Harrison Hotel, was simply referred to as "FH." The Clearwater Building, where the kitchen and dining facilities were located, was known as "CB," and so on.

I came across a confidential issue, which shed some light on the real nature of Scientology. The bulletin was a description of a special auditing process, which was only available in Clearwater (and consequently, it was rather expensive), called the "Fixated Person Rundown." Basically, it consisted of asking two questions repeatedly of the patient. Two questions. I remembered these two questions from another Scientology publication – a compilation of the most simple and basic auditing processes of Scientology.

I realized that the behind the grandiose names ("Fixated Person Rundown," "Prosperity Rundown," "Super Power Rundown" etc.) one found very simple processes, taken from the basic books of Scientology, yet sold for exorbitant prices with a lot of effort put into marketing. The processes were simply repackaged – just like taking a cheap plastic trash can, giving it nice packaging, renaming it "Super Trash Container Extra 2014" and selling it for five times the normal price.

After working there for a week or so, I was told by Kathrin that they managed to find an auditor to deliver the Pain-Drug-Hypnosis check. I received it, passed and then waited for the Security Office to make up their minds. Kathrin was trying to do her best to keep me calm and patient – she told me a story about a Hungarian recruit. He arrived to Flag, and while he was waiting for the paperwork, he went out to smoke a little bit to calm his nerves. He was anxious about the whole adventure, and mistakenly threw a burning cigarette stub into a trash can. It caught fire and the fire alarm went off. Church Security grabbed him, put him into a car and announced their intent of putting "the Communist arsonist" on the next plane to Hungary. The recruitment office successfully thwarted the attempt, though and managed to get him approved by Security in the end. The guy eventually graduated basic training and was now posted as a security guard.

In addition to the print shop, I also had to help the recruiters. One day, I was instructed to get Hubbard's bust from one of the ground floor storage rooms to the so-called Crystal Ballroom on the top floor. It was a tad heavy, so I put it on the floor in the elevator. Unfortunately, there was a Sea Org executive travelling with me. He got really upset, accused me of "degrading LRH" and had me pick up the bust. I quickly grabbed it and laid it on my shoulder, with its face down. He did not like that either. In the end, I had to carry it in my hands, holding it in front of me. According to official Church communication, Hubbard was considered to be a simple man, who happened to the greatest friend of mankind. In reality, he was worshipped much like a god.

I had another interesting experience. When I had signed the Sea Org contract in Budapest and the recruiters told me all the conditions of working for the Sea Org, they were very clear about one point: you cannot have children in the Sea Org. Should a female Sea Org member become pregnant, she either had to undergo an abortion or face dismissal from the organization. Earlier, it had been permitted to have children, but the couple had to agree to be moved to a small, non-expanding Scientology org. According to the recruiters, it did not work out very well, so for the sake of saving the planet, not having children was a necessary sacrifice.

All Sea Org members in Clearwater had labels on their shirts, giving their name, rank and post. One day I bumped into a very young girl (around 10-12 years old), who had a striking resemblance to David Miscavige, the *de facto* leader of the Church. According to her lapel, her name was Jenna Miscavige. I asked Kathrin about her later that day. She told me that Jenna is the daughter of Miscavige's brother, a member of International Management.

Naturally, this was not in alignment with the aforementioned internal policies, but I had learned to ignore this type of contradiction by then.

Meanwhile, the Security Office made a decision and wanted a tailor-made security check to be done on me. This was again a lengthy interrogation, conducted using an E-meter. The intent of the questions was obvious: they wanted to know if I had ever committed any crime and they wanted to know every little detail about my relationship with the members of my family.

It came up during the interrogation that back in high school, I had read some Scientology materials on the Internet that the Church considered to be "confidential, upper level" material.

I got the feeling that they were glad – they finally had an excuse to get rid of me! I was told by a security guard that I had to prove that I was a good and dedicated Scientologist – but in Hungary. He told me that I had 24 hours to leave the "base." In order to resubmit my application, I had to have a good "production record" outside of the Sea Org to make up for my unfortunate adventure in Munich and looking into confidential materials.

I did not have much choice, so I rebooked my ticket and boarded the next Tampa – New York flight. Upon arriving at JFK airport in New York, I discovered the next Budapest flight was cancelled due to security reasons. So, as the only major positive moment of my ill-fated visit to the States, I was able to spend a night in New York, all paid for by the airline.

THE FLAG WORLD TOUR

Upon arriving in Budapest, I reported to László and told him what had gone down. We agreed that I would help him in the office to build up a production record and I would be ready to assist the personnel of the upcoming "Flag World Tour" event (a promotional show of the organization in Clearwater) if needed. Eventually, we would try again to get my application approved.

I started to work for László. As a part of my duties, sometimes I had to pay a visit to the local Sea Org unit in Budapest called "OTL Hungary," and I was unimpressed with what I saw.

(Note: as a good Scientologist, I dutifully asked László what OTL stands for, so I would not go past a misunderstood word. He explained that it is an abbreviation of Operations and Transport Liaison. This name did not sound too religious, so they had to work out an acceptable one that was also abbreviated as OTL. Finally, it was incorporated as a religious order of the Church of Scientology Hungary called "Országos Tanács és Lelkészség," i.e. "National Council and Clergy" in English.) It was good enough for the wogs, and they were satisfied with knowing the truth.

They rented two apartments – one was used as the main office in the day and as a berthing facility in the night. The other one was the "training org" (and staff berthing No. 2.). The office equipment had been obtained in a rather economical fashion – most of the desks were the familiar green school desks I spent so much time sitting behind in elementary and high school. The rest looked like "repurposed" furniture, most likely brought by staff members straight from their garages and sheds. One of the rooms featured a weathered couch and two armchairs, too (I was sure that the set was older than me). The loft was crowded with sleeping bags and mattresses.

One day I went there around noon, so I had the opportunity to check out the food. They were eating something yellow that remotely resembled rice. I did not even want to know what it was. The attitude was also less than charming – one of the deputies of Miklós, the "commanding officer", made a derogatory remark on my tenure as a mission staff member, stating that all mission staff were doing all day was "dev-t" (short for "developed traffic," i.e. unnecessary work) . Unsurprisingly, I decided that I would never become a Sea Org member at this base.

A few weeks later, the personnel of the Flag World Tour arrived to set up the big event. The tour consisted of a young Dutch lady (responsible for invitations and attendance confirmations), her Italian husband (tasked with setting up the event itself) and a Swiss couple, Mr. and Mrs. Alan Juvonen. Alan was responsible for the most important aspect of the tour: sales and gross income, while his wife was charged with delivering free e-metered "case assessment interviews," a ploy to get people to come in for Scientology's trademark hard sell "registration" (sales) interviews. The original plan for the event was simple enough – they were to show a promotional video of the Mecca of Scientology in Clearwater (which had a distinct '80s infomercial style that closely resembled similar videos produced by US MLM groups), then the public would be assaulted by a horde of makeshift "Registrars," aiming to sell as many Flag services as possible. Compared to their American counterparts, the majority of the Hungarian Scientologists were not really wealthy, so Alan was not exactly enthusiastic about this trip to Budapest. He knew that he had to meet his money quota no matter what, so he started to speak to the locals to get some ideas. He asked me how one could influence Hungarians concerning spiritual matters, what are their buttons. I gave him a brief summary of the 1000-year history of the Hungarian nation, the effects of the two world wars and the Treaty of Trianon and how proud we were of the numerous Nobel laureates we had produced. He listened intently and came to the conclusion that Hungarians consider themselves the spiritual leaders of the region, and he would mention this in his introductory speech to gain the affection of the locals. I was a bit baffled by this, as according to the basic tenets of Scientology, we were all spiritual beings and nationality supposedly had absolutely zero significance inside the Church. But then I figured he was a mighty OT and a veteran Sea Org member after all, so he must know best.

Alan also talked to László frequently, trying to figure out how he would survive the extremely low income he predicted for the event. He had very high quotas for each event held, irrespective of location. As I wrote earlier, there were only a handful of rich men in Scientology in Hungary at that time, and they had not done enough auditing and training services to be eligible for the advanced ones delivered by Flag.

As they say, necessity is the mother of invention, so Alan finally came up with an idea to save his skin. He would give his speech after the video. In the speech, he planned to give high praise to Hungarians, followed by his trick: he would invite every attendee to pay around 5 USD in cash to Flag for a future service as a down payment to "start the flow." He had us put an envelope on each chair for that purpose. This would not amount to much financially (around 300-400 attendees were expected), but it would mean 300 new names to the Central Files of Flag. He hoped to escape the wrath of his senior for the lack of significant gross income by sending another important statistic into screaming affluence.

The event was scheduled for the following Saturday, but there was a slight logistics issue (and as I found out later, it was a rather common occurrence in the Sea Org) – the package containing the VHS tape of the event video would arrive on Friday morning, and it had to be dubbed before the event. The Italian Sea Org member gave me the task of getting the tape through Customs. I did not know that he was just looking for a fall guy, as Customs officials told him that it was IMPOSSIBLE to complete all the paperwork on Friday.

At around 11:00 AM on Friday, I was dispatched to the airport to get the videotape, as it was stuck at the Customs office (as predicted). I was definitely not a popular person, as the customs men were already clock-watching and making their weekend plans. After a lengthy conversation with the officials (I told them, among other things, that this was going to be a historic event that would literally save the world), one of them finally got bored with my enthusiastic lecture and grudgingly filled out all the papers, likely just to shut me up.

I triumphantly returned to the office. The Italian guy was genuinely surprised. He thanked me quickly and rushed to a nearby studio to get the dubbing done.

Meanwhile, László was talking (shouting would be a better word to describe it) with someone on the phone.

"Csaba, this is called SABOTAGE!" he screamed at the top of his lungs. He was talking to my ex-boss in Pécs Mission, who did not really want to bring people to the event. I was startled by the situation, as I had never before witnessed a Sea Org member doing something like that. László assured me that this is pretty common in the Sea Org, and there is even a policy letter from Hubbard stating that you would need to shout at the dumb ones if that was required to get your job done. He told me a few stories to illustrate that from his days at Flag. It was a strict rule though that your higher-up were not allowed to do this in front of public Scientologists, so his boss usually brought him to a basement office for the 10-minute yelling sessions.

He also told me about what happens to those Sea Org members whose statistics are down for three weeks in a row. They are humiliated in front of the entire crew of Flag at the weekly staff meeting – they have to stand on a stage as the "saboteurs" who destroy the fruits of the hard work of the rest. László had to go through this ordeal two times while he was serving there. It was obvious from the manner of his retelling that it had a profound effect on him. He said that it was a harrowing experience to stand as the focal point of the raw hate of over a thousand people.

The next day, I was sent to the dubbing studio to find out how the Hungarian version of the event was coming along. When I arrived the first 10 of the 45 minutes were ready. The head of the studio, also a Scientologist, laughed at my questions and told me that it would be impossible to do it properly in the available time window. He was probably right, but I have learnt my lesson from the Sea Org members – the right attitude is to get the job done no matter what obstacles one encountered. It was called "making it go right."

We completed the whole video as best as we could, even I had to lend my voice as not everyone showed up who was called in (everyone involved was a Scientologist).

The dubbing (along with the necessary editing and remixing tasks) was completed half an hour before the scheduled start of the event. The end product turned out to be rather faulty. There was no time to mix the audio track properly and the volunteers (including me) were subpar as dubbing actors. It was watchable, but it also needed some extra concentration and effort on the part of the viewers to understand what was said.

We hopped into the Lada of the studio owner and rushed through the city to the event hall. Fortunately, it was at the end of August, and traffic was light so we made it just in time.

The event went along nicely just as Alan planned. He managed to win over the Hungarians (he already won the battle by stating that he was an actual OT VII – an unlikely sight in Hungary at that time), and got the attendees to stuff some cash into the prepared envelopes. The trick worked and his bosses appreciated the solution, too. Nevertheless, he was not yet off the hook. He still had to rake in a sizeable amount of dough. Alan managed to get the Executive Director of Budapest Mission to turn over the "rich person list" and called these in for "interviews," and he also got the Registrar to name anyone with sizeable assets. I could see with my own eyes that he was under tremendous pressure – he received regular phone calls during the day, his seniors were constantly demanding (either nicely or in a threatening manner, depending on the progress made) the "product": sign-ups and more importantly, money. It definitely worked, as Alan managed to squeeze a nice amount of money (around 45,000 USD) out of the few who were qualified to go to Flag for services. They were then allowed to leave Budapest for their next destination.

László resubmitted my application to Clearwater. The Security Chief was still unimpressed and it was clear that they would not let me join the Sea Org there anytime soon. Therefore I decided to look for another Sea Org unit, which would take me in regardless of what I had done in the past.

CHAPTER FOUR

A New Sea Org Member is Born

TO BERLIN!

I continued to work for László, still trying to figure out how to continue in Scientology. I had not completely given up on the idea of working in Clearwater one day, but I did not see how I could accomplish it in the near future. Despite all the negative experiences I had there, I was still a dedicated member of the Church. I still thought that being a Sea Org member was the ultimate way to help humanity and to achieve the aims of Scientology. The utopian "new civilization," a very attractive promise of the movement, seemed to be worth any sacrifice.

Earlier I decided against joining the local Sea Org unit in Budapest, but now there seemed to be no other way to become a Sea Org member.

A protest at the German embassy, organized by the infamous Office of Special Affairs, gave me the final push. László was asked by the OTL to "loan" me for the protest. I was an actual minister of the Church, so I was an ideal candidate for the little act they planned for the protest. I was to dress in a ministerial garment, complete with a large Scientology cross and then two muscular guys would restrain and silence me. That was supposed to symbolize the suppression of our "religious freedom" in Germany. As far as I know, German authorities did not recognize Scientology as a religion and their national security agency kept us under constant surveillance. I was told that there were one or two pending lawsuits, with dire financial consequences should they be lost.

László was also invited to attend the protest, but he just sent a message to Miklós, the CO (Commanding Officer) of the OTL, stating that a) he was officially on a recruitment mission in Hungary, and b) he was under strict orders not to get involved in any local mess or problem.

When I relayed this message to Miklós, he had a laugh (he actually said that László must have misunderstood the phrase "local mess"), and did not pursue this any further. Around a hundred people attended the demonstration. I had an opportunity to talk with some of the OTL staff members and I was pleasantly surprised, they seemed to be genuinely decent people. Though my first impression of the Hungarian Sea Org outfit was rather unflattering, I had to admit that there was no other realistic option for me to lend a hand to "saving the planet." I overcame my critical thoughts, and went into the OTL. I told them I wanted to work here and told them my story. My application was accepted and I moved to the OTL berthing spaces a few days later (naturally, the only condition I got was that it had to happen before Thursday, 14:00).

Since I spoke English, I was assigned to the translations unit. The schedule mirrored the "it's a calling, not a job" idea. The official working hours were between 9:00 – 22:30 plus overtime if something needed to be completed, so we rarely finished working before 11:00 PM. As around twelve of us were living in the flat that we also used as the main office and there was only one bathroom, it was practically impossible to get on a mattress or bedroll before midnight. Saturday was the only exception as we had the whole morning on that day for our personal hygiene and cleaning needs.

The money allocated for food was the lowest priority, so we had to get creative in that regard. The Deputy Commanding Officer taught me the recipe of the "OTL special." He put a slice of buttered bread into the microwave oven (which was made in the Soviet Union by the look of it), waited until the butter melted and then put some powdered condiments on it. I will never forget his face when he ate this delicacy and said "It's better than McDonald's!"

When I joined them, the whole OTL was busy getting people confirmed for a demonstration organized by OSA International. It was to take place in Berlin, on the 27th of October. The Church planned to protest against the suppression it was experiencing in Germany, using the religious persecution card (and to a smaller extent, the Holocaust card, as they tried to find similarities between the persecution of the Jews and the situation Scientology found itself in).

Miklós totally switched into his enthusiastic freedom fighter mode and wanted to bring 2000 people from Hungary to aid in the battle against the damn Nazi suppressives. Practically everyone was working on this target, neglecting all other duties. Miklós was coordinating the entire effort and was on the phone constantly, calling and activating all missions, along with the local representative of Scientology Mission International, a young girl named Melinda.

On paper, they had the same rank and Miklós was not her boss, but that had never stopped Miklós from giving orders to her and anyone working in OTL for that matter. The organizational chart of the Sea Org was a very complex one, probably "Byzantine" is the best word to use. Though Miklós was the commander of the Hungarian Sea Org "base" (two rented apartments and 20 people), the executives or representatives over the various areas of the network of Scientology (missions, field auditors, Scientologist businessmen etc) were not directly under him - he was just supposed to "coordinate" their activities, as their bosses were their European counterparts located in Denmark.

As far as I knew, this system was the brainchild of David Miscavige, the supreme leader of the Church of Scientology, and it was introduced in 1996, causing a great deal of chaos. Nevertheless, the sheer force of personality of Miklós was sufficient to get what he wanted, no matter how these "executives" tried to resist his orders or avoid any unpleasant or labor-intensive tasks by quoting these policies.

In order to improve our efficiency, Miklós explained to us the "principle of five phone calls" during our weekly staff meeting. This principle was valid only for getting Scientologists into action, who were not as dedicated as Sea Org members. According to Miklós, you had to call someone five times, before he or she would actually start doing something effective.

After the first call, he would forget the whole thing and would not do anything. After the second call, he would remember that you called him earlier for the same reason, but would stop at this point. After the third call, he would realize what you wanted from him. After the fourth call, he would seriously contemplate that he should do something, but only after the fifth call would he take any action.

Miklós even fired a two-man mission to crank up the pressure on the so-called "field" (a collective name for all non-staff Scientologists). The missionaries were almost glued to the phone to get everyone agreeing to attend and bringing others. The goal of getting 2000 people was constantly hammered into their heads. Whoever picked up the phone at the OTL had to yell this slogan ("Berlin 2000!") into the receiver (imagine the surprise of my father when he tried to call me there once). Miklós was, in turn, called regularly from the European office to provide the number of people confirmed and paid for their tickets on the buses rented by the Church.

The situation rapidly escalated into an all-out effort to reach every Scientologist and to get them on the buses. In the final few days before the protest, two-man teams were formed and sent to all the missions in Hungary to get them enthused by holding small "activation" events.

Miklós told them to lock the doors and not to let anyone leave before he or she promised to be in Berlin.

The tools of persuasion included a famous Hungarian poem by Mihály Váci, called "Not yet enough," especially this part (a rough translation, it sounds much more fluid in Hungarian):

> "Don't just wish for good things,
> but really-really want them;
> and it's not enough to want,
> but you have to do things to have them!"

Another part of the toolset was a memorable scene from the Mel Gibson movie *Braveheart* (the passionate speech of the protagonist before the Battle of Stirling), which was shown as a part of the event. The main point was the idea of freedom and that Scientologists are now fighting for freedom (although in a peaceful manner).

One week before the event, Miklós got an order to contact other minority religions to swell the numbers, as the demonstration was about religious freedom after all. Small groups of three Sea Org members were formed and the smaller religious organizations in Hungary were assigned to them. My task force got the Mormons and the Jehovah's Witnesses. Our visits were completely ineffective, as the Hungarian religious minorities were completely uninterested in our problems.

Miklós got a call from OSA Europe that he should tell the Hungarian Hare Krishna community that the "great Sharma" was confirmed to attend the protest, as that might get them to come. Miklós did call their spokesperson who politely asked, "Which Sharma?" as apparently there were thousands of Sharmas.

Finally, we managed to get together around 600 people. When we arrived in Berlin, I was a bit disappointed to see that the protest was not such a big deal after all, considering the effort we put into it. Around 3000 people attended from all over the world. We marched from the rallying point to the Brandenburg Gate, where Church musicians performed a small concert, and the whole crowd sang together the unofficial hymn of the Church, a song called *We Stand Tall*. To be fair, this was a really uplifting experience and a fantastic feeling to sing along with a crowd of thousands and believe in a better future.

Mike Rinder, the head of OSA International gave a very passionate speech and sent a clear message the German government: "we are here to stay!" The whole event ended around 18:00. We stayed there to help dismantle the stage, as (unsurprisingly, I might add) no preliminary plans were made for that.

CONFRONTING THE PHYSICAL UNIVERSE

A few days after the Berlin protest, we got a new ultimatum from the European Scientology headquarters in Copenhagen. They somehow found out that there were some people posted in our Sea Org base who had not done proper Sea Org basic training yet. Miklós was ordered to handle this immediately.

Hubbard called this basic training "EPF," which stands for Estates Project Force. The name comes from the nature of this boot camp, as new recruits do 8-10 hours of manual labor ("estates work") daily. The stated purpose was to learn to "confront" the physical universe, i.e. to face it comfortably and be able to handle it, as its Scientology definition states. According to Hubbard, one had to be able to handle inanimate objects properly in order to graduate to handling people. In addition to this type of work, EPFers had to complete 5 basic courses. The targeted completion time for the EPF was 3 weeks, but it was not uncommon to take months if the candidate had study problems. No days-off, leaves etc. were allowed, and even spouses had to move into separate berthing (sleeping) spaces for the duration of the program.

The Hungarian Sea Org unit could not deliver this properly for a simple reason – there was no place to do manual labor. As I said earlier, the so-called "base" consisted of two rented flats in downtown Budapest. Ironically, the owner of the flat used as office space was the CEO of the largest economic newspaper in Hungary, which had published several anti-Scientology stories in the past. But this did not seem to bother the contracted parties. Money has no religious affiliation after all.

Note: The rental contract did have an interesting liability clause included – the person who signed it in on behalf of OTL had to personally and financially guarantee as a private individual that any damage to the apartment would be fully repaired. Naturally, Miklós had his deputy (who else would take the fall for the big boss?) sign the contract, which provided perfect joking opportunities as well. Any time a staff member bumped into a door or managed to damage a wall, he was ready to crack a liability clause joke on his unfortunate deputy.

But orders in the Sea Org were supposed to be complied with, no matter what it took, so the EPF was started and I was assigned to it. The manual labor part was "solved" by doing some cleaning work in a nearby building. Apparently, it did not satisfy our higher-ups in Copenhagen, so the local boot camp was cancelled and every trainee was ordered to report to Copenhagen, to the European Sea Org base.

Miklós pulled me aside before we left. He explained that there would be attempts in Copenhagen to "rip me off," i.e. to keep me there as a staff member. He told me some names who had been sent to Copenhagen for training, but never returned. So, basically I was supposed to ignore any promise/order/ threat they made and come back right after my EPF was complete. I was a bit baffled by all this, but I assured him that I would come back no matter what.

The facilities in Copenhagen looked like a proper Sea Org base for a change. Three large Scientology organizations were located in the city, employing hundreds of Sea Org members. The administrative headquarters of all Scientology activities for Europe was called Continental Liaison Office Europe, abbreviated as CLO EU. New Era Publications, the European publishing corporation of the Church was also housed in the same large building. The third was the Advanced Organization & Saint Hill Europe, or AOSH EU, which was located in another building owned by the Church. The "Saint Hill" designation referred to a range of services offered by the organization, which were identical to the ones available in the original international central service organization of the Church, located at "Saint Hill," an estate near East Grinstead, England. The Advanced Organizations were the ones authorized to deliver the "OT" levels.

The security office checked my papers, but surprisingly they did not make a big deal out of my misfortunes in Munich. Off I went to work and study.

The Church also owned three hotels in the city, which were used as staff berthing. I was sent to Hotel Corona, located near the harbor. When I was brought to my small room (which I had to share with seven other EPF'ers), I thought "Rather Rundown Workers' Hostel Corona" would have been a more appropriate name.

The glass of the only window in the room was broken, but for some reason the maintenance staff did not care to replace it. The entire room was about 16 square meters, and the majority of the space was occupied by three cupboards and four two-high bunk beds, leaving a small corridor in the centre to navigate among the towering cupboards and beds.

The so-called hotel looked like it had not had any proper maintenance for decades – broken windows, rickety old two- and three-bunk beds, worn wooden floor everywhere. The serious overcrowding of the building caused an ever-present distinct odor as well. The number of shower stalls was very inadequate, so normally I had to stand in a queue for 20-30 minutes, and I had a maximum of 3-4 minutes under the water. And you had to make it to the hotel really fast after work if you wanted warm water.

To be fair, it was clean and orderly, as any such offences were dealt with rather harshly. Regular inspections were conducted by Security and Ethics personnel, and if someone had not made his bed or cleaned up his part of the room, he received a chit. After the third chit, the offender was moved to the so-called "pig berthing." It was also a Hubbard policy, if someone did not maintain order and cleanliness in his room, then he must desire bad living conditions and who were we to stand in the way of his wishes. The pig berthing was a room with the occasional cockroach or two, which was either undergoing renovation or was in a decrepit condition, sometimes even lacking a window. The offender then had ample opportunity to consider the advantages of regular cleaning. The poor Sea Org member usually realized the error of his ways soon enough and wanted his old room back (which looked pretty nice compared to the pig berthing), but he had to demonstrate his commitment first by keeping "pig berthing" as clean and orderly as possible.

As I found out, all Sea Org members (except married couples and top executives) lived in similar conditions.

The other berthing building was called Hotel Nordland. It was in a bit better condition (the hallways were in much better shape), but the smell was the same. Room spaces were similarly utilized to the hilt. They had larger internal height though, so they used big three-level bunk beds (which I had never seen before) to maximize capacity. The ceiling was within arm's reach from the top bed.

The menial labor we had to do as EPFers was varied enough – mostly cleaning, maintenance and construction jobs (apparently, there was some push from the international church "uplines" to fully renovate the hotels). Sometimes we moved furniture.

As I mentioned earlier, five courses had to be completed as part of this basic training. The first was a course of Hubbard's study technology, called "Basic Study Manual" or BSM. It was kind of a heavily dumbed-down version of its big brother, the Student Hat (which I had already completed in Munich), so I did not have to do it. The second course was called "Welcome to the Sea Org." It consisted of five taped lectures of L. Ron Hubbard, all from the late '60s. In these lectures, he told his audience about his various exploits and adventures as a master mariner, and also explained his vision and plans for the Sea Organization. The last lecture was on the subject of public relations, where he savaged all major governments of Earth to make his point that Scientology was the only hope for the planet. He also made a bunch of predictions for the political future of various nations, but almost none of those came through (which planted another seed of doubt, but it was not enough at the time to shake my blind faith).

The audiovisual property production unit of the Church called Golden Era Productions had produced the lectures in Hungarian, too. A Hungarian D-list celebrity, who happened to be Scientologist, was cast as the voice talent. (Note: for some unknown reason, he was later replaced with a Hungarian Sea Org member with a slight speech impediment.) They made sure that he recounted the lecture in exactly the same style as Hubbard. It was clear that he had to emulate the old man, laugh when Hubbard laughed, raise his voice when Hubbard raised his etc. It was a bit bizarre, but apparently it was "what Ron wanted."

The "Introduction to Scientology Ethics" course came next. I had to study the book of the same title as well as a few internal Sea Org directives. Basically, the internal code of general conduct and discipline was taught on this course.

I learned two new things about the Sea Org. One was the peculiar way of addressing one's seniors. All of your higher-ups (including any and all staff members of organizations considered to be higher placed in the Byzantine internal network of Sea Org organizations) had to be called "Sir," regardless of gender. I did not really know why it was – I thought it was in alignment with the Scientology doctrine that we are genderless spiritual beings (i.e. only the body had gender).

The other was the rather draconian regulations regarding romantic relationships. Due to PR reasons (Hubbard's own words), it was forbidden to engage in sexual relationships out of wedlock. He also forbade any "heavy petting" before marriage. Any violation of these policies was to be dealt with severely, i.e. the offenders had to be thrown out of the Sea Org (or, as he put it, "beached").

Ironically, he did not give any definition of what he meant by "heavy petting," so the interpretation of policy was different in the various Sea Org outfits. I remember having a serious dispute about touching breasts and dictionary definitions of "heavy," "petting" and "heavy petting," between the Hungarian Sea Org unit and the Continental Liaison Office. A male Sea Org member touched the breasts of his girlfriend while kissing, and one overzealous guy in Copenhagen wanted to get the guy kicked out of the Sea Org for that heinous offence. Fortunately, it happened just before the "evolution" to translate the *What is Scientology?* book to thirteen or so languages hit the European base, so the whole issue was quickly forgotten.

Having and raising children was absolutely forbidden, and if a female Sea Org member got pregnant, she had to leave the Sea Org immediately or have an abortion (and they were often persuaded to do so, as unsurprisingly it was pretty hard to get someone to join the Sea Org in the first place).

There were severe consequences associated with violating the disciplinary codes. On paper, there was an internal justice system complete with courts, committees, hearings etc. to curb the excesses and people in the organization had certain rights, but I found this more or less a sham. The whim of those in positions of power was the dominant factor in justice proceedings. The so-called protective mechanisms were reduced to paperwork to make such decisions look right and show that they were in alignment with the policies of Hubbard.

The Sea Organization also had a sort of a "penal company" for repeat offenders, "chronic non-producers," "repeated stat-crashers" and those who violated the rules regarding romantic relationships. It was called the Rehabilitation Project Force (RPF). It was virtual imprisonment coupled with forced labor and mental reprogramming. The stated purpose of the RPF was to find and handle the underlying evil purposes of the individual which made him/her to commit such crimes, so he/she would become a productive member of the group once again.

Everyday life in the Sea Org, as bad as it was, looked like a walk in the park compared to the RPF. While on the basic training, I saw the "men in black" (RPF members were only allowed to wear plain black or gray clothing) running around (they had to run everywhere), and naturally, they were strictly limited to areas inaccessible to public Scientologists. I saw them mostly in the kitchen, doing the dirty work. If any of them made any grimace or talked back, the Sea Org members working in the kitchen were allowed to send them to run a few laps around the building as punishment.

A few more chilling facts about the RPF: a maximum 7 hours of sleep was allowed, the rest of the day was mostly taken up by either working or studying. RPFers were not allowed to initiate communication to anyone outside RPF and had to address any Sea Org member as "Sir," no matter how lowly the position or rank he or she held. Any personal belonging that would have interfered with the "rehabilitation" (non-Hubbard books, walkmans, radios, mobile phones, laptops, cartoons etc) were confiscated for the duration of the program. No holidays were allowed, every day was a working day, including Christmas and other traditional holidays. They had to have a security guard present when they spoke to their family members, giving only carefully worded and scripted answers. Outgoing letters were monitored to ensure that nothing went out which cast the Church in a negative light, and incoming letters were opened to filter out any "external influences."

Freedom of movement was also restricted, as they were not allowed to leave their place of work without supervision. They also had separate berthing spaces and married couples were separated for the duration of the program. If one's spouse was assigned to the RPF, then more often than not he or she was transferred to another country, and the word "divorce" was frequently mentioned. RPF dormitories were usually in even worse condition that the normal Sea Org ones; usually crammed with three-story beds and even more restricted shower and bathing options.

They also had to study 5 hours a day. They were twinned up and had to complete a simplified, "read it - drill it - do it" version of the auditor training courses and complete a series of e-metered confessionals on each other, uncovering all of their so-called crimes and underlying evil purposes. Their pay was also reduced (one quarter of the normal Sea Org pay, which was also a pittance) for the duration of the program.

It usually took at least a year for someone to get through the entire RPF lineup, but I heard of people who were on it for several years. Additionally, if your twin deserted from the Sea Org during the program, then you had some tough luck, as you had to restart the whole thing from scratch.

I fortunately was never assigned to the RPF, but I met a few people in the Sea Org who had done it. Unfortunately, they were rather tight-lipped, so I could not learn anything other than what I already knew from Hubbard's writings.

In retrospect, the whole RPF and the idea behind it was really horrific – the real purpose was to mentally break and reprogram someone and give them a new personality. It can even be called brainwashing as the desired end result was a Sea Org member with an unconditional belief in Hubbard and his "tech," who follows orders blindly and does whatever it takes to serve the Church.

The ethics course was followed by the Basic Sea Org Member Hat. It was a short course, explaining the communication and command channels within the Sea Org (all compiled from the writings of Hubbard).

The final one was called the Personal Grooming Course, which taught the unsuspecting wannabe Sea Org member the proper way to wash his/her clothes and brush his teeth (seriously), and introduced a whole lot of various uniforms and insignia. I learned something new here – it was strictly forbidden to use any scented deodorant, shampoo, soap or any perfume. The same applied to any and all cleaning agents and detergents. Sea Org members were only allowed to use the unscented versions, as their scented counterparts could "restimulate" unpleasant memories, claimed Hubbard. (Note: I found out after leaving the Church that it was part of Hubbard's paranoid mindset. For some reason, he hated scents and odors, and went to extraordinary lengths to dispense with them.)

At the end of this last course I had to put together a so-called personal grooming kit, and there went the rest of the cash I brought with me for emergencies (naturally, no one told me beforehand that this would be a requirement). Finally, I had to appear before a Fitness Board[12], which looked into my eligibility to join the Sea Org. The three members of this panel again looked through all the folders they had on me. I got the familiar set of questions about what happened in Munich, but then I was found fit for service.

I became a full member of the Sea Organization.

---

[12] Every Sea Org base has such a board for reviewing eligibility for Sea Org membership, theoretically operating by the relevant policies of Hubbard. Sea Org members had to appear before that board after completing their basic training, and any time circumstances warranted it. The committee usually consisted of three members, chaired by the head of the qualifications (quality control) division.

BECOMING A HEARTLESS BASTARD

The basic training did start me on a spiritual journey, but it was a far cry from the one I originally signed up for, I was slowly turning into a cold, calculating, merciless and rather manipulative person, with the occasional streak of cruelty. Hubbard actually recommended ignoring traditional values in his voluminous policy letters and bulletins about the Sea Org, citing the paramount importance of the mission of the Scientology movement, which overrode any other aspect of the situations in question.

The personality of the ideal Sea Org member was exemplified by the supreme leader of the European branch of the Church (his official title was "Commanding Officer of the Continental Liaison Europe"), Walter Kotrič. At that time, I had only seen him in action for a brief period, but he definitely had an air of absolute confidence, determination, toughness and extreme dedication. He behaved like the great warlords and generals of history. He had zero tolerance for slackness, poor job performance and to put it mildly, he was not particularly fond of excuses. He was also rather tall and muscular, and had a deep, booming voice coupled with a strong Austrian accent, which added an extra punch to his orders and threats.

He also had a special ability: he was able to yell with incredible volume, intensity and intention, a skill he used frequently if he was not satisfied with someone or wanted to get instant compliance to an order. He had no reservations about getting physical if he thought the situation warranted it. He usually grabbed his victim, smashed or pushed him against the nearest wall and screamed at him. He exuded such raw intention and determination that the loudness of his voice probably did not even matter.

I saw him do this a few times while I was on my basic training. One time, when we were working in the courtyard, he had a go at someone on the fifth floor. Every word he uttered was clearly audible five stories below. According to our boss, Walter had worked with Hubbard earlier, and he possessed the same skill, and likely had taught Walter how to do it properly.

So that was the ideal attitude one had to have in mind when adjusting to life in the Sea Org. Hubbard even wrote a separate policy regarding yelling & screaming. He approved this as long as it forwarded production. He preferred it to the "graveyard calm" of silent, peaceful places, where nothing happens.

Walter had two deputies. They were both women, but handled their affairs in a similar fashion to their master. In addition to the screaming "tech" (they were similarly talented at that skill as Walter), sometimes they were nice and charming, if the situation necessitated that sort of approach.

Anne, the deputy responsible for "operations" (whatever that meant), heard about me and the list of major courses I completed in Munich. She paid a visit just after I completed the EPF and tried to find a way to keep me from returning to Hungary. She was very nice and polite, and highlighted some empty positions in the Copenhagen organization. Keeping the promise I made to Miklós in mind, I respectfully declined her offer.

A bit later, I received a call from the OTL and was given a new assignment. Apparently, there was an ongoing international project to implement an internal memo system throughout the Scientology network called the "telex system," by setting up a secure private network for the Church on the Internet. All Church organizations received a special computer, with a software application called "External Comm," which was developed in-house as a special add-on to a commercial software called Lotus Notes. In a nutshell, it was a digital implementation of a communication system designed by Hubbard for telex machines. The internal memos were numbered in the same way telex messages were numbered back in the '70s, and the application tracked the replies and unanswered communications. The Church had staff members, who had the sole duty of getting these "telexes" answered. The communications about a specific subject could only be closed by the senior party.

As I had a bit of IT training, I had to learn how to use the system, so I could train our "telex" operator in Budapest. As an additional duty, I had to find a way to get the computer to Hungary and avoid paying customs duty (I was handed a letter of donation from the European Church). After completing the short software training, I started to look for a way to return to Budapest. Fortunately, I found two new Hungarian Scientologists (they were doing their first steps), who were about to leave Copenhagen by car. They were unwilling to bring me free of charge though, especially with the computer. I had to find a solution, as unsurprisingly, OTL was not willing to pay a dime. Necessity was again the mother of invention: The simplest way to raise money was to sell my return airplane ticket to some sucker. Theoretically, it was not transferable, but I had already learned to ignore this kind of moral dilemma. I approached a fellow Hungarian EPFer with the idea. I chose him because I remembered his name from László's list of degraded beings. He was on it and even received 5-star rating in that category. This helped to suppress the remaining doubt over what I was about to do. I told him that he could use this if he was persuasive enough at the airport, which was a convenient half-truth. He bought my ticket and I had the money to pay for my seat in the car.

My travelling companions were not especially happy about the extra baggage. It was a fairly large computer, complete with a big monitor, a printer and an uninterruptible power supply. On top of it, it was rather valuable, and they did not want to get stuck in Customs (they had their doubts about the letter of donation). The whole setup was put on the back seat, next to me, covered with a blanket.

We were nearing the Hungarian border, when one of them suddenly asked me a question: "Hey, Peter, isn't it a problem that I used to regularly smuggle merchandise through the border? I learned from Ron that if someone commits overts [harmful acts] in a particular area, then he can pull in some tough situations. So, my past offences might catch up with me now and we would be stuck here with the computer."

The other one was tired so he announced to me that he was not going to wait just because of me and in case of any problem, they would leave me there with the computer and I would have to find a way to get to Budapest.

We crossed the border and drove to the Customs booth. The officer on duty looked into the car and waved us to proceed. There was a long silence in the car, then a bit later the driver laughed and said loudly: "Hey, we have a computer here!" Fortunately, the windows were rolled up. The rest of the journey was uneventful, and I made it to the base safely.

Miklós was glad about the successful delivery and the money spared on transport. A few days later, I got a new position. I became the Dissemination Chief, responsible for getting translations and promotional materials done.

I became familiar with the org board [organizational chart] of the OTL, which looked like this:

OTL HUNGARY

Commanding Officer (CO) of OTL

Division 7 Executive	OSA, top management representatives

Deputy CO for Internal Matters

Division 1 HCO	personnel, ethics, communications
Division 2 Dissemination	translations, promotional materials
Division 3 Treasury	finances, accounting, records
Division 3A Base Crew	food, berthing, maintenance, cleaning

management entities (not under the CO OTL) led by their respective COs

FOLO	supervision of orgs
SMI	supervision of missions
IHELP	supervision of field auditors
WISE	supervision of Scientologist businessmen and their companies
ABLE	supervision of "secular" social betterment organizations

Deputy CO for Operations

Division 4 Operations	data collection and evaluations, sending and managing missions
Division 5 Training Org	staff training and auditing
Division 6 Public	public relations in the immediate area, crew morale, compliance with legal regulations

The functions of the various divisions were as follows:

Division 7 – though it was part of the OTL on paper, it was not under the supervision of its CO. Representatives of the various top-level Scientology organizations constituted this division, including OSA, New Era Publications and the Finance Network[13].

Division 1 – (traditionally called Hubbard Communications Office or HCO) all personnel matters, all internal justice and disciplinary matters, internal communications.

Division 2 – translations of Hubbard writings as well as orders, magazines, videos etc. issued by upper management; design and production of promotional materials.

Division 3 – finances, records, and accounting.

Division 3A – providing food and berthing for Sea Org members, maintenance and cleaning of facilities.

Division 4 – collecting data and statistics from the field, sending missions to Scientology organizations (in case of emergencies or when ordered by upper management) and managing these; managing telexes.

Division 5 – training of OTL staff members as well as staff members from Scientology organizations.

Division 6 – internal (crew parties etc) and external PR (handling neighbors, local authorities etc.).

The representatives of the five organizations (called entities) responsible for the main areas of Scientology activities were also part of the Hungarian base. Their immediate seniors were their European counterparts, and as I mentioned, this accounted for a pretty chaotic operational pattern.

Here is a short description of these entities:

Scientology Missions International (SMI): responsible for the missions, i.e. small Scientology organizations which were originally called "franchises" (which was a pretty exact and rightful name for them).

International Hubbard Ecclesiastical League of Pastors (I HELP): responsible for the field auditors.

Flag Operations Liaison Office (FOLO): responsible for Church organizations or "orgs," which delivered major Scientology services.

Two theoretically secular organizations were also part of the liaison office of the Church (which, as I mentioned, was officially a religious order). A non-profit organization called **Association for Better Living and Education (ABLE)** was, for all intents and purposes, an integral part of the organization

---

[13] Finance Network: a separate network inside the Church, responsible for monitoring finances and collecting the management and licensing fees for top-level Church organizations.

structure of the Church. Additionally, all of its staff members were also Sea Org members, so monks of the Church in a legal sense.

ABLE was a theoretically secular management entity responsible for the social betterment activities of Scientology, with four subsidiaries under its umbrella (Narconon – drug prevention and rehabilitation; Criminon – crime prevention, rehabilitation of criminals; Way to Happiness Foundation – handling the moral decline in society; and Applied Scholastics – providing tools for educators and educational institutions.)

The other secular organization was the **World Institute of Scientology Enterprises (WISE)**. On paper, it was a membership organization for Scientologist business people and it also licensed Hubbard's administrative methodology for a fee. The Hungarian branch was officially registered as a non-profit association, but it did not stop the Church from having Sea Org members work there on a Sea Org schedule.

So, I became the head of Division 2, and thus, a member of the so-called Advisory Council, a body comprised of the division heads.

One of the key duties of the Advisory Council was doing the weekly financial planning on Thursday nights. Miklós made one thing perfectly clear to us – the preferred way to get the resources needed for our job was to "obtain" (it was a code word for getting something free or donated by a public Scientologist) them somehow, as he absolutely hated spending money when there was any other way.

This habit of his tracked back to the founding of the OTL, which he told us during one particularly long night. It turned out that it was a rogue, unauthorized action. He was working for one of the Sea Org organizations in the USA, but his visa had expired and he had to return to Hungary. He then had the idea to form a Sea Org unit here, as there was sufficient potential manpower. He submitted a request to the international management of Scientology, but then did not wait around for the answer. He simply had Tamás Nagy, the Hungarian leader of the Church, register OTL Hungary as a religious order of the Church of Scientology Hungary and started to operate with the tacit approval of the mighty Walter Kotrič (he actually liked the idea, as it was maverick enough for his taste).

The problem with his bold initiative was the lack of economic foundation supporting it. He did not think about how the OTL would survive financially. Theoretically, it was supposed to receive a percentage of the income of the Scientology orgs it managed. But there were no orgs in Hungary, just a few missions. He found a rather unorthodox solution, and became in his own words, a "money retrieval expert." He began to track down ex-Scientology staff in Hungary and collect their so-called "freeloader debts." (When these

74

poor sods left their respective orgs, they received bills for all training and/or auditing services they received while on staff. The prices charged were outlandish. For example a full EPF of 5 courses in Copenhagen cost around 3000 US dollars, and it was rather easy to rack up a 5- or 6-figure bill, if someone was on staff for a longer period of time.) All Scientology organizations paid 10% commission to whoever collected these so-called debts. Miklós took a simple but effective approach. He sat down with his deputy and started to phone and relentlessly hound these ex-staff members, employing the entirety of Scientology's sales and manipulation techniques to squeeze every last penny out of the poor suckers.

He then quickly established a course room and ordered every mission in Hungary to send people to the OTL for various training courses, which were then billed to the missions and the fees were collected with the usual take-no-prisoners approach, which he called "putting the pressure of God on them" and using "ironclad control."

Money was still tight, though. Therefore, office supplies were usually to be "obtained" – brought in from our unsuspecting families or donated by a Scientologist. Most of our computers were provided by a Scientologist management consultant, who got them cheaply from one of his clients, but there were quite a few which were originally personally owned by new members, who handed these over to the OTL. The kitchen appliances were originally owned by our cook. The main thing was to spare any expense for the Church.

The attitude of international Church management did not help either. They insisted on implementing a "standard" financial system, which meant that around 35% of our gross income had to be sent to various international Church organizations and we were required to spend 14% on promotion, so we had only around 50% of the income to spend on everything else (including rent, staff pay, food, etc).

After appointing me as Dissemination Chief, Miklós wasted no time with formalities and started to push for compliance and products in true ruthless Sea Org officer style. No excuses were accepted, and I was supposed get the statistics up (i.e. higher than last week's) by Thursday 14:00, no matter what. I had two men under me (one for the promotional materials and one for the translations, who mostly worked with Scientologists volunteers).

One of my fellow "monks" summarized the most basic survival trick: if bricks start to fall, you better jump aside so they hit the guy directly under you. The classic "lick upwards, kick downwards" policy applied. In order to survive as a member of middle management, I had to name a person responsible if the stats did not go up or downright crashed or there was a problem (called a "flap" in Scientologese), and I had to present a handling (an ethics order, a punishment, ordering overtime etc.) which satisfied my seniors.

The favored method of getting compliance was "you do not go to sleep until it is done" and I learned to use it fast. Otherwise I would have to take the fall and suffer the consequences (overtime, reduced rations, no days-off etc.).

It took just a short month to detect troubling changes in my personality and attitude. I became a bit like Miklós, who, was the alpha male in our little group. I was tough on my juniors, learned how and when to scream and yell at them and I was constantly standing over them, demanding products. Non-compliance was not tolerated – so if a translation was set to be completed that week and the translations director was behind his target, I was supposed to take over, call in some additional translators and keep them working throughout the night (Wednesday nights were usually very long) until the target was reached. Naturally, this rather compromised the quality of the translations, but no one seemed to care when the all-important stats were up by Thursday 14:00.

I also developed another unfortunate characteristic: a disdain and contempt for anyone considered to have a lower status than Sea Org members.

The lowest stratum on this imaginary list was occupied by non-Scientologists. They were called "wogs," defined by Hubbard as "someone who isn't even trying [to achieve spiritual freedom]." It was also used as an adjective. An example of this might be "wog" parties, where "wog" music was played and "bodies are squirming" as opposed to L. Ron Hubbard's inspirational music, which addressed the spiritual beings and had real aesthetic qualities. Wogs were looked down on the most in the Sea Org.

The next group on the list was the public (non-staff) Scientologists. They were held in a rather low regard as they did not take real responsibility and did not join the Sea Org. They were not giving their all to Scientology, and were involved in various wog things. They were considered "dilettantes," who "had other fish to fry" and they were "not on-purpose enough" (these were the actual expressions used).

Org and mission staff members were next. They were looked down on, too, but perhaps with not as much disdain. They had realized the necessity of saving the planet, but they were too lazy and/or cowardly to sacrifice everything for the cause. They took the easier way – working only 40 hours a week for a Scientology organization, and had time for their own hobbies and businesses on the weekend.

Only two months had passed since I joined the Sea Org, but I had already changed in a profound manner. Christmas, every Sea Org officer's nightmare (usually the stats go and stay down in the holiday season) was right around the corner and to make matters worse, 25th of December was a Thursday. Miklós told me that he does not care how, but the completed translations would have to be sent to the European Sea Org base before 14:00 on 25 December. He was just executing orders, as Walter had sent a telex to him a week before, stating that he was still not interested in the "Christmas dramatizations" and we had to be upstat[14], NO FAIL.

I went to my hometown for Christmas anyway. My parents were a bit freaked out about my creepy new personality and how I bragged about handling my subordinates. And they looked at me like I was an alien when I repeatedly called the translations director on the 25th to ensure that enough translations were completed to get the stat up.

Sea Org tradition called for organizing a few parties between Christmas and New Year, and for once, we were happy to oblige. The first was the Kris Kringle / Secret Santa party, which was unsurprisingly abbreviated in the Sea Org as "KK." Our Secret Santa was definitely meaner than its wog counterpart – playing high-school grade practical jokes on each other was somehow a part of the culture. The target person was to receive three gifts, but he or she had to complete three tasks to learn where these were.

This was a good opportunity to discharge frustrations and dish out some payback for the inevitable conflicts that arose from living and working so tightly. One of the female Sea Org members got a weird assignment for her gift – she had to go to another female Sea Org member who had rather small breasts and convince her to massage them, stating that "British scientists" discovered that massaging breasts might make them bigger over time. And if she managed to accomplish this task, she would be told where her gift was. Each year, I always found a way to avoid getting involved in this, as I considered it disgusting, but some shipmates did enjoy this sort of depravity.

The second was the "Bosun Party," which was basically a costume ball (this was not always held) and the third one was called the "Beer and Cheese Party." According to Miklós, Hubbard ordered international Church management to supply us with candies and chocolate each year for that party, as we got a package each year for that purpose, sent by international courier services from Los Angeles. The other necessary ingredients (i.e. beer and cheese) were procured locally.

These (and any and all other crew parties) mostly revolved around gorging on any available food (as money spent on food had the lowest priority and these parties represented a rare occasion when a Sea Org member could eat a proper amount of food) and watching movies (it was forbidden to own or

---

[14] upstat: Having upward trending production statistics and/or performing well.

watch TV regularly, as according to Hubbard, it made zombies out of people and reduced productivity).

As for movies, Sea Org members in Hungary had a particular taste. At my first party, Miklós brought a VHS tape, so we could all enjoy his personal favorite, an American comedy called "*Brain Donors*." Another frequently shown film was a recording of Michael Flatley's *Lord of the Dance*. That performance was looked upon as the right mixture of discipline, agility and professionalism, which was expected of all Sea Org members.

There was another educational tape for us that we had to watch from time to time. It was a parade by the Honor Guard of the US Marines, which was extremely well-choreographed and they performed amazing stunts. This was shown as the proof of Hubbard's maxim: "the key to professionalism is drilling."

The next year (1999) brought me to a new job – Miklós decided to promote me to a higher position.

CHAPTER FIVE

Personnel Psychosis

RECRUITMENT

Miklós appointed me to the position of Executive Establishment Officer (or Exec EstO). This was a so-called network position, located in the aforementioned Division 7. My boss was the European Exec EstO, who was located at the Sea Org base in Copenhagen. I had to send my statistics and a report of my activities to him on a weekly basis.

According to the Hubbard policies describing my post duties, my first and foremost duty was the recruitment of new Sea Org members. Actually, this was the primary reason Miklós wanted me in this position, as his deputy Tamás, had to leave the Sea Org. Tamás had an interesting career. He had joined the Sea Org in Clearwater and worked as a recruiter there. His US visa expired and he was caught by US authorities, sent back to Hungary and banned from entering the United States for 10 years. He had a wife in Clearwater, who had to stay there. With no other option to remain in the Sea Org other than to join the Hungarian outfit, he reluctantly agreed to do that. His tenure was short-lived though. His wife called a few months later and informed him she was pregnant and intended to keep the child, against the wishes of her seniors. According to Sea Org policies, they had to leave the Sea Org (and pay their freeloader bills). Tamás wrote a petition to international Church management and tried to get himself and his wife transferred to Budapest Org, referring to an earlier policy which allowed for that. His petition was denied.

Miklós now had to find a new deputy and train him. He decided to send two of the original OTL crew members for officer training aboard the cruise ship *Freewinds*, operated by the Church in the Caribbean. One of them, the head of Division 1, would take over as his deputy after completing training. I had to take over recruitment until he returned.

Miklós also installed the 15-year old son of the President of WISE Hungary as the temporary head of Division 1. He was probably the saddest example of the application of personnel policies used in the Church. Hubbard did not consider general eligibility or diplomas and non-Scientology education important. Age was also not a factor to consider, as children and young adults were considered to be "big thetans [spiritual beings] in small bodies." The recommended approach was to give someone a position and train him on his post and duties (he called this *hatting*), and the incumbent would begin to perform properly sooner or later. Hubbard did author some contradictory policies which set eligibility rules for certain (mainly executive) positions, but usually the first approach was followed as this was more dominant in his writings.

The boy was visibly struggling under the weight of this enormous task. And in addition to Miklós, now he had another product-oriented boss over him. Me. I got down to business immediately.

Our major recruitment targets were Scientologist teenagers and young adults (mostly in the 16-21 age range) whose parents were either Scientologist or their relationships with the parents were so good or so bad that joining the Sea Org did not cause too much upset. They were targeted for a simple reason: it was rather easy to convince and manipulate them. Our main weapon was picturing an idealistic future, and with that in mind we could steer the whole conversation onto the level of emotions, where enthusiastic endorsement of a bright future suppressed any rational qualms or misgivings. They were usually receptive to this approach. Ironically, I was also in this category, though I did not fully realize it at the time. My new personality was already well in the making: I was becoming more and more Peter Bonyai, the Sea Org member, and less and less Peter Bonyai, your average Hungarian teenager.

The first recruitment target I zero'd in on was Krisztina, the 16-year old daughter of a Scientologist couple. She had already signed a billion-year Sea Org contract. There was only one problem: on paper, she was the Executive Director of Mission Kalocsa. As there were no other staff members in the mission, she was basically picking up the phone (95% of the calls came from Scientology management) and doing paperwork in the short time she spent in the mission after school. There was a mission holder, who signed the license agreement with SMI International, but he was too busy with his "wog job" to spend any time at the mission. According to Church policies, the mission should have been closed long ago, but no one in management wanted that as it would have brought down the "number of missions" statistic, which was considered to be very important.

So, I had to find a suitable replacement for Krisztina. It was a virtually impossible task as there were a grand total of 4 Scientologists in her city, and three of them were unqualified for staff. The fourth had absolutely no intention of becoming a staff member. Miklós did not care much about these problems and called me every hour, demanding I come up with a solution. He told me I could not return to the base without Krisztina, and I had better get her there before Thursday 14:00 (and it was already Wednesday morning). There was only one way to go – convincing the parents to allow her to leave and simply bringing her to the Sea Org while ignoring the threats from the SMI Representative. I sat down with the Scientologist parents that afternoon. I listened while they explained to me all of the problems they had with the Church so far, and I in turn told them the great uplifting sales pitch about the noble mission of the Sea Org and what it means for the planet and its survival. I was pretty good at it by then. The Mission Holder joined the conversation when he came back from work and I started to work on him, too. I used all the tools I learned from Hubbard and Miklós, which was ultimately a fine-tuned and very effective mix of flattery and threats. We finally came to a resolution at 2:00 AM and they agreed to let Krisztina go. I had the feeling they simply gave up, knowing that the Sea Org would not leave them alone until their daughter arrived. We boarded the first bus in the morning together and I physically escorted her to the Sea Org base, to ensure she would not change her mind. Miklós was very happy with the catch.

Two new prospects (called Balázs and Viktória) came next, fortunately from Budapest this time. Unsurprisingly, both were minors and wanted to join the Sea Org, but the parents were non-Scientologists and understandably opposed the idea (quite vehemently in fact). This looked like quite a challenge, as I had to convince angry parents to let their kids join a "cult." Balázs was the so-called "hot prospect," as he wanted to join yesterday and his parents represented the only barrier. I managed to get them to agree to come in and talk about it. Surprisingly, the father did not seem to care much about the whole thing, he just shrugged and stated that Balázs could do whatever he wanted, and he would not stop him. The stepmother on the other hand was furious. I remained polite and tried to get her to tell me what her real problem was. It turned out that little Balázs had tried to convince his parents in a rather unorthodox manner by literally telling the truth (at least what Scientology considered the truth). He informed his parents that he was a spiritual being and he looked at them as the biological creators of his material body, since he considered himself at least a million years old if not more. He also mentioned that he had already signed an employment contract for the next billion years, which forced him to work for the Sea Org.

This was the point where I had to pick up the pieces and get Balázs arrived. I had a long conversation with the stepmother and I managed to decrease her level of hostility. She even said at one point that they would reconsider letting Balázs go. Nevertheless, it took two more weeks until Balázs managed to convince his parents to allow him to join. We spoke almost every day and I coached him on what to say and how to reply to their questions and alleviate their concerns. He finally arrived to the base and became a Sea Org member. Ironically, he then married Krisztina, my first recruit and eventually they wound up working in the international headquarters of the Church in Hemet,

California. Later on, Balázs, who was apparently a "voice talent," became the Hungarian voice of Hubbard on the translated lectures and Krisztina was assigned as his assistant.

The other prospect was named Viktória. Her parents were divorced and her mother was raising her alone. The family already had a history with Sea Org recruiters, which made the situation much harder to handle (her mother actually chased one of the more insistent recruiters out of their house with a broom). I used a similar approach to get her to arrive. I handled the main objections of the mother and then I coached Viktória how to speak to her, so she would allow her to join the Sea Org. It took a few weeks, but eventually her mother resigned herself to what she felt was the inevitable and let her go.

The next target was considered somewhat of a coup. I was tasked with getting a computer programmer (a known Linux expert) into the Sea Org. His non-Scientologists parents adamantly refused to let him go, so I was sent to the remote Hungarian village they were living to speak with them in person. They turned out to be nice country folk, who just wanted to protect their son and his career as an IT professional. I told them about INCOMM (the international IT division of the Church responsible for the eventual computerization of management) and I told a half-truth about his potential bright future as a programmer if he was posted there. Our Sea Org unit did not plan to send him there, but knowing the complete insanity surrounding personnel matters in Scientology, it was not impossible that he would wind up there one day. So, I got him arrived by tricking the parents, but I knew he would have to stay in constant communication with them to avoid trouble in the future.

After completing basic training, he started out as an office assistant, and photocopying, procuring office supplies and other minor errands. Naturally, if he failed to submit a purchase order for any of the items before the purchase was made, Miklós made him pay for them out of this pocket with his usual coy smile. The poor guy regularly withdrew money from his bank account to literally pay for his mistakes. Unknown to us, his parents also got text notifications of all debits on his personal account. Their worst fears were confirmed – their child was apparently handing over his money to the Church and he did not even have time to call them now and then. So, I made him visit his parents and talk to them more often so the situation would not escalate.

A few weeks later Miklós handed over Viktória and the programmer to the Advanced Organization in Copenhagen (Walter Kotrič was personally pushing this in his usual forceful way) as a part of some weird personnel exchange deal. I found out about it after the fact and was very upset, but I had no choice – I had to accept it as a good Sea Org member and move on.

The Advanced Organization had a recruitment tour in Budapest and the IT expert was assigned as a translator for them. Therefore, I had limited opportunity to help him regarding his parents. Two or three weeks later his entire family showed up at the OTL – around 10 close relatives arrived in three cars. They demanded to see the boy and wanted to take him away right then and there. The recruiter from Copenhagen ran around the OTL trying to find someone to help. His face was red with a mixture of fear and anger, and he obviously blamed us for not handling the family situation. I told him to get lost when he asked me to help (I was still not over the entire deal which resulted in losing my recruit). As a last resort, the recruiter called in Péter Kárpáti, Director of Special Affairs of the Budapest Mission, who was also the spokesperson for Scientology in Hungary. We did not think much of him as he was not a Sea Org member, but that didn't prevent us from dumping this sort of situation on him to handle. He talked to the parents a bit and managed to calm them down, but nothing could have changed their minds and they took the boy. Péter Kárpáti summed up the situation by stating the obvious: these people had no one to talk to regarding their son and Scientology.

I still had to wrap up the matter, as Péter Kárpáti was not a Sea Org member. I called the father and made an agreement with him to come in with the boy a week later, so we could "complete the paperwork." I secretly hoped that I might turn this around still as we badly needed new recruits. The father did came in, but he was armed with a dangerous "weapon" – a critical book on Scientology, written by the No.1 enemy of Scientology in Hungary, Dr. András Veér, a prominent psychiatrist and a key target of attacks by the local chapter of Scientology's antipsychiatry organization, the Citizens' Commission on Human Rights. He even contacted Dr. Veér and asked for advice. The battle was obviously lost, as at this point I had no choice but to turn the matter over to OSA due to the involvement of the good doctor. The father even wanted to help me leave the Sea Org. He told me that he could get me out anytime, as he had Dr. Veér's private phone number and if I ever wanted to leave, I should just call him. I politely refused his offer (by then, my indoctrination and knowledge of Scientology had formed an effective shield which nullified all such attempts) and we went our separate ways.

I briefed Péter Kárpáti on what went down. He told me that I should not worry as OSA had implemented serious programs to neutralize Dr. Veér. He was considered such an important enemy that he even had a code name in their telexes – he was simply referred to as "V." He could not tell me more about this though, as it was "confidential."

The really hard part came after that incident. I ran out of so-called hot prospects (who had already decided to come but were unable to for some reason), so I had to do the full work with future ones – starting from convincing them to join the Sea Org in the first place.

Miklós managed to find a full dress "navy blue" Sea Org uniform (we did not even have proper uniforms at that point) in one of the cupboards, which was apparently left behind by one of the many foreign recruiters that visited Hungary. This so-called "Class A" uniform was eerily similar to the standard US Navy dress uniform. I looked sharp in it, so I had to wear it from then on. All dressed up, off I went to recruit some fresh meat at the nearby Budapest Mission.

I asked the staff members whether they knew anyone who wanted to or was ready to join us. One of the staff members in the test center (a 12-year old daughter of one of the Course Supervisors, charged with entering personality test results into a computer) told me that she had completed the EPF in Copenhagen, but had to leave Denmark as her visa expired (Hungary was not a member of the European Union at that time). She then joined Budapest mission to work together with her father.

I mentioned this to Miklós at the daily "product conference" (which was held every day at 22:30). He reacted just like I expected he would: if she completed basic Sea Org training, she should work in the OTL and she was not to be allowed to work in the mission. Then he added that I was to bring her over and have her started before Thursday 14:00 to count on the weekly stats. So, I ordered the girl to come over. I told her that she could not continue to work in the mission, as she has completed the EPF and she has to move in to the female dormitory and start working as a Sea Org member right-now. She told me meekly that she would not want to do that and she would rather work together with her father in the mission. I told her coldly (keeping in mind the Hubbard teaching that children are big beings in small bodies and they were on the same terms as the rest of us) that I would be forced to resort to disciplinary actions, which in her case would be a Court of Ethics for disobeying a legal order.

She began to cry shortly after the words "Court of Ethics" left my mouth. I was not moved by the obvious manipulative trick to gain my sympathy and told her that I did not care how she felt and I would go ahead and start typing the ethics order right now. She looked at me with a sad, resigned expression and told me that she would then move in and start working she wanted to avoid a Court of Ethics. She came in the next morning with her luggage and reluctantly filled out all the forms and signed everything we put in front of her. At that time, I was rather proud of myself and thanked Hubbard for giving me such effective tools to maintain order and discipline among Scientologists. Today I look back at this incident with a great deal of regret and shame, but at that time I was quite proud of myself. I even got a written commendation for it.

I continued to frequent the mission, hunting for new potential Sea Org members. On one occasion, I noticed a short, stocky guy, who complained to the Receptionist about a course he recently completed in the mission and made critical remarks about the Church. I remembered what I learned on my basic training – "the primary purpose of the Sea Org is to get ethics in on this planet and the universe." This person was attacking the only hope of mankind, the Church of Scientology – therefore he must have been a criminal! I went to him in my recently dry cleaned and pressed navy uniform, complete with the standard issue silver chain for petty officers and towered above him (I was 6'4" after all). I looked him in the eye menacingly and told him that he needed to stop right now. He told me to shove off but that did not scare me and I stepped even closer to him. He lost his courage and started to run and I chased him down the stairway (the mission was on the 5th floor of a large apartment block). He ran out of the building and disappeared into the crowd on the street.

US IMPORTS

While I was busily recruiting and hunting for new crew members, Miklós was trying to find a way to get two of his old acquaintances transferred to OTL Hungary. He wanted to send them on a lengthy technical training program, to eventually become Class VI auditors and to audit us to Clear.

At that time, they were posted in one of the Sea Org units in Los Angeles. The couple (Charlie and Judith Miklán), had joined the Sea Org in 1991, in the heyday of Scientology in Hungary. Charlie even had a short stint on the RPF. He spent a few months running around in black clothes, but then a review board found his assignment unjustified and he was released from the RPF and reinstated as a regular Sea Org crew member. I did not know anyone else in the Sea Org who had such an easy stint in the punishment camp.

According to her communications, Judith had somehow managed to conjure up a replacement plan and she came back to Hungary (it was a bit suspicious why they let her go so easily, and unfortunately, later on certain events confirmed my initial fears), but Charlie was supposedly holding an important position, so we had to send a quality recruit who could replace him. Our outfit was on the lowest level of the Sea Org food chain, so we naturally had to adhere to every policy Hubbard had ever written on the subject of replacing outgoing staff members. Sadly, it did not apply in the other direction, as higher-level Sea

Org units were more or less authorized to take our personnel as we apparently had a duty to "flow up." The official post title of Charlie was Director of Disbursements, Continental Liaison Office, Western United States. Among other things, geography was also somewhat revised by Hubbard. He delineated the following continents on Earth, accompanied by the inevitable abbreviations:

Europe (EU) – contained Europe (except the United Kingdom), Israel, Middle East and the entire area of the former Soviet Union.

United Kingdom (UK) – contained India and Pakistan in addition to the United Kingdom proper.

Eastern United States (EUS), Western United States (WUS), Canada (CAN) and Africa (AF) – surprisingly, these ones more or less matched their real life counterparts.

Latin America (LATAM) – included Central and South America plus the Caribbean (except Puerto Rico which was "EUS").

Australia, New Zealand, Oceania (ANZO) – Australia, New Zealand, China, Japan, Vietnam, Thailand etc. belonged here.

Miklós carefully chose a very promising recruit as the replacement for Charlie and sent him to Los Angeles. As this was clearly a personnel matter, I felt I had to weigh in and do what I could to get Charlie arrived. I was a still a bit naive and idealistic and I sincerely believed that straight and honest communication would be the solution. After all, we were all working for the most ethical organization on Earth, with the common goal of saving this planet, so I was certain that the folks at the Western US unit would be sympathetic to our request and cooperate with us in the matter.

I wrote a telex to the personnel director of CLO WUS and asked for cooperation. The next day a reply arrived, signed by the unnamed personnel officer, stating that she did not even hear about this, who am I to try and rip off their staff member and most importantly, WHERE IS THE REPLACEMENT who is fully trained in that position and qualified to take over?!

I panicked at the infuriated response. The last thing I wanted was to cross our mighty Commanding Officer, so I tried to calm the WUS person down. I wrote back to her that the replacement was enroute to Los Angeles and would be trained by Charlie.

A day later Judith approached me. I could tell by the look on her face that something was very wrong. If looks could kill, I would have been carted off to my grave immediately.

"Peter," she shrieked, "what the fuck were you thinking? Do you know what you did?" And then she launched into full-blast yelling mode – "You have destroyed months of hard work with your fucking telex, you stupid motherfucker!!!"

She then started to throw around wild accusations, claiming that I must have a hidden agenda and I simply did not want Charlie to come back to Hungary. She then stated that obviously I was sitting on major CRIMES and Charlie was a trained auditor and he would find out. She then told me angrily to "spit out my crimes now," as if she discovered them at a later date (and she would do that eventually), I would face SERIOUS consequences. After finishing this rant, she stormed away.

I was completely baffled. I could not decide if she was serious or she was just overtaken by her anger and said things she did not really mean.

The next day Tamás, the deputy commanding officer who was just about to leave the Sea Org, tried to give me a last and final lesson on the personnel situation in the Sea Org.

"Peter, you cannot imagine what sort of PERSONNEL PSYCHOSIS is going on in Los Angeles," he said, putting careful emphasis on these words. He then told me that the West US does not have a personnel director, nor anyone posted above that position, so the duties of the post are directly managed by the Commanding Officer and that's who answered my telex. He added that the CO could interpret my telex to mean that we just gave someone to them and they can put him on any post they want. So Charlie was now forced to hide the recruit from the top executive of the base, while he turned over his job to him. Tamás also told me that the Commanding Officer hated Charlie, so they would get the replacement approved by International Management, without involving the CO, so she would be powerless to stop it.

I did not really know what to make of this new information. It was completely at odds with the image of the Sea Org as depicted by L. Ron Hubbard. In an elite, effective, completely rational and sane organization, which was tirelessly working on the salvation of the planet and used the best organizational technology (and the only one which actually worked) in the world, such a situation should never have happened – the Commanding Officer of a large Sea Org unit is forced to handle personnel matters on her own? Unusual solutions are required due to petty feuds between staff members? It did not make any sense until I got the universal explanation of such situations: *the administrative technology of Ron works perfectly if known and applied.* Apparently, any and all such situations stemmed entirely and only from the ignorance or non-application of Hubbard policies. Miklós was also a bit angry about the whole mess I had created. Especially when Judith told him all about the "damage" I had caused. He told me his opinion in his usual direct and coarse style: "No more fuckups like this, understood? Personnel cycles[15] NEVER go on telex lines."

---

[15] short for *cycle of action*, a Scientology word for matters or projects

Fortunately, he was too busy with another situation to be too preoccupied by the Charlie replacement business. Péter, our future Deputy CO, had just completed the Sea Org Officer Training School aboard the *Freewinds*, along with his study twin, the Deputy Executive Director of ABLE Hungary (which effectively resulted in a secular, social betterment non-profit organization being led by a monk, who had just completed a civil version of naval boot camp). There was a slight problem though – the senior officer of the training program refused to let them go until OTL paid their room and board expenses in full. This amounted to 4000 USD, which was a hefty sum to a small unit like ours. The first plan was to have them escape from the ship and we would pay the bill in installments. Sadly, that senior officer was a wily old fox (he was apparently one of the original Sea Org members, who worked with the Commodore directly) and they had confiscated the passports of the trainees for "security reasons" at the beginning of the program. So we had no choice but to come up with the money.

After a day or so, Miklós came up with a solution. We printed a bunch of management training materials for a WISE company, using our internal translations (as they were not officially available in Hungarian), and the amount we charged for this service covered the bill. We had no right or authorization to do so, but as always, the ends justified the means. The owners of that company were dedicated Scientologists, so a few months later Miklós even got them to finance a targeted PR campaign, which consisted of sending a copy of the freshly translated book *What is Scientology?* to each member of the Hungarian Parliament.

BECOMING PRODUCT ONE

Product One was the name of a series of courses to be done after the completion of the EPF. This was theoretically a prerequisite to being officially posted, but due to the chronic lack of personnel, it was never enforced.

I completed these courses in the daily allotted 2.5 hours study time, in Spring, 1998. The first two courses were Staff Status I and II, which I had already completed in Pécs Mission, so I was routed onto the four courses exclusively available for Sea Org members.

The first one was called *The Keys to Competence Course*. It contained around 20 *Flag Orders* and *Central Bureaux Orders*, which were policies written by Hubbard exclusively for the Sea Org. The essential message of the course was fairly simple: all Sea Org members, no matter where they were on the Scientology Bridge to Total Freedom, had to be able to do any and all tasks and perform any duty. According to his reasoning, every Sea Org member was an immortal spiritual being, existing for millions of years. Therefore each human being who was now serving in the Sea Org, had accumulated a vast, yet hidden knowledge and was theoretically able to do any job. Therefore no excuses such as "I am not trained for this," "I have never done anything like that" etc. were acceptable and were in fact lies. In one of the policies he made a remark regarding the Sea Org officers assigned to managing orgs, stating that they had been running planets earlier, so they should stop telling him that they did not know what to do.

According to this theory, if the external pressure was sufficiently high, abilities would be reactivated. He called this "necessity level," and according to him, if one increased this necessity level by demands and threats, virtually any order would be complied with. If someone was apparently unable to do something, then we had to suspect that he was out-ethics (Hubbard defined out-ethics as "his own concept of ethics is inadequate to his survival" meaning he lacked self-discipline, was lazy, had other fish to fry, or was an outright criminal, which prevented him from functioning effectively). He summed the whole concept up by stating that the only real prerequisite to being a staff member was to have one's breath visible on a mirror.

He expected Sea Org members to put aside all negativity, be effective under any circumstances and comply with orders given, no matter what. Sea Org members were not supposed to accept any excuses from others or themselves as to why something could not be done. I learned a bit more about the advantages of yelling at one's subordinates. Hubbard stated that a calm and peaceful working environment is far from ideal. If someone had to shout to get something done, it was completely acceptable and the right thing to do rather than just silently watching while others did not do their jobs.

Mission School Third Class was the name of the next course. The theory part and the training exercises definitely had a distinct "Secret Agenting for Dummies" feeling about it. The basics of the so-called "Sea Org mission tech" had to be studied on this course. A mission was a 2-3 man group of Sea Org members, usually sent to remote locations to handle a situation that could not be addressed on normal administrative lines from a distant control center. A few examples: a Scientology organization that was on the verge of bankruptcy and was thousands of miles away, a serious lawsuit against the Church which the local officials were unable to properly handle etc. Missions were also fired to complete large special projects such as registering and establishing the Church in a new country where Scientology was not present at all, or collecting millions of dollars from local Scientologists for purchasing a building for their organization.

The main idea behind Sea Org missions was the strict adherence to the mission orders. The mission orders were theoretically the result of a very thorough analysis of the situation, therefore the missionaries were only allowed to execute their orders in the given sequences, and absolutely no deviations were tolerated. They were given a series of exact targets to complete, and they were supposed to send a daily report each night, reporting what target was completed and what targets were started but not done yet. They received a response the next morning from their mission operator, with further directions and orders as to what targets to work on and complete, with exact deadlines.

At the end of this course, there were a few practice missions to complete. The final one was to write a shopping list and to visit three supermarkets and compare their prices for the items on the list. I enthusiastically started on it, but in one of the shops they did not really appreciate that I was conspicuously marking down prices on a clipboard and had me escorted out by security. I learned my lesson and did this in a more clandestine way in the other shops.

I was really excited. It was fun to fool around as a make-believe James Bond. In my fantasy world, the dumb wog shop assistants in the malls did not even suspect that the nerdy guy, who looked like your run-of-the-mill systems administrator and was busy taking notes was secretly a special agent in-training for the planet-saving Church of Scientology and was destined to ensure that they and their children had a future at all.

When I completed the mission, I had to write a final report and report to a trained missionaire for debriefing. In my case, it was Imre, the President of WISE Hungary, who also happened to be the oldest Sea Org member in Hungary. He was in his fifties, a relic in the OTL. When I told Imre that I was kicked out of the first supermarket on my list, he made a sly remark that I should have told them that I was drawing up a shopping list for a wedding with 500 guests, but I could take my business elsewhere if they insisted. I was a bit annoyed that I was not smart enough to come up with this elegant, James Bond-esque caper on my own.

The mission school was followed by two courses addressing what were considered to be important Sea Org basics. The first was called the *Sea Org Etiquette Course*, and it contained a set of rules derived from maritime traditions and American naval etiquette (for example, officers were not allowed to issue orders during meals).

The *Sea Org Cleaning Course* was the last course in the Product I lineup. It contained lengthy essays from Hubbard on the various harmful effects and drawbacks of dirt, dust and smell. Unsurprisingly, he also developed cleaning and grooming technologies. I was sharply reminded again that it was absolutely forbidden to use any scented products, perfume or cleaning agents. Everything had to be absolutely undetectable. Windows were to be cleaned with cold water and black and white newspapers, no cleaning agents were allowed. Furniture had to be cleaned with diluted ammonia. These regulations were a bit baffling (the policies were written in the '70s, and a number of effective cleaning supplies were invented since then), but severe penalties were associated with using anything for cleaning that smelled. I resigned to adhere to these new rules and as part of the practical assignment, I cleaned the windows with wet newspapers, no matter how ineffective it looked when compared to modern solutions.

As a part of my on-the-job training, Miklós tried to teach me how to get things done, using selected Hubbard policies. There was even an expression for denoting everything related to obtaining compliance: the *product officer duty*. All executives were considered to be product officers, even those assigned to positions that had only organizational and/or personnel-related duties. The expected attitude of a product officer is best summed up by this internal joke:

– What is the difference between a product officer and a terrorist?

– You can negotiate with a terrorist.

The so-called product-oriented approach, which was expected from Sea Org members, was even more applicable to product officers. The targets had to be met OR ELSE, and the stats had to go up no matter what. Hubbard had a rather low opinion of what he called "worker-oriented" executives, who were apparently mindful of the needs of their subordinates, and lost sight of the paramount importance of achieving the goals of Scientology.

This is what he wrote on the matter:

"A worker-oriented executive is trying to be liked by not requiring work from his organization: What is he actually accomplishing? He is lowering their living standards; he is pushing them into poverty; if he keeps on failing to persuade them to produce, he will kill them off. It categorizes as a suppressive act. 'Go on, Joe, take the day off.' 'Oh, you poor fellow, you shouldn't work so hard.' 'Who cares about the stats, let's only work from eleven A.M. to noon.' 'Are you all comfortable as you doze? Oh, that's good, snore on.' Such a person is surely not an executive: He's an impostor with a pistol leveled at the staffs' head. For surely, surely it is HE who has them drawing such low pay and it is HE who will at last, through their tolerated indolence, get them fired. It is HE who will lose the org. That's a pretty high price to pay for 'being a good fellow'.

...

"It is a maxim that crews, staffs and employees respect only those in power who do their jobs and get them to do theirs. Oh, yes, they will elect people who tell them they don't have to work. But it's interesting that the first ones they blame when

things go wrong are these worker-oriented softies: In the chaos of their wake, the next one people will support is a tough, strong one who knows his business.

"The only executives that staffs and crews really respect are those who get them to produce and get the job done.

"Look at Carter, the past unlamented president. Although he talked a lot about leadership, although he was the darling of the working man and all that, in office he was so wishy-washy, soft and incompetent 'everybody's pal' that they eventually threw him out with a landslide victory for his opponent, a very tough talking man who was actually antisocialist.

"However one tries to coat the pill, there is no substitute, in an executive, for the ability to get the crew to produce.

"The fire-breathing product officer will be followed and supported when the wishywashy old pal guy will be stepped all over in the rush to follow a real leader."
– L. Ron Hubbard, Policy Letter of 17 January 1982

Now I knew the basics. I was ready to assist the expansion of Scientology with brutal efficiency and blast all barriers away.

THE SPECIALISTS OF ETHICS

A new training program was released in spring 1998 for Sea Org members, entitled the *Sea Org Ethics Specialist Course*. It was a comprehensive course containing the majority of the ethics and justice policies of Scientology, which meant that one could learn all about the internal justice system on this course. It did not take long for Walter Kotrič to order Miklós to do this course immediately and he ordered him to do it in Copenhagen AND bring a twin with him to help him through the practical assignments. Miklos chose me as I was a fast student like him. I was not particularly happy to spend several weeks at the European base, as I had just started a new romantic relationship with the local representative of I HELP.

She was a very likeable and attractive girl, born in Oradea, Romania to an ethnic Hungarian family. She left her family when she turned 18 and moved to Budapest. She tried her luck as a singer, and then joined one of the Scientology missions near the capital and worked there until Miklós recruited her for the Sea Org. She was very enthusiastic about achieving the aims of Scientology – a trait which we had in common at that time.

She was three years older than me, but due to the increasing amount of stress I was under as the main recruiter, she looked younger than me. I heard that one of my fellow crew members remarked that he did not know why this pretty young gal was interested in that old geezer.

Our relationship remained platonic due to the strict Sea Org regulations, but we were very much in love. So, we did what we could in the precious small amount of time we could spend together – we took walks together for an hour or two each day, after 23:00.

As a faithful Church staff member, I considered my career and progress in Scientology to be more important than my romantic interests, so I departed for Copenhagen with Miklós.

We quickly completed the course as both of us spoke good English, were fast students and were able to progress roughly at the same rate. It turned out that Walter actually liked Miklós and sometimes had us visit him in his office. He showed us his other side – the likeable but overloaded executive, who could be very funny, especially when speaking about the annoying problems he encountered. So, when we showed up, he either told us some good stories about his exploits – apparently he worked close to Hubbard earlier and he was the one who did the mission to set up the Sea Org base in Moscow, Russia and to start the expansion of Scientology there, or he talked about his problems. Hamburg Org was one of his favorite subjects, starting with the first conversation we had. He said he did not know what was going on, but he was sure there were a lot of SPs (Suppressive Persons) among the public and the staff because they were not even able to keep their shiny new building in reasonably good shape. International Church management had sent two missions there – one was hunting down SPs and issuing "goldenrods" (ethics orders were issued on goldenrod-colored paper), and the other was apparently watering the flowers in the building. He added that he sent a 5-man command team to take over the org, all of them were good, proven and experienced Sea Org members, but they failed miserably and had to be recalled a few months later. He explained that they "turned into fucking vegetables" down there.

While he was talking about Hamburg, he quickly glanced through his incoming telexes on his computer. He noticed something, his face turned red, he bolted out of the office and ran to one of nearby rooms and started banging on the door and shouted loudly until they let him in. He came back 10 minutes later, grinning. He told us cheerfully that Senior HCO (one of the upper-level networks in Scientology, responsible for various personnel matters) wanted to steal one of his staff members again. He told us in confidence that if he were not so alert, they probably would have ripped off his entire crew already.

I was shocked to hear that from our European boss, but then I recalled my misfortunes and the conversation I had with the Deputy CO OTL about personnel psychosis.

Another thing about Walter was his absolute hate of "downstats" (people who were lazy, unproductive or spectacularly unsuccessful in life). One day we joined him as he went to eat in the Sea Org dining room in a separate building. A beggar approached us, asking for money. Walter looked up and snapped at him: "Fuck off! Get some work!"

The attitude was familiar – it was an application of Hubbard's "rewards and penalties" policy letter. According to Hubbard's theory, the key to success was rewarding good performers (upstats, he called them) and penalizing bad performers (the downstats). The idea was not just applied to organizational matters, but to life in general. Therefore giving money to a beggar would have been to reward a down statistic.

Walter paid us a final visit a day before we left. He approached us with a very stern look on his face, which scared the hell out of me. I feared the worst – I thought he was going to press us against the nearest wall and yell in our faces. Luckily, somebody else was the target day. Richard, the Deputy Executive Director of ABLE (the same one who had recently been on officer training) had returned from Stockholm, after a failed recruitment tour and was about to do his debrief. Walter, using an awful lot of four-letter words, told us that though he was aware that it was not an easy task to recruit for the Sea Org in Sweden, this "dickhead could not even get a single person to sign a fucking contract." He added that he had been in the Sea Org for a long time now, but he had never heard of a recruitment tour that came back completely empty-handed. Even in the worst places (Hamburg, Lyon, Oslo etc.) at least 1 or 2 contracts were always signed. Miklós thought over what he knew about the guy, then told Walter that Richard had just married recently, and his wife (who was also an OTL staff member) had long phone conversations with Richard in the night. I confirmed that I had also seen daily phone calls. Walter immediately lost his temper and shouted: "the out-ethics motherfucker must have spent the tour money on fucking phone calls to his wife!"

Then he ran off to ABLE offices. He was back 10 minutes later, dragging Richard along with him. The poor guy was quivering with fear, sweating and his face was completely red. So I assumed the full blast yelling phase had been completed by then.

Walter shoved the guy at us with such force that Richard almost fell over, then barked his order: "Handle him and find all of his other crimes!" and stormed away. Miklós dutifully did an ethics interview with Richard, but could not find anything other than the private phone calls he made using Church funds.

We had one more brief chat with Walter before we left. He told us that now it was our turn and we were to root out any out-ethics in the OTL by applying what we had just learnt.

After arriving in Budapest, we divided all known situations between the two of us and got rolling on the tough ethics interviews in the "spit out your crimes already" style. Our new ethics campaign had one major victim: the local representative of Scientology Missions International, who was a bit of a withdrawn young woman. Miklós did not like her because he perceived she lacked drive (he called her "1.5 voltage girl" behind her back), so it was an opportunity to demote her and promote one of her juniors, who was generally livelier. Our attitude became considerably tougher, and we treated new or badly performing crew members with ever more disdain. Miklós, for example, said half-jokingly to the student administrator in the training organization, who was responsible for scheduling students by phone: "You need to do two things: First, stop being so fucking miserable. Then you need to start calling people in." I was running similar lines on the personnel department people and resumed my recruitment efforts, but in a tougher style.

As an ethics specialist, I had to pass up forbidden fruit. Before the course, I was seriously contemplating breaching the Sea Org rules and taking a step or two further with Kriszta. But now I had to set a good example and I had to suppress my hormonal urges.

We could not enjoy this new situation for long, as a huge project hit us like a meteor shower – the translation of the huge (hundreds of pages long) *What is Scientology?* book that had to be done NOW, NOW, NOW.

THE BACKFIRED MISSION

We received the order in the usual Sea Org manner: no prior warning, zero chance to prepare and without any known or issued plans: translate the new edition of the English *What is Scientology?* book, containing a description of every single part of the Church, a detailed account of Hubbard's life and a good part of the philosophy and theory of Scientology. We had to virtually ignore all other tasks. The translation was to be done, then verified using a strict methodology and finally edited by a professional editor. We had one month to do it, so we were supposed to fire a mission to accomplish the task. We made a quick calculation; we needed about 160 part-time volunteer translators to get it done within the expected target. We received no funding, and had none of our own, so we had to rely on volunteering Scientologists. The situation was further complicated by the methodology we were supposed to use: there was a huge emphasis on exactness and the translation had to be as close to the original as possible, enforcing a very literal approach. Paraphrasing or altering the original meaning in any way was unacceptable. It had to match the English original, sentence by sentence.

A day later our misery was compounded by a new order – at the same time, we had to translate Hubbard's *Introduction to Scientology Ethics* book (itself an 800-page tome), which had been newly recompiled.

Miklós decided to send me on this mission together with the "Director of Personnel," a 15-year old boy. We had to get the books translated by the deadline, no matter what. The mission operator was one of Walter's deputies. We had to send a report to her every day at 22:30. She replied each night with her instructions and orders, so we could begin the next day accordingly.

Miklós tried to cheer me up by telling me about his most memorable mission. I was not too enthusiastic, as it appeared to be an impossible task and I was being set up as the sacrificial lamb to take all the blame should we not achieve the miracle. He told me the story of the unauthorized foundation of the OTL. The idea behind it (which he worked out with Walter) was to register the OTL and then do an important mission to prove that its existence was indeed required. Walter had an idea, and as all great ideas in the Church, it included collection of large sums of money.

At that time, the Budapest Mission was using photocopied unauthorized translations as course materials, as except for a few basic books, no Scientology materials were officially available in Hungarian. According to one interpretation of the relevant policies, the Budapest organization should have paid royalties on the pirate copies to the publishing corporation of the Church called New Era Publications International in Copenhagen. So Walter fired a mission, formed from the staff of the freshly established OTL, to calculate all the royalties owed for the course packs locally produced in the past 7 years and to collect all the backlogged monies owed, complete with interest.

According to Miklós, his first task was to "get in ethics" in the Budapest Mission. According to Sea Org logic, if someone does not pay royalties, he is stealing directly from L. Ron Hubbard, the biggest crime of all. So Miklós and his cohorts called a special staff meeting and announced that everyone had to do an overt/withhold write-up. Walter warned Miklós beforehand that during the initial briefing there would be staff members who would try to stop this by stating that such actions had to be approved by the Case Supervisor[16], so they were to prepare to address this eventuality head-on. One of the missionaires was supposed to take photos of any such elements, and another was to conspicuously take notes on a black clipboard.

---

[16] the person responsible for supervising all auditors and auditing actions; the sum of all individual aberrations, fixed ideas, painful memories etc. was called one's "case"

Just as Walter predicted, one of the staff members stood up and voiced his concerns about Case Supervisor approval for such actions. Immediately, a photo was taken and notes were written. This proved to be enough to dissuade anyone else from protesting. Miklós then summoned the executives of the mission and briefed them on his task. He asked them how much work would be required to collect all the invoices written for course packs in the last seven years (they were stored in big cardboard boxes). One of the Mission executives responded with an answer that became a running gag in OTL later (almost always mentioned when we faced seemingly impossible tasks or deadlines): "100 people working for 10 days fulltime!" Miklós just smiled and said: "OK then, let's get cracking on those boxes!"

Naturally, this meant that every staff member in the mission (they had almost 100 staff at that time) had to stay there for the night to sort and collect invoices. They managed to get it done by the following morning, the debt was calculated and Miklós and his missionaires relentlessly pressured the executives until the organization paid the bill in full, mainly by forcing them to rake in as much cash as they could.

So, now it was my turn to produce a similar miracle. I had to mobilize all Hungarian Scientologists who knew enough English to translate and to get as many paid "wogs" on board as needed to get it done in time. I went to all the larger missions in Hungary, appointed translation liaisons and got volunteers working for us, while constantly calling English-speaking Scientologists in Budapest to come in and help.

There was enormous pressure on me – if my mission operator was not pleased with our progress, she would accuse me of sabotaging the expansion of Scientology and threaten me with dire consequences (demotion, a lengthy ethics program or a trip to the RPF). I tried to pass on the pressure as much as I could, mainly to the other missionaire on the project (yes, the 15-year old). He could not take it and after a while ran away, never returning to the Sea Org and in fact he left Scientology altogether. His father was the President of WISE Hungary, and he was very upset with me and (somewhat correctly) blamed me for driving his son away from the Sea Org and Scientology. He never forgave me, so I managed to make at least one lifelong enemy during the impossible mission.

But that was the least of my worries. The situation quickly got out of hand in Copenhagen, as they were supposed to translate both books into all European languages. As the order came directly from Miscavige, Walter had to take over the entire operation personally. Miklós was also ordered to do the same in Hungary. He was now personally pushing the translations in his usual forceful style, but he had only two Sea Org translators and four fulltime qualified volunteers to work with, while I did my best to round up new people as volunteers. They were already pushed to the limit, sleeping 2-3 hours a day for weeks. The editor of the materials, who was a Scientologist, was moved into the OTL apartment which had been turned into translations HQ. He was constantly given coffee to minimize his need for sleep. After a while some of the translators fell asleep while typing. One day, when I came to the apartment with contact information for new volunteers, one of the Sea Org translators was lying on the ground sleeping. Miklós, also looking very tired, tried to wake him to find out if he achieved his target during the night. Walter was calling to find out about the progress, and Miklós just replied: "Sir, I do not know how much of his target was done. The Translations Director is unconscious right now." Walter was also half-asleep, so luckily for us, he was too tired to go into beast mode. He just sighed and said that we should send a report when the translator regained his senses.

As the pressure increased, every OTL staff member who spoke English had to do some part of the translations – first, outside of the official working schedule (9:00–22:30), and then later they were ordered to ignore their normal duties and translate all day long. Another problem was the unfinished nature of the English material itself – it kept changing as we progressed, so sometimes we had to redo sections.

The net result of all this rush, changes in the English materials, overworked staff and sleep deprivation was mass confusion. Miklós had to be at his absolute best to maintain any sort of control over the situation.

The Translations Unit staff had no way to properly train or control the new volunteers recruited by me, therefore there was no noticeable increase in the volume of translations being accomplished. Anne, my mission operator, noticed this after two weeks and wanted an explanation.

She stated that either I was lying about the newly recruited translators or the Translations Unit had sent them away. In my reply to her, I gave a detailed list of all the translators I had recruited and what happened to each. I was terrified of becoming the fall guy for the failure, so I decided to shift the blame to the OTL. I described the executives as lazy and out-ethics and asserted they had failed to assume the required level of responsibility for the project.

I gave some examples of OTL staff members who had tried to evade the mandatory translation jobs assigned to them by stating that "it is the job of the Translations Unit, and they should be doing it."

I poured all my accumulated bitterness into that report, as well as the frustration I felt due to the stark contrast between the ideal scene described by Hubbard and the reality. As a result, the report suggested that the situation was worse than it actually was.

Anne wrote me a lengthy reply and based on the data I provided, decided to scrap the current translations mission and transform it into an ethics (i.e. punishment) mission. According to her analysis, "the OTL had sabotaged the project, so it was time to hit them hard with old-fashioned Sea Org justice." I had to remove Miklós from running the translations, I had to take over while "putting in ethics" in the OTL and I was now responsible for the deadlines.

Since Anne did not bother to do any fact-checking on what I wrote, I realized that she probably did not want to. The new situation had advantages for her, too – she now had a scapegoat for not making the deadlines (the out-ethics OTL) and she was off the hook for being an ineffective mission operator. I also realized that finding a target to blame was a way to survive in the Sea Org, where impossible deadlines were an everyday occurrence.

There was one more realization I had. I knew I was way over my head. I had developed a profound respect for Miklós, as he was undoubtedly the most talented person in the OTL. I felt that it would be impossible to do a better job than him. Anne was not interested in any of my concerns. She wrote me that I would either root out any and all out-ethics in the OTL or I would be targeted for them – according to her logic, if I were not willing to hit the locals hard, then I must be in agreement with the lazy and out-ethics saboteurs, and thus deserving of even harsher punishment.

So, trying to be a good Sea Org member, I did what I had to do. I assigned the so-called "Danger Condition" to Miklós and all OTL executives. This consisted of a) bypassing them, i.e. taking over the translations project, b) having them write up their "crimes" (and implementing the appropriate punishment) and c) reorganizing the entire area, so the dangerous situation would not occur again. This ethics cleansing did not stop at the executives though. I was instructed to find the crimes of the two Sea Org translators as well. I looked through the contents of their computer hard drives and found that both had the popular computer game *Starcraft* installed, and they were playing it over the local computer network (to be fair, they did not have much time for this). I made a huge scene about it (I could not find anything else), using the yelling & screaming tech I learnt from Walter. I (unjustly) accused them of playing the game all the time I was not present, which impeded the progress of the translations. They also had to write up their crimes. Anne was satisfied with the level of terror I introduced, and I made two new enemies. Meanwhile, Miklós tried to get back in good graces of the European HQ, and forced every English-speaking crew member to work in the translations unit almost full-time. This included Judith Miklán, my worst enemy, who never forgave me for the telex I sent and hated me with a passion. I sensed she was waiting for her opportunity to get her revenge.

I became increasingly unpopular with the Sea Org members working day and night on translations as well as with the executives who were subjected to all the punishment I was ordered to dish out. I always made sure to sleep at least 6 or 7 hours and spend some time with my girlfriend, which irritated the hell out of the crew members who were sleeping very little for weeks. I had a bad feeling – I felt that something was being plotted against me.

A few days later, the new Director of Special Affairs in Budapest Mission, Marika Szamper, approached me. She told me that she just got an order from OSA Europe and I had to get a metered ethics interview. They wanted to check if I was a potential trouble source of any kind for the Church. I told her to go to hell and never come back, as I was a Sea Org member and she had no authority over me. This was not the end of it though, as the next day my mission operator confirmed that it had to be done. The interview was done by one of the auditors in the mission, which I found very odd (and demeaning, as a proud Sea Org member). Nothing came up, and I thought this was behind me now over.

I could not have been more wrong. The next day I was stopped by Péter, the deputy Commanding Officer of OTL, who waved a telex in my face. It was sent by the European OSA office. In short, I was removed from the mission and my position as Executive Establishment Officer, and I had to travel to Copenhagen in 24 hours for a lengthy Security Check[17]. Miklós got a separate order from Walter that I had to be under 24-hour watch and someone had to physically escort me to Copenhagen, so I could not escape.

It was so surreal that at first I thought it was a practical joke. I tried to get more information out of Péter. He told me reluctantly that I was considered to be a spy sent by the National Security Office of Hungary. I thought that I was now the fall guy and somebody must have misinterpreted what I said in Munich. It seemed it would be simple to clear up this confusion, so I did not protest much and went along with it (not that I had much choice).

I said goodbye to my girlfriend and packed my things. She was very worried, but I told her nothing bad could happen. We were members of the most ethical and rational organization on the planet after all, so this matter would be treated with fairness and justice.

So, at the end of April, 1998, in the middle of a huge translations evolution, I went to Copenhagen to face my accusers. Miklós managed to negotiate the buddy clause, so I boarded the plane alone. I was told that I would be picked up at the airport and I should not try to do anything stupid.

---

[17] metered interrogation, which is not protected by priest-penitent privilege; everything the suspect said was actionable

Chapter Six

Under Watch

THE DISCIPLE OF THE DARK ONE

Three Church security guards were waiting for me at the airport. They escorted me to a car and I was brought directly to the European OSA office. Two female Sea Org officers were awaiting me. They introduced themselves as Wahida Hickey, investigations director of OSA Europe and Natália Nemes (a young Hungarian lady of my age), who was the senior investigations and reports officer for Scientology in Europe. I knew I was in bigger trouble than I had expected. The presence of these two senior executives confirmed this was not just a misunderstood situation to clear up. They told me briefly that I was considered to be a covert informant, sent by the National Security Office of Hungary. Wahida added that the game was over as a Scientologist had recognized me as one of the students of Dr. András Veér, the No.1. enemy of Scientology in Hungary. According to their theory, Dr. Veér had joined forces with the National Security Office and they sent in one of his best students (i.e. me) to spy on the church. In their view, the "destructive actions" I supposedly committed on the translations mission and my "suspicious behavior" (I was caught a few times reading communications addressed to other people, when my curiosity got the better of me) confirmed the accusation. Therefore they were conducting a full and thorough investigation.

At this point Natália took over. She called in a security guard (a young Hungarian named József) and informed me that from now on, József would escort me everywhere and I would be under 24-hour watch until all my security checks and interrogations were complete. Also, we were to move in together in a separate room in one of the crew berthing buildings. I was forbidden to go anywhere alone; a security guard had to accompany me wherever I went. Note: security personnel had additional duties in the Church, not just the safeguarding of assets and personnel. They were also supposed to watch whether crew members were working hard and send back to work anyone they found loafing or taking unauthorized breaks. If someone slept in, it was security that sent a guard to get him out of the bed and drag him into work.

Natália also told me that I would receive a very long, e-metered Security Check called the "Germany Sec Check." It was originally developed for Germany, where infiltration attempts by their national security agency were supposedly common. A specialist was flown in from Germany – a man trained by Miscavige's direct underlings to conduct such special interrogations. The questions were not limited to suspected espionage activities – I had to confess every harmful act or transgression that sprang to mind during the sessions, even if these had nothing to do with the main line of questioning. Priest-penitent privilege did not apply, so they could use anything I said against me. Finally, the sessions were videotaped.

I was also told that the whole procedure might take several months because a) my auditor had other suspects to interrogate, so he had maximum 2-3 hours per day for me; b) all questions had to be fully cleared, i.e. the auditor asks the question repeatedly and extracts every associated harmful act of commission or omission until the question fails to produce any reaction on the E-meter; and c) the so-called Case Supervisor reviews the notes and worksheets of the auditor each night and if he made a mistake, then he had to restudy and/or drill certain procedures. In other words, they really wanted to make sure that nothing was missed.

Natália left the worst for last: as I was officially a suspicious individual who had caused a lot of problems for the Church and because they were being forced to provide food and shelter for such scum, I had to work in exchange for their generosity. For such untrustworthy lowlifes, heavy manual labor was the only option. The security guards were the appointed taskmasters and they were always briefed what I should do next.

The first major task was the construction of the new security office, scheduled to begin in the next 3-4 days. I had a fleeting thought that it was like forcing the inmates to build a new prison, but I dispelled this ill-intentioned idea from my mind at once.

It was already late, so József escorted me to our room. I already accepted the fact that I was now, in Scientology terms, an ethics/security particle[18], so I had no illusions regarding the quality of the berthing space I was being assigned.

When I first entered the room, I knew instantly that I was considered a very dangerous operative. It was likely the worst room in the worst of the Sea Org hotels. The room was clearly targeted for renovation. All the plaster had been removed and the resultant debris was lying all over the floor, along with and a bag of cement, a bucket of paint etc. The solitary light source was a single light bulb hanging from the ceiling. The room was otherwise empty. József

---

[18] in Scientology, everything is considered a "particle" that travels on communication lines (including people)

brought me to the attic to look for mattresses. We found two mouse-chewed mattresses and two sleeping bags, which were probably World War II vintage (or perhaps earlier). It was better than sleeping directly on the floor.

Then I learnt the bathroom/shower usage rules for people like me. When I used the bathroom or shower, József waited outside until I finished; when he had to use the facilities, he called another guard to watch me until he was done.

So, I cleaned up the room a bit and prepared my mattress and sleeping bag. It turned out József had special nighttime orders: he had to place his mattress right in front of the door, then lock it and place the key carefully under his mattress.

I gave some thought to this whole new situation I found myself in. I was still a true believer, so I reluctantly accepted my fate and decided to fully cooperate. I thought that I now had a chance to fully clear my name and I would not have any barriers later to progress on the Bridge and achieving total spiritual freedom. I did not want to lose this opportunity, thus I had no other option.

"NOT THE USUAL COMM EV[19] BUNCH"

The next day József introduced me to the other "inmates." As it turned out, there were three fellow disgraced Sea Org members who were also under 24-hour watch. As I mentioned earlier, we were to participate in the preparatory work on the new security office, scheduled to begin in the next few days. As a warm-up job, we were sent to help out the ongoing renovation of Hotel Corona. I was on window painting detail, with the occasional wheelbarrowing of debris.

I tried to get to know my fellow inmates and learn how and why they got themselves into the same type of mess I now found myself in. As it turned out, three of them were also victims of the translations evolution, and the fourth had felt up his girlfriend without marrying her first.

The undisputed leader of our gang was Ralph Pieters-Kwiers, formerly the Establishment Officer of the European Scientology translations unit, responsible for the recruitment and training of Sea Org translators. He was a very tall middle-aged guy, and his happy and easy-going nature was in stark contrast with the aura of dread surrounding our situation. According to him, he had

---

[19] short for Committee of Evidence, a kind of a Scientology trial by jury, which is supposed to be impartial, establish all the facts and come up with a ruling

major disagreements with the incredible pressure and terror tactics employed by the executives. Apparently, Miscavige did not trust the European Sea Org outfit to complete the translations in time, so he sent an 8-man (!) mission to get everything completed by the deadline. The missionaires exemplified the take-no-prisoners attitude glorified by Hubbard, mercilessly setting brutal targets and not letting people leave until those targets were met. The situation was even more dire than what I experienced in Hungary. Translations personnel hardly got any sleep at all, the atmosphere was dreadful and severe retaliation followed even the smallest mistakes. Ralph was at odds with this approach from the beginning and tried to use internal PR methods to raise morale (and thereby production).

He ended up in a major fight with the chief missionaire and was subsequently removed from his position and sent to do manual labor under 24-hour watch. He also had a so-called Non-Enturbulation Order issued on him – a kind of last warning, printed on goldenrod paper like a Suppressive Person Declare. Non-Enturbulation Orders essentially forbade the recipient from making critical remarks about the Church or its management, or "causing trouble" in any way. Even a single report of any such remark would result in being instantly declared a suppressive person. He was also to be given a lot of Security Checking just like me, possibly in the hope of getting him to see the error of his ways and change his way of thinking. At that time he showed no sign of any change of heart, he was still critical about staff members adhering to the party line, sometimes making crude jokes about their subservience.

Ralph was still loyal to Hubbard and his teachings, but had a damning opinion about the current state of affairs in the Church. He told me he was worried about a new trend in executive appointments – unquestioned loyalty to top management seemed to be the new requirement. The percentage of executives who had mercilessly executed orders without asking questions had increased steeply. People who objected or had different ideas were swept aside. After leaving the Church, I realized that this attitude was based on a principle of Hubbard. He defined organizational ethics as a tool to remove "counter-intentions" and "other-intentions." So, according to him, the key to success was the dismissal of people who had minor or major disagreements with the intentions of top management. Robert Dale was another permanent fixture in our little group. The Englishman found Scientology in Birmingham, became a Dianetics auditor and then joined the Sea Org in Copenhagen. He seemed to be a very competent person, almost a genius, as he demonstrated exceptional knowledge of architecture and computer technology as well as martial arts. He did not like to talk about his career in the Sea Org, so I never really learned why he wound up assigned to manual labor.

The third member of our team was a middle-aged Norwegian lady, who had been the Executive Director of the Scientology Church in Oslo. After joining the Sea Org, she was assigned to the translations unit as "Norwegian Translations In-Charge." She had achieved the State of Clear, which meant that theoretically she was completely devoid of aberration or irrational thought that concerned her personal survival. The reality was in stark contrast with that though. She was assigned to our group because she entertained suicidal thoughts and tried to jump out of a window on the fourth floor (for some inexplicable reasons, the security guards were frequently made crude jokes about that in her presence). The Norwegian translation of the two books was going rather slowly (mainly due to the lack of workforce – the number of active Scientologists in Norway who spoke English and were willing to translate as volunteers was very limited). Walter was not exactly moved by the facts and put the "pressure of God" on the poor woman. She eventually cracked.

She told me that one time Walter yelled at her for minutes and while watching her reaction, announced this to the entire translations crew: "Somebody is stopping the book and that somebody is working hard to prevent it from being completed." It was not hard to guess whom he meant. She became even more depressed when the Miscavige people arrived and the situation deteriorated even further. Lack of proper sleep and nutrition combined with the constant pressure and working 18-21 hours a day in front of a computer monitor took its toll. She felt so worthless that she started to contemplate suicide. She confessed this to one of the security guards when she was caught looking out of a window for too long.

She was immediately sent to do manual labor and was told that she would get a little auditing to fix her up a bit and then she would be offloaded from the Sea Org. One of the security guards told me in a casual manner that she was constantly watched so she could not harm herself. They were apparently more concerned about preventing any PR and legal problems than her wellbeing. The auditing she was given was intended only to ensure she would not commit suicide in the near future. At that time, I had no real problem accepting that way of thinking. I sincerely believed that only the Church had the secret of the route to total spiritual freedom, therefore it had to be protected at all costs. People were expendable for the greater good.

A few days later we were transferred to the basement of the central building, where we began construction of the new security office. The first task was the destruction of the old furniture stored there. Robert seized the opportunity to show off his martial arts skills and demolished a few cupboards with his bare hands and feet. He also told us how he was attacked by a gang of seven in college. He got through the fight with a few scratches, but his attackers wound up in hospital. Judging from his demonstration of strength, I was inclined to believe him.

A few uneventful days followed – I went to confess my sins for 2-3 hours every day, then I rejoined the ethics particle brigade, working until nearly midnight. After we demolished the floor with pickaxes and cleaned out all rooms, we were supposed to destroy a set of concrete steps using a jackhammer. We really enjoyed this part, but I was pretty sure that we breached a number of work safety regulations by using that piece of equipment after a minute-long demonstration (called "instant hatting"). It was getting late, but as good Sea Org members, we were not interested in how we might disturb the wogs. 5 minutes after 6 PM the Port Captain (who was, among other things, responsible for maintaining friendly relations with the neighbors) of the Sea Org base arrived, a very nice and attractive young blonde girl called Magali.

She thoroughly reprimanded Ralph for making so much noise as the neighbors had specifically and repeatedly asked that all construction work cease at 18:00. The OSA PR person also arrived and told us that from now on, we were only allowed to work indoors after that time. When they left, Ralph in his typical style commented that they had it all backwards, as Scientologists were supposed to "be causative over wogs" and not the other way around.

A new ethics particle arrived the next day – man called Cif, who was the Birthday Game[20] In-Charge for Europe.

We asked our guard about him and he was very eager to share the juicy details. According to him, Walter was doing his usual daily inspection and found out that the stats of the European orgs were crashing for the week. He then towered above the poor 5'3" Cif and proceeded to deliver an old-fashioned Severe Reality Adjustment (that's a Sea Org term meaning to adjust the person's thinking so they understand how terribly they have been performing their duties and vow to reform immediately). For some reason, Cif lost it and assaulted Walter. Naturally, Walter was not the kind of person to pass up a good tavern brawl style punch-up. Finally the security guards had to intervene. Cif was sent to do menial labor and had to appear before a Committee of Evidence for sentencing. Upon hearing this, Ralph shouted to Cif that our gang

---

[20] a competition in which all Scientology organizations around the world participate. It is basically a year-long production contest, starting and ending on Hubbard's birthday (13th of March) each year. It was launched by the man himself in 1983. The production and performance of Scientology organizations is measured on a weekly basis (which ends and begins at 14:00 every Thursday). Points are awarded for rising statistics (1 for small, 3 for large increases). The calculation is based on the degree of expansion happening locally. All continental Sea Org bases have a person responsible for calculating the weekly points and sending the standings to each org. In addition to that, they are also responsible for getting the org staff members enthusiastic about the game and to produce more.

106

was not the usual Comm Ev bunch, so he should not bother trying to join us, the really hardened criminals.

Shortly after that, my daily schedule was changed. The Case Supervisor of the Norwegian lady ordered 1-2 hours of daily walks to accompany her auditing. As she needed two escorts to make sure she could not get away and no more security guards were available, I was ordered to accompany her and her guard for the walks. For some mysterious reason, we had to take these walks in Christiania. I did not know at that time why this district was so famous, but it became clear after a few days that it was not your garden-variety Western European suburb.

Alessandro, an Italian teenage boy joined us a few days later. His "crime" was being involved in some heavy petting with his teenage girlfriend. As Robert and I preferred to keep to ourselves, he mainly talked to Ralph as they discussed the internal problems of the European base.

After a few weeks, I became acquainted with all the eight security guards of the base. Oddly, five of them were Hungarians. Our shared nationality made it easier for me to learn more about the base than I should have been allowed to. During our conversations, they dropped a few hints about a recent purge in the security ranks. Apparently, there was a huge security flap[21] and the entire security unit was sent to the RPF. A recently recruited contingent of Hungarians was used to replace the majority of them. According to Ralph, a female crew member was raped after walking home from the office building to her Sea Org hotel late at night. Naturally, the security guards refused to talk about it, so all I knew was this piece of news from Ralph.

Nevertheless, I was able to get some information out of my fellow Hungarians. According to them, Robert Dale was placed under watch as "he knew too much" about the security system of the base (apparently, he was also a security expert). He shocked the European RTC[22] Representative by showing her various ways someone could steal the precious OT materials from the European Advanced Organization, due to incompetent placement of security cameras. Therefore, he was personally audited by Miscavige's European enforcer, Ms. Antonella Tisi.

Only the senior executives were allowed to have cell phones "for security reasons." Everyone else had their phones confiscated. Therefore security personnel used walkie-talkies. As it was relatively easily listen into such commu-

---

[21] serious issue or problem

[22] short for Religious Technology Center; in theory, this corporation is the holder of all Scientology trademarks and copyrights, and has no management duties or rights. In actual fact, it is the top organization in the Scientology hierarchy; its chairman/CEO is David Miscavige, the *de facto* leader of the Church.

nication, they used super secret codes so that the "enemy" would not find out about our plans. I found out later that the system they used was the ten code system used by US law enforcement. Naturally, the young European Sea Org members had no clue about this, so they were very proud of top management who had found a way to annoy the various secret services who were attempting to spy on them at all times. Unfortunately for them, even I was able to work out what the codes meant after listening to some of these communications. Some code.

I completed and passed the security check by the end of July, 1998. I thought, somewhat naively, that there could only have been one conclusion – I was not a spy. OSA submitted the entire documentation to the European RTC Representative. She was not convinced and demanded further auditing and interrogation. She ordered a review of the PDH Check I received in Clearwater and I also had to receive a tailor-made security check, comprised of questions based on all the things I had said during the session. She also ordered that all that auditing should be videotaped and the Senior Case Supervisor of the Advanced Organization had to personally watch all these tapes to ensure nothing was missed.

I was not exactly liked by Security and OSA personnel before, but now they positively hated me for being such an incredible nuisance. They thought it was over when I completed the Germany sec check and they could finally reassign my personal security guard to more important tasks. But instead they now had to solve an even bigger problem. It turned out that there was only one auditor on the entire Sea Org base who was qualified to deliver the review of the PDH Check and he was a leading auditor of the Advanced Organization. The executives of that organization flat-out refused to allow him to audit me, as he was fully booked auditing paying public.

There was no immediate solution. Additionally, the Security Chief was no longer able to provide a full-time guard to watch me, so he implemented a "solution" – the security guards took turns and when no one was available, I had to sit in front of the Security Office, facing a camera, for a "maximum 1-2 hours per day."

This quickly turned into 5-8 hours, and I was given Hubbard books so I would not get bored. This continued for two weeks. One of the guards told me half-jokingly that there had been someone like me earlier, who had sat there for weeks, and finally he had a sort of a mental breakdown). Time quickly went by reading the copious volumes of Hubbard, so I survived this latest ordeal relatively unscathed. They took me out for 20-25 minutes at each meal, so I could spend some time outside. Nevertheless, it was rather depressing to sit idly for hours, basically watching a camera watch me.

My girlfriend, Krisztina, also tried to keep my spirits up. Though I was not allowed to speak to her on the phone, I could send her letters and receive her replies. All these letters were read by the Security guards though, so I could not write what I really felt. But knowing that somebody was there who cared for me helped immensely to get through the rough patches.

My family also tried to get through to me – I was invited to attend the wedding of one of my cousins. I had no choice but to politely decline by writing an acceptable truth that I was on an intensive training program which could not be interrupted.

My predicament was fortunately over in two weeks. The RTC Representative spotted me sitting in front of the Security Office and asked about it. She was furious when she learned that nothing had happened to carry out her orders. She gave 24 hours to the Security Chief to arrange the auditor to deliver the action and assign a full-time guard to me. My popularity broke new negative records, but somehow they managed to arrange the auditor and the guard. This new security check took another three weeks and I was again found to be innocent.

The 24-hour watch was ended and after all these months I was a free man again. To be honest, I learned to appreciate some basic human rights as a side effect of my nightmare. After the last auditing session was completed, I was sent to OSA. Wahida, the investigations officer greeted me and handed me a pile of lengthy legalese declarations to sign. I glanced through them. They were various declarations wherein I had to promise not to reveal any confidential data I learnt while in the Sea Org, and I also agreed to pay 100,000 Danish Kroner for each and every violation of these agreements. I gathered my courage and asked Wahida why that was necessary. She told me that I should not worry and this was just a formality. I signed everything she gave me. The only way out was to cooperate. She could have given me anything to sign at that point and I would have done so. I was on the verge of being able to go home.

She then told me that I would have to appear before a Fitness Board, which would review all the documentation and the result of my auditing. They would make sure that I was qualified to be a Sea Org member and wrap up the whole matter.

Obviously, there were two ways to interpret this; I tried to convince myself that they intended to keep me in the Sea Org. Nothing came up during the lengthy sessions that would disqualify me and I was not a spy. The behavior and attitude of the security guards told me otherwise, though. As soon as I came back from the OSA office, I was told that I need to leave the base before Thursday 14:00, so I would not be a minus point on their statistic (it was Tuesday afternoon). They called OTL and got them to pay for my bus ticket.

Thursday morning I was escorted out of the Sea Org base and I was told that I should go back to the OTL where I would be informed what my next step was to be.

QUALIFIED OR NOT?

I got a rather cool and tense reception at OTL. I was assigned to odd jobs around the office, as no one seemed to know what my exact status was. Miklós and the Hungarian OSA representative tried to get some information from their European counterparts, but all they got was the usual brush-off reply "we will send you all the data by mail, don't call us again" etc. Thus, the bizarre story dragged on. Meanwhile, I was addressing a gigantic stockpile of unfiled documents, which occupied me for about 2 months. In the eternal struggle to push up the stats every week, there was no time left for such organizational tasks as filing.

At the end of November, the scheduled mailpack of letters and folders arrived from the European base. I was responsible for distributing the internal communications, so I went through it. There was a big red folder in the packet, labeled "Committee of Evidence – Peter Bonyai." Apparently, OSA had secretly arranged a Comm Ev behind my back. I read through the folder to find out what happened after I was sent home. Judging from its contents, OSA had valiantly tried to get me kicked out of the Sea Org. The Fitness Board was supposed to find an acceptable reason to dismiss me by exploring one or two of the flexible qualification requirements. However, they rejected that plan, stating they could find no real reason to offload me, and only a Committee of Evidence might terminate my service in the Sea Org. OSA then convened this disciplinary body. They in turn, according to the minutes of their meetings, reviewed the so-called evidence provided by OSA. This consisted of a knowledge report stating that I was a student of Dr. András Veér and acted "suspiciously"; my statistics, graphed and shown in a way to seem downtrending; all of my auditing folders and documents, containing everything I had ever done all the way back to the first mischief I was involved in as a small child. They decided that I did not meet the high ethical standards required to be a member of the Sea Organization and I was to be offloaded immediately. The "fact-finding body" concluded all that without asking me a single question or confronting me with any of the accusations or making any effort to establish the facts of the case. They sent their findings and recommendation to the International Justice Chief (the head of the internal justice system of the Church) in Los Angeles for approval. Surprisingly, the reply was what one might have expected from an impartial and highly trained Church official. He rejected their submission stating that "acting strangely" in itself did not constitute an eligibility problem for the Sea Organization. He also reprimanded the committee for failing to provide proper evidence for their generalized statements. The committee did not respond and apparently, that was the end of it.

I got the picture – because I was found innocent, it looked really bad that they had wasted so much effort and so many resources on auditing me for months and placing me under 24-hour watch. It would have been easier to rationalize if I was found ineligible for the Sea Org.

I was really pissed off. I considered myself a mild-mannered fellow. I fully cooperated with them to clear my name, did everything they asked and all I got in exchange was their repeated efforts to secretly stab me in the back. OSA did not even bother to send a short message to clarify my situation – they just sent the rejected Committee of Evidence findings and the folder.

Apparently, they blamed me for the whole mess. Had I not "acted strangely," the whole ordeal could have been avoided.

Nevertheless, Miklós was glad that it was finally over and found me a new position in the training division of OTL.

CHAPTER SEVEN

The Training Center

CLIMBING UP

I started work in the training center in December, 1998. The "center" was a rented 80 square meter (about 700 sq ft) apartment, used as a course room/office space in the day, and as berthing space at night. It had three staff when I was assigned to it. A Course Supervisor, a Registrar (salesperson) and an administrator (who happened to be the 12-year old girl I had brought over from the Budapest Mission a year earlier).

In order to understand the role of the training center, a brief summary of the income sources of OTL Hungary is in order. I wrote about it earlier, but I will reiterate for the sake of clarity.

As the establishment of the OTL was a rogue action, there were no clear policies on how it was supposed to sustain itself financially. As a temporary measure, the rules designed for continental liaison offices were adapted for us. In 1996, these policies were revised and codified by Miscavige, then implemented as the "New Era of Management" throughout the entire Scientology network. These policies were considered just as sacred as anything Hubbard wrote, so we had to apply the system without the slightest deviation.

There was one problem – the continental organizational scheme was built on the idea that there were several Church organizations and one Advanced Organization located in its area of responsibility. The continental office would receive a certain portion of the income of these organizations, and this "management fee" was designed to be its main source of income. The role of the continental training center was to train the Sea Org members on the base for their jobs (almost exclusively Hubbard materials) and to audit them (which usually meant security checking). Additionally, non-Sea Org org executives were sometimes brought in to do intensive management training there.

This model was unworkable in Hungary, as there were no orgs (let alone an Advanced Organization) and only a handful of missions. So, we had two income sources left: collecting freeloader debts of ex-staff and selling courses in our training center to Scientologists. Anyone who left the Sea Org before his billion-year contract was up was considered a freeloader, and had to pay for all the training course and auditing he received for "free" as a Sea Org member. In order to increase the potential income, the courses were way overpriced.

For example, we billed 3,000 USD for basic training, which was normally completed in 3-4 weeks, and between 500 and 1,000 USD was for charged for each subsequent course. We did not have too many freeloaders at that time, but due to this pricing policy, we could collect hefty sums from these traitors. We were relentless and ruthless and pursued even penny. Even minors were charged for every service they received (though they got a 50% discount – Hubbard even had a policy for this).

Theoretically, we would not have any income from the training center, as we had no orgs in our area of control. But Miklós was not the type to let any money-making opportunity pass, so he arranged with Walter that we could deliver paid courses to mission staff and to "VIP" non-staff Scientologists.

As these public Scientologists were allowed to receive courses that were translated in the Translations Unit, but not yet officially published for anyone else to use, we soon had a comfortable monopoly on higher-level Scientology courses in Hungary. This was a source of much friction with the Budapest Mission, as our training center took the people they turned into Scientologists to enroll them on our premium services.

One of our key services was the Student Hat course, which I had completed back in Munich. We delivered it, using an amateur translation produced by volunteer Scientologists. Another popular service was the Basic Course Supervisor Course, which was delivered to mission staff and to companies run by Scientologists who wanted to set up their own Scientology course rooms.

My first position was Delivery In-Charge – my job was to call all students who had unfinished courses and help them complete by applying Hubbard's study technology. According to him, the only reason a student left a course incomplete was that he had gone by one or two words he did not understand. My job was to find those words and get them cleared.

I note that it is relatively easy to rack up unknown words on a Scientology course. Hubbard liked to tell tales and anecdotes about his various adventures around the world and he liberally spiced them with the special terms of the subject in question. Ironically, in the same lecture where he announced his discovery of the power of the misunderstood word, he went into a lengthy tale about his studies as a photographer. Poor students had to look up the various photo development methods used in the '50s if they wanted to understand what Hubbard was talking out. The hundreds of abbreviations used in Scientology as well as the special terminology containing over a thousand new words created for the subject significantly deteriorated the general accessibility of the materials.

There was one distinct advantage to my position in the training center – I did not have the vast workload I had in my previous position and I was actually able to finish off each evening by 22:30 and have some leisure time till midnight, including spending quality time with my girlfriend. The strict Sea Org rules did not exactly help our relationship blossom, as we were both around 20 and our hormones were in overdrive. Therefore, it seemed that the next logical step was to get married as soon as possible – there was no other way to live and be together. Krisztina was reluctant at first, as despite having a good understanding of each other she still felt there was something missing from our relationship. After a prolonged period of courting, she eventually surrendered and agreed to marry me. The wedding was arranged, and we were married in February, 1999. My close relatives as well the executives of the OTL were all invited. The atmosphere was rather tense as the two camps did not really speak to each other. Imre, the President of WISE and the eldest of the Scientologists, tried to get into communication with my family, but he did not have much success. My "wog" relatives did their best to ignore my fellow shipmates, who left the party early before it really became good thanks to the alcohol that was present. In their minds, the planet would not clear itself and the stats were waiting to be pushed up starting again first thing the following morning.

I was a bit disheartened by these events – if I was not able to get my closest relatives to accept Scientology, what chance did we have for clearing the entire society? But then as a good Scientologist, I quickly banished these doubts too.

I had more important things to do than trying to convert my family. Imre, observing the quality of service in the training center, decided to use his considerable sales skills to convince some specifically selected people to do some courses there. His targets were "wog" businessmen or media people who had came into contact with Scientology, but had not yet taken a first step.

The first was a reporter who worked for RTL Klub, the largest commercial TV channel in Hungary. She was dating a WISE member at the time and Imre sold her on the idea of doing a communication course at the OTL. He even volunteered to help her through the drills. She came in a few times, Imre was always with her, but she did not really like the course and left for good after a few visits. I did not call her or try to handle her as Hubbard had a rather damning opinion about newspaper and TV reporters.

The second big catch was a pair of businessmen, the owner and CEO of Premier Pension Fund, a large private retirement fund. Imre was trying to get them to implement Hubbard's administrative technology in their corporation and he hoped that success there would be an excellent advertisement for WISE and the Hubbard methods. He sold them a training package and started them on the first course, the Student Hat. He wanted them to eventually study the entirety of Hubbard's "admin tech," and helped them along by conducting small seminars and providing personalized coaching for them. They progressed well on the course, but then the Hungarian securities commission shut down the retirement fund due to accounting irregularities and suspected embezzlement, and the owner stopped coming. The CEO did complete, but then never showed for any other service.

The collapse of the fund made headlines and Imre was forced to defend Scientology and WISE on national television when the connection was discovered. He pulled the Church's favorite rabbit out of the hat, claiming that not all WISE members are Scientologists, and WISE was simply a membership organization that could not be held responsible for all the activities of its members. As a matter of fact, the shady dealings started before the owner and the CEO were introduced to Scientology. But then again, they did not become ethical businessmen by joining WISE and learning more about Hubbard's methods and philosophy.

The next target, this time sent by a Scientologist management consultant, was another wog CEO – the manager of the Hungarian branch of Stiefel Eurocart, a German cartography firm. Big plans were in the making for him. We hoped that he would implement the Hubbard admin tech and then the inevitable success would convince the German owners to adopt these methods, in turn leading to an improved opinion about Scientology among German businessmen. Unfortunately, our plot failed miserably. Upon hearing that his Hungarian CEO spent company money on Scientology management consultation and courses, the German owner promptly fired him. He then had a failed stint as a Scientology management consultant, tried to get himself into better shape by spending his remaining money on auditing at Vienna Org, but did not get the results he expected. He eventually disappeared from Church lines altogether.

A few months later, Walter found out Miklós had created a "non-standard" position for me (Delivery In-Charge) which did not appear on the official organizing board of OTL. He ordered Miklós to assign me to a standard post, and so I was appointed the Director of Correction, theoretically the head of a department in the training center. In non-Scientology terms, I was now responsible for quality control. I had to find the real reason (or "Why" as Hubbard called it) behind the bad job performance of staff members who made mistakes or were downstat. Hubbard had a rule for that, too – if someone did not perform well, he was either unaware of his policies on the matter or did not apply them.

My job was to interview the failing crew member and discover what they did not know or apply. Then I had to write a study order, containing the materials to be (re)studied as well as practical drills to be done, which in theory would then mean they could do their jobs properly thereafter. This was also my statistic – the number of fully corrected staff members. A staff member was deemed "corrected" if he completed the study order AND the problem he caused was resolved AND the relevant statistic was uptrending, all in the same Scientology week.

It was not an easy job, as most of the crew had minimal specialized training for their posts, so most of the time I simply had to order some on-the-job training for them. Unfortunately, I was not very knowledgeable about most of these training materials, so I had to start studying the thousands of Hubbard and Miscavige writings and policies on organizational matters.

My stint as "Dir Correction" did not last long, as Miklós had other plans. It turned out that he just wanted to see the reaction of the European Sea Org executive when he promoted me to a department head. As there was no backlash, he promoted me again and made me the head of the entire training center/division, so I was officially now the "Commanding Officer of OTL Training Org" or CO OTO, for short. He did this mainly so he could dump the money-making duties on me.

He had plenty of other problems of his own at that time. *What is Scientology?*, the book that had been translated to all major languages started to become a problem again. New Era Publications, the publishing arm of the Church, contracted one of the major Hungarian retailers, Alexandra Books, to publish the book and put it into its stores.

The CEO of Alexandra agreed on one condition: they wanted a guaranteed volume of sales, meaning if the specified quantity were not sold commercially, then New Era would buy those books in bulk from the publisher. The Hungarian New Era Representative signed the contract and the book was published in Hungarian. As the Alexandra CEO predicted, only a handful of copies were sold, so the publisher requested New Era to buy the amount specified in the contract. New Era sent a reply that their Hungarian representative was not authorized to sign that contract so they would not pay. Alexandra Books then threatened to sue.

As the Hungarian New Era Representative was technically a Church staff member in Hungary, this whole mess put the Hungarian Church in danger. Miklós was ordered to find a solution to the problem. Miklós then called in the New Era Rep and the head of OSA and ordered them to see the richest Hungarian Scientologist and get the money to buy the books. They were under actual orders not to leave his house until he gave them the full amount of money Alexandra Books demanded (around 10,000 USD). The mission was accomplished, the money was obtained and the publisher was paid off. We used the books as "dissemination material" – all Hungarian libraries, government agencies and even all members of Parliament got a free copy.

After the dust had settled on the *WIS?* fiasco, Miklós made my new position official. It was good to feel that he really trusted me and he even convinced the incumbent head of the training center to resign (who was also his wife), so my appointment would go through smoothly. Walter was not exactly thrilled to hear about the promotion of the blackest Hubbard sheep in Hungary, but he decided to allow Miklós to do as he wanted and did not intervene.

"MAKE MONEY, MAKE MORE MONEY"

The start of my career as a division head was somewhat overshadowed by the almost instant failure of my marriage. It simply did not work out as I expected. Divorce was not uncommon in the Sea Org – the almost complete lack of free time, extreme performance demands, the ever-present ethics problems or the difference of status of the members of the couple eroded even the best of marriages (not to mention lengthy absences as a result of RPF assignments or being posted to another part of the world). The extremely Social Darwinist attitude fostered in the organization brought out the worst in me – the woman did not meet my expectations, the woman had to be dropped.

As I spent more time as a Sea Org member, I became increasingly cold and perfectionist, I cared less and less about the individual private issues of other people. Kriszta became the first major victim of this change in my general attitude. I felt that she would never progress in Scientology as fast as I would. I was a fast student and she had difficulty progressing through her courses.

I tried to look up Hubbard's writings on marriage, but those just strengthened my belief. I felt that we were not compatible because our emotional tone levels were different, and according to Hubbard, such marriages were not workable.

I decided to deal with the situation with the speed and resolve expected of a Sea Org member. I told my wife that I was going to divorce her and I would submit the papers to the court in a week. She was devastated, tried to convince me to give her another chance, but I was adamant about my decision.

My family was shocked by this news. It was apparently the last straw for my relatives and I could see the last vestiges of goodwill evaporate. Even those who had tolerated my beliefs up to that point now angrily questioned my decision. Some of my fellow Sea Org member were also outraged (rightfully so, I admit), that I had just discarded my wife after two months. Nevertheless, I was convinced that I was doing the right thing, doing what Ron would have done in the situation and I looked for a Scientologist attorney. I told him that I wanted it done fast so he should name his price to get the divorce hearing scheduled within 48 hours. As we had nothing to divide, I convinced Krisztina to agree to everything and list the reason for the divorce as "irreconcilable differences." The whole procedure was over in 15 minutes the following day and we were officially divorced. I was proud of myself. In my view I had effectively handled the situation and remained at cause, not letting my emotions and feelings influence my judgment.

There was a drawback though -- as I was no longer married, I had to move back into the overcrowded men's berthing. I did not want this and managed to get authorization to sleep in my office (which was converted from the larder of the apartment we rented for the training center), under my desk on a mattress. This was still better than sleeping on a three-story bunk. Four more people lived in the training center, so only the five of us had to share the shower and the bathroom, a much better proposition than those living in the men's or women's berthing.

In my work, I felt a bit lost on the "income line" (as we called it). The very reason I became a Scientologist was the lack of interest in the material things of life. I was attracted by the advertised spiritual side of Scientology. I was not particularly enthused by the idea of extracting the hard-earned money of others. Naturally, I had to overcome these mental barriers quickly. Miklós tried to help me, gave me advice and more Hubbard materials to complement what I had learnt about selling in Pécs Mission.

According to Miklós, there were two basic rules. The first: no report usually means noncompliance; i.e. the lack of reports usually means lack of compliance or movement. The second was actually Scientology Axiom #43: *Time is the primary source of untruth.* According to Miklós, the more time passed between the setting of a target and its realization, the less chance it had to be successfully accomplished.

These were the primary factors I had to keep in mind when I talked to the executive directors of the Scientology missions in Hungary. My job was to get them to send their staff to the OTL for training and pay for those courses. It was not easy, as they usually had no money. There was a solution, though: they could get a local wealthy Scientologist to donate the money for the training of their staff member. In keeping with the second rule of Miklós, I had to give a tight deadline (1-2 days) for them to collect the money by calling those on the local rich person list. If the executive director did not report back to me, then I had to conclude that he had done nothing and I contacted him again, rekindled his enthusiasm to get the donation and told him I would contact him the following day and I expected a result. If he got the money, then I was supposed to get him to send it to us immediately, so time would not enter into the equation and make it untrue.

Emotional manipulation was also an important tool in getting the heads of the missions on board with our ideas. Miklós advised me to refer to the Hungarian freedom fighters of our glorious past and to clearly define and present a threatening image of an enemy. For example, one of the mission holders (who was born in Transylvania as an ethnic Hungarian) was known for his patriotism. It was enough to remind him of the Revolution of 1848 and to sing its unofficial anthem to get him into action – he managed to get the money donated for the training of his staff member in a day.

The concept of help was also a button we exploited to the hilt. When the push for money hit a snag, I was supposed to suggest to the reluctant mission holders that their payments would help Scientology expand and ultimately become victorious in the end. Therefore, they would not only forward their own spiritual development, but indirectly they would also make their environment a better place.

The main thing was to divert the matter to an emotional level and make it a question of belief. This was an excellent way of dispensing with rational computations and common sense. After half a year of relentlessly practicing the aforementioned principles, I became quite good at getting the money out of the pocket of Scientologists. Miklós helped me become better at raking in the cash – he showed me relevant Hubbard writings from time to time to fine-tune my approach. He was working on one of the longest courses in Scientology, the Organizational Executive Course, which contains the entirety of Hubbard's admin tech and he always shared the wisdom with us when he came across something useful. One of the memorable additions to my repertoire was the importance of selling training or auditing PACKAGES – the idea was to get the public to pay for multiple services always. Hubbard even recommended Scientology sales personnel develop a loud and derisory laugh for when a poor Scientologist wanted to pay for one service only. The laugh was supposed to overwhelm the public, and then the request for payment of the package had to be repeated.

There was one more important thing that Hubbard (and therefore Miklós) repeated over and over again. It was a simple rule: CONTROL = INCOME (in capital letters like that). This was also the primary qualification point for people working anywhere near income lines – they had to be willing and able to control people. Control freaks were favored for sales positions. Due to the insane demand for money on the part of the executives ("he has to pay right now or latest by Thursday 14:00" etc.), sometimes the Registrar had to physically escort a prospective buyer to the nearest ATM or convince them to leave their place of work in the middle of the day to pay for their next course. Having no inhibitions or considerations about doing this sort of thing certainly helped in these positions.

The favorite mantra of Walter when he was talking about getting in money or dissemination or recruitment was the "invasion of privacy." This meant to show no respect for the private sphere of others. For example, if someone did not want to come in Thursday morning with the cash, then he had to be questioned why and interrogated as to exact details – what time did he get up in the morning, where would he go next etc. and then point out a solution. The ideal registrar was like an attack dog which locked his jaws onto the victim's leg and could only be removed by hacking off that limb.

Here are a few Hubbard quotes that were shown to me repeatedly, containing the correct approach and method for sales:

"It is necessary in writing an ad or a flier to assume that the person is going to sign up right now. You tell him that he is going to sign up right now and he is going to take it right now. That is the inference. One does not describe something, one commands something. You will find that a lot of people are in a more or less hypnotic daze in their aberrated state, and they respond to direct commands in literature and ads.

"If one does not understand this, and if he doesn't know that Dianetics and Scientology are the most valuable service on the planet, he will not be able to understand hard sell or be able to write good copy.

"So realize that you're not offering cars or life insurance or jewelry or stocks or bonds or houses or any of the transitory and impermanent things which are based on things not surviving or on things that are in fact being destroyed. You're offering a service that's going to rehabilitate the thetan and that is lasting.

"Hard sell means insistence that people buy. It means caring about the person and not being reasonable about stops or barriers but caring enough to get him through the stops or barriers to get the service that's going to rehabilitate him." – L. Ron Hubbard, Policy Letter of 26 Sept 1979, COPYWRITING

"The results of Dianetics and Scientology are fantastic enough to please all but the most psychotic in the society. These results have never before been seen on the planet. But there are always SPs out there who don't want people to get well and who use literature to get you in trouble.

"The art of hard sell is you tell people to do something. Hard sell is based on knowing and promoting in the line of truth and not being reasonable about people who want 'other things' and 'other practices'. There is nothing to compare with Dianetics and Scientology. They are infinitely valuable and transcend time itself." – L. Ron Hubbard, Policy Letter of 19 Sept 1979, PROMOTION

"Before 1949 man's knowledge of himself, the spirit and the mind was a black barbarism. Look over the psychology, psychiatric and religious texts of the 30s and

40s. Man could not change. He was a degraded animal. The way you applied ther-
apy was dreams or drugs, ice picks and ice baths.
"Only Dianetics and Scientology began the road out of that witch pit.
"But the witch pit is still there for almost all the world!
...
"Those billions are still in the witch pit. They are still boiling.
"Dianetics and Scientology are NEW NEWS.
We are the only road out." – L. Ron Hubbard, Policy Letter of 20 Aug 1979,
DIANETICS AND SCIENTOLOGY ARE NEW
  "Erase from our org patter 'Which do you want, Mr. J?' Don't ask which course,
or what pin or what book or which auditor or what door or what time he or she
wants to start anything or which door or which road or which membership.
  "Cultivate totally on a staff a didactic but pleasant approach. 'Your intensive
starts...' 'This is your next book...' 'Your next course should be taken on...' 'Go to
the third door.'
  ...
  "Erase even the banal 'What do you wish?' or 'What can I do for you?' as even
that throws confusion into it." – L. Ron Hubbard, Policy Letter of 16 April
1965, Issue III, HANDLING THE PUBLIC INDIVIDUAL

I was not the only one who worked on selling courses. Miklós sometimes
mobilized Imre, the President of WISE, if we were strapped for dough. He
linked me up with the co-owners of Admiral & Escorial Consulting (a management consulting company that implemented a streamlined version of Hubbard's admin tech in small and medium sized enterprises). At that time, I was
one of the few people in Hungary who had studied a relatively large amount of
Hubbard's organizational policies. They wanted specialized courses compiled
which would properly educate their staff in these methods. I put together a few
courses for them, generating some extra income.
  A language school called LightHouse was another steady source of income
and new students (we trained some of their teachers). It did not last long,
though. This school was originally founded as a nonprofit organization (initially called LITE Language School) by the Church and five private individuals
(including Péter Kárpáti, the first OSA director in Hungary) with the purpose
of teaching Scientologists the English language by employing Hubbard's study
technology. At that time, it seemed easier than translating the entire Hubbard
library. The language school was later converted into a for-profit corporation
and the Church was no longer a co-owner. Nevertheless, the new corporation
was still paying 10% royalty of their gross income to ABLE Hungary, a Scientology entity responsible for licensing Hubbard's study technology. The rela-

122

tionship between Scientology and the language school became strained after a few years. The majority shareholders were Scientologists, but they did not like the extortionate royalty percentage. The language school was doing very well, had hundreds of students and they paid huge amounts to ABLE without receiving much in exchange. ABLE could not even issue proper invoices (being a non-profit organization they could not really do that), they expected the owners of LightHouse to find a solution to pay the royalties as a kind of religious obligation.

The owners finally rebelled and stopped paying royalties, and replaced each and every course they offered which contained any of Hubbard's tech. The Church did not let it go easily; a lengthy and bitter battle ensued, which ended predictably – the Church declared the owners Suppressive Persons and expelled them from the Church.

Imre even took advantage of a friend (and hunting partner) of the President of Hungary's biggest bank. Imre convinced this friend (who was a Scientologist) to get the bank to donate to the Church for the training of Scientology Course Supervisors. He got 2,000 USD, which was an impressive feat. I had to write an invoice for unspecified "training" which only contained the short and innocent name of the Church ("OTL Hungary") but made no reference to Scientology.

It took about a year to for me become very good at parting Scientologists from their money. By applying what I had learned, I was usually able to push someone into his biggest problem (or ruin, as we called it), and sell him the solution (which was always one of the courses we delivered). There was one remarkable event that fully convinced me about the workability of these sales techniques. I was talking to a university professor about his financial problems. For the sake of this story, it is important to know that my office was close to the restroom. The professor was really under the effect of my carefully manipulative questions and communication tricks, and was fully immersed into his ruin – which was his apparent inability to hold onto money. When he reached this point, someone in the restroom broke wind in a rather lengthy and loud fashion. It took real effort on my part not to burst out in loud laughter, but the professor was so stuck in the ruin that he apparently did not even hear it and went on talking about his predicament. Naturally, he bought the course at the end of our talk.

As part of my daily moneymaking activities, I encountered an interesting phenomenon – certain Scientologists pocketed nice profits from the system. The Church paid sales commissions to so-called field staff members or FSMs (who were the closest things to field representatives in Scientology) on fees paid for services or donations made to Church projects. The percentages were: 10% for auditing, 15% for training and 10% for direct donations. Two methods were used to evade taxation (to be fair though, not every field staff member resorted to this): they either had an offshore company, which was the beneficiary of the commission payments or they simply considered themselves to be ecclesiastical personnel and did not pay income tax. This mentality was prevalent among the field auditors, who considered themselves to be doing charitable activities and therefore in their minds at least, they had deserved tax exemption.

OSA tried to find a legal way for the tax-free payment of commissions and the tax exemption of auditors, but they could not work out anything in the 10 years I spent there.

MANAGING THE CENTER AND OTHER DUTIES

As I became better at making money, the Registrar of the training center was transferred to another division because I was thought to be able to get in enough money without any assistance.

On paper, the generation of income was not listed among my official duties. But as I learned, it was a default basic duty of all Sea Org members (along with recruitment). Nevertheless, my performance was judged on my real position – the head of personnel enhancement. I had to make sure that staff members attended the mandatory 12.5 hours of study time each week, had a training line-up to progress on, dealt with any medical problems and corrected flubbing crew members.

Staff training was a daunting task in the Sea Org, as one had to somehow navigate between the unrealistic production targets, the borderline insane fixation on getting everything done NOW NOW NOW and the almost complete lack of proper training materials for the non-Scientology aspects of various Sea Org positions. There was certainly no shortage of Scientology administrative training materials, but in retrospect, it was an outdated and cumbersome system, and the extreme pressure just made its shortcomings even more glaring.

L. Ron Hubbard wrote this in his policy letter of 23 July 1972: *"Admin training with no org experience to relate it to is a waste of time."* Let's give credit when it is due – he was completely right. As I mentioned earlier, most of the recruits were enthusiastic teenagers (including me) who had never had a real job before joining the Sea Org. And most had never seen an actual functioning Scientology organization. So, most of the administrative training they received was a colossal waste of time – that's why that quote burned into my mind when I first read it. It matched my experience exactly.

The difficulties were compounded by the incompetent application of Hubbard's personnel selection policies (which were pretty stupid in the first place), leading to some disastrous appointments. Miklós and the personnel division took Hubbard's advice seriously (under the circumstances, they really had little choice) by ignoring any "wog" skills or education but simply sticking to the qualifications invented by Hubbard. The net result of this "unorthodox" method was a completely ridiculous distribution of personnel, demonstrated by the actual education levels and "real-world" professions of our executives:

Commanding Officer of OTL	– telephone repairman
Deputy CO for Internal [Matters]	– high school + 1 year in economic university, left it for Scientology
Deputy CO for Operations	– high school + 1 year in light industrial college, left it for Scientology
Commanding Officer of OSA	– cook
Division/Department Heads	
Personnel	– biology/geography teacher
Dissemination	– cook
Translations Unit	– mailman
Treasury	– livestock breeder
Accounting	– singing/music teacher
Operations	– mechanic
Public Relations	– retired police major
President of WISE	– smelting engineer
Deputy President of WISE	– registered nurse
President of ABLE	– seamstress
Head of SMI office	– high school + 2 year in Buddhist college
Head of I HELP office	– high school

For example, we had two professional cooks, but both of them were assigned to administrative positions, and we wound up with a painter in the kitchen due to the lack of other options.

This phenomenon of craving statuses not normally or easily attainable in the real world was also noticeable among public Scientologists. According to Hubbard, Scientologists constituted the elite of Planet Earth, and this was quite a strong motivation for them to stick with the Church, no matter what they experienced. In retrospect, quite a few Scientologists were affected by the glory of their bestowed status (i.e. gratification of their ego) and this is what kept them there, not their spiritual progress or the even the complete lack thereof.

Entrepreneurs who made their fortunes from shady business deals, drove luxury cars and evaded as much tax as they possible could were despised in the wog world, but were valued and respected members of the Scientology community, earning standing ovations for their generous donations during Church fundraising events. Unknown, D-list actors were heralded and treated as famous celebrities. Successful members of MLM systems became stars in the Scientology sky by bringing new people into the Church to spend their money on Scientology.

Meanwhile, I had a new problem on my hands – I had to find a school for my Course Administrator (the 12 year old). Wog schools were naturally out of the question, so she was sent to a school with ties to ABLE called The School of Ability and Creativity. They were applying Hubbard's study technology the same way we did – they used checksheets, and instead of having classes for various subject each day like a normal school, they studied only one subject at a time. Thus they studied math for weeks until they completed the annual study requirement, had an exam and then moved on to the next subject.

As the commanding officer of the training organization, I also became a division head and a member of the so-called Advisory Council (which consisted of the heads of the divisions of the OTL). Our main duty was to have a meeting each Thursday night and dream up an income plan and do the financial planning for the next Scientology week; i.e. we had to propose to the top executives how to spend the money that came in. Half of it was already allocated before we even began the meeting – we had to send roughly 36% to international and continental management and 14% had to be spent on "promotion." We had to figure out how to pay the rent & utilities, staff pay & berthing as well as three meals for each crew member per day from the other 50%. Usually it was no small feat –staff pay averaged 0-5 USD per week per person, and we usually allocated 8 USD per person per week for food. This was just enough to prevent starvation, but by no means adequate. Consequently, almost everyone hit up his or her family for extra food.

The financial system was set up so that any incoming big sums eventually found their way to International Management.

The OTL was usually so broke at the end of each year that only the state-sponsored income tax 1%[23] donations to charities and religions saved us from bankruptcy.

---

[23] Since 1996 the Hungarian Personal Income Tax System has included the possibility for individual taxpayers to personally allocate 1%+1% of their income tax. Individuals are entitled to request the Tax Authority, via their tax return, to transfer 1%+1% from their tax liability to an officially recognized good cause e.g. a charity. Based on the law, 1% can be transferred to a Hungarian foundation, non-governmental organization, institution or funded plan, and the other 1% to a

For example, income from book sales in all Scientology service organizations had to be kept in a separate bank account and the income could ONLY be spent on restocking the books, promotion and sales commissions. It was forbidden to spend book income on operational expenses. Additionally, it was a duty of OTL to translate all Scientology materials to Central European languages free of charge, which then were published by New Era at a huge profit. They paid a pitiful amount as a contribution to OTL expenses. As far as I remember, it was 1% of all Scientology book sales in Central Europe. New Era Publications was staffed by Sea Org members, who worked day and night for a pittance, like us. The profit of this in-house publishing outfit also went to International Management.

WISE management consultants followed the pattern set by the Church – they sold extremely overpriced services to unsuspecting marks. The consultants had to pay 10-15% of their income to WISE, the "secular" licensing entity. As Hungarian WISE consultants were doing surprisingly well, the local WISE office collected 15,000 – 40,000 USD per week in royalties (they had to send 95% of that money to WISE International). Interestingly, according to extant Hungarian legislation, companies were free to use "Hubbard tech" without paying royalties. One of the consultants went rogue in 2001 and sent a letter to WISE, stating that he had a million-dollar cognition and would not pay any royalties for using Hubbard tech as it was "illegal." He quoted – among other legislation – Act LXXVI of 1999 on Copyright, Article 1, Section 6, which said *"No idea, principle, concept, procedure, method of operation or mathematical operation may be the subject of copyright protection."* Imre, the President of WISE wanted to sue the guy, but the Church attorneys told him that it would be unwinnable.

Hefty sums were also collected in the name of the International Association of Scientologists, supposedly for major promotional and dissemination campaigns as well as for covering the costs of "battling the SPs and psychs." We could not touch these funds; they had to be sent straight to an entity called IAS Administrations.

In retrospect, the reason was clear – the structure of the Church was carefully shaped by Hubbard to maximize the amount of money and power at the disposal of the one who sat at the top of the organization. Initially, he was that man; after his death, David Miscavige grabbed control after a series of internal battles, and he is still the head of the Church today. His power is as unlimited as was Hubbard's (there is no one to hold him accountable and there is no means to remove him from his position).

Hungarian church registered by the court or under a preferential budget heading.

Due to the shortage of funds at our management level, financial planning meetings sometimes turned into lengthy squabbles over the necessity of purchasing certain items. The most memorable moment was the grand show of Dezső, the head of the Base Crew Division (the service & maintenance crew worked here – cooks, drivers, cleaners etc.), which he put on for purchasing two wheeled shopping bags. He gave an emotional speech about how he and his crew could not cope with the heavy lifting when purchasing the weekly food items and they simply could not go on without these wheeled saviors. Miklós tried to shut up him, but Dezső would not let this go. Finally he went down on his knees and began literally begging that we purchase these two bags. At that point, most of us were laughing in disbelief, so we granted his wish and added these to the weekly authorized expense list. Next week, Dezső was very silent throughout the meeting. Miklós asked him at the end whether they managed to buy the wheeled bags or not. Dezső replies with an abrupt "no." Miklós asked him why not. He responded in a resentful voice: "The driver was in a hurry and would not let me buy them."

With that pronouncement we had to have a 15-minute break, as most of us burst into uncontrollable laughter. Sadly, the mood was not always so jolly. As funds were always very tight, we often ended up in tense and heated arguments which usually ended in traditional Sea Org-style shouting matches.

Lack of proper funding also made it rather hard to push up certain statistics, so we became creative so our numbers did not look as bad. One of our statistics was the "percentage of operational equipment." The inspection was done every Thursday morning and it had to be 100% or else. One Thursday, around noon, one of the refrigerators broke down. There was no money to replace it and no time to get it repaired before 14:00. There was only one solution to keep the stat up – remove the fridge from the base immediately. Dezső hesitated as the fridge had originally been brought in by one of the staff members and she was still considered its owner. The Deputy Commanding Officer for Internal Affairs (the immediate senior of Dezső) asked him about the stat at 13:30. Dezső explained the fridge situation. The D/CO did not hesitate to do what was necessary to save the statistic. He grabbed Dezső and they threw the fridge from the balcony into the street – literally.

There was no such simple solution when the one and only gas stove malfunctioned on a Thursday morning. Dezső had two hours to get it repaired. The handyman he found told him that he could only come the next day, as he was already booked for Thursday. Dezső could not let the "lazy wog" destroy his statistic, so he began to beg. He told him that we were a commune and eighty people would be hungry if he did not come right away. The handyman reluctantly agreed to see to it immediately but wanted an extra 100 USD as a rush surcharge. Dezső now had to find the money. Such an expense was obviously not allocated in last week's Financial Planning, so he had to get a donation from a Scientologist. Dezső chose a WISE member at random (the owner of a headhunting company) from the list and called him on the phone. He started to pressure him to donate 100 USD. At first the guy could not believe what he was being asked to do, but he soon came to realize that the annoyingly tenacious Sea Org member was actually serious. As this particular CEO was heading to an auditing session, he realized that it would probably cost more to handle his rejection of the donation in session than to give the money. He was in Vienna, so Dezső persuaded him to have one of his employees in Budapest bring the money in immediately. Imre, the President of WISE, was not happy, but Dezső was the hero of the hour, for he had saved his statistic "in an OT way."

Handling the medical problems of the crew was also my responsibility. Needless to say, Hubbard was also an expert in this field. He wrote several policies on vitamins and antibiotics. Referring to various sources and his so-called research, he strongly recommended (mandatory in practice) taking high doses of certain vitamins when getting auditing (supposedly to aid the auditing process). He suggested 600 mg of Vitamin E, 200 mg of Vitamin B1 and 1000 mg of Vitamin C. Due to financial constraints, I could only buy Vitamin B1 and C in powder form, so I devised a "cocktail" by adding the specified amounts to a glass of water and called it "gummiberry juice" (in reference to the Disney animated series).

Hubbard had two rules for antibiotics and drugs – the first was a total ban on aspirin or any of its derivatives, stated in a technical bulletin called "Drugs, Aspirin and Tranquilizers," dated 17 October 1969:

"By actual clinical test, the actions of aspirin and other pain depressants are to:

"A. INHIBIT THE ABILITY OF THE THETAN TO CREATE MENTAL IMAGE PICTURES

"The thetan is rendered STUPID, blank, forgetful, delusive, irresponsible. A thetan gets into a "wooden" sort of state, unfeeling, insensitive, unable and definitely not trustworthy, a menace to his fellows actually."

Regarding antibiotics, he wrote the following in a technical bulletin called "Antibiotics, Administering of," dated 29 March 1975:

"The trick is to get the temperature subnormal with antibiotics within the blood leveling period. Blood leveling means when the anti-biotic has gotten into the blood and is actually holding the infection.

...

"More of the same antibiotic is given approx 2 hours prior to blood leveling time. This then brings the temperature right on down to subnormal; continue the

*antibiotic so that it keeps the temperature subnormal until it just can't keep it
subnormal anymore and it comes up to normal. It will be found that the patient is
now well and not likely to relapse.*

...

*"98.6°F or 37°C is normal. A thermometer can be a bit off (.1 or .2 high or
low) and temperature can vary a bit for "normal" one person to the next.*

*"Rising temperature (above normal) is a reaction to a disease. Lowered tem-
perature (below normal) is a reaction to a disease being handled by the body or the
antibiotic plus the body.*

...

"The general rule when administering antibiotics is:

1. *One gives antibiotics until the temperature comes down past normal to
   subnormal and comes up to normal again with anti-biotics.*
   *After blood leveling time of the first antibiotic the temperature should
   break (go normal or below), the person going into a sweat. If it doesn't,
   then it's either not enough antibiotic or the wrong kind.*
2. *After dosage if the temperature just came down a bit from where it was,
   that type of antibiotic probably will handle the illness but enough has not
   been given. Increase the amount being given.*
   *If after blood leveling time from the first antibiotic the temperature did
   not go lower or even rose, it's the wrong anti-biotic. You change off to
   another and start all over again."*

I do not know how scientifically sound this reasoning is (this note was
added to it later by the Church, possibly to prevent lawsuits – *"This data is
given for information alone and is not intended to prescribe or otherwise treat an
individual. All prescriptions and treatments should be done in due accordance with
the medical laws of any country in which a person seeks treatment"*), but since
Hubbard wrote it, it was holy scripture for us.

The resolution of medical problems and health-related issues was hindered
by another Hubbard axiom – according to him, all illnesses (and accidents)
exclusively stemmed from present or past suppression. So, after the physical
symptoms of a sickness were treated, the underlying suppression had to be
found and rooted out.

For example, when the seasonal flu epidemic hit us and half the crew fell
sick, I was tasked with getting them back on their feet and working in 1-2
days. Megadoses of Vitamin C and garlic were administered, and we had an
effective way of dealing with fever – adding cayenne pepper and honey to hot
water and drinking this spicy cocktail. After that came the harder part – the
so-called PTS-handlings to find the past or present suppression.

130

To be honest, I did not believe in this, even as a hardcore Scientologist. So I had to get creative with paperwork to report the required PTS-handlings completed. Almost all Sea Org members in Budapest were financially dependent on their parents or brought food regularly from home to avoid malnutrition. This was a so-called "effect situation," a kind of a PTS-situation. So, this was given as the reason for becoming or being PTS and getting the flu. The affected crew members got programs to get their "effect situations" handled, which naturally were never executed.

In Autumn 1999, a new campaign was launched by International Management. We were required to put heavy emphasis on and strengthen our religious image and identity as a Church. A large tome had been published in the major languages of the world for that purpose, containing scripts for various ceremonies (weddings, funeral and naming), prayers and sermons, written in the early '50s by Hubbard to add to the religious nature of Scientology. Also, Sunday Services were made mandatory for all Church organizations and missions.

A new course had also been published for the delivery of these Sunday Services, which consisted of reading a Hubbard writing to the "congregation" and then giving them some "group auditing" (basically, it was a similar to a lite group therapy session). Every Scientology mission and organization had to train at least one person to deliver this new service. So, Miklós delegated this problem to me – I had to get every Hungarian mission to IMMEDIATELY send someone for that training. It was not easy, as quite a number of the missions consisted only of a local Scientologist who sometimes held lectures to a few interested people in his or her living room. Nevertheless, we put relentless pressure on the bigger missions until they sent someone. Miklós also saw an opportunity to make some extra cash, so I shook down a few wealthy Scientologists to pay for the training of mission staff members or got the local Mission Holders to get the course fees donated by their local rich public Scientologists. After a while, the demand from above subsided, and consequently we also put this project on the back burner.

At the end of 1999, we ran out of office space. So did Budapest Mission. Miklós joined forces with the Executive Director of the mission, Tamás Nagy (who was also – at least on paper – the President of the Church of Scientology Hungary, though he had no authority over the OTL as we were Sea Org and he was not). They started to look for a suitable location where we could all move in together. Due to the nature of getting new people, it had to be near a street with a lot of pedestrian traffic and in the central business district. They managed to locate a suitable property: a large, two-floor rental in an apartment block, big enough for both organizations. Miklós was a shrewd negotiator and managed to get a significant discount on the rental fee. We then moved in together, the OTL took the upper floor, and the mission the lower one. As we could no longer use the office spaces to sleep in, we converted our former offices into berthing spaces. The training org was too large to fit in, so we stayed in the same separate flat, saving me from having to move to a crowded crew berthing. I continued sleeping under my desk each night.

After we finished moving in, we were assigned a new task by International Management. Budapest Mission had to be converted into a full Church of Scientology organization ("org" for short), so it could be presented at one of the upcoming international Scientology events as proof of unprecedented expansion. It was to be the first organization in the former Eastern Bloc. As Budapest Mission was doing rather well and had over 100 staff at that time, this was not particularly hard to accomplish. We had to rush and push a few auditor trainees through their courses (done in Copenhagen, supervised personally by Walter to make sure they completed as fast as possible) and find suitable candidates for a few positions that were mandatory for orgs, but not for missions. I was quite busy with the day-to-day affairs of the training org and making money for daily operations, so I was not really involved in this project.

In fact, I only had one job related to this org-making. In order to open an org, two Sea Org members had to be added to existing personnel. One of the was the Flag Banking Officer, the chief financial authority and decision-maker in an org, and the other was the Flag Representative, who was an observer, representative and enforcer for international church management. That person had to send a report each week about what exactly happened in the org, and he was also responsible for getting the programs and orders of international management completed.

Both positions were equal in rank to the executive director of the org, and due to the mandatory Sea Org membership required by these posts they were even somewhat senior to the actual head of the organization. Hubbard envisioned the operation of an org like this: the Executive Director would take care of the day-to-day matters, the Flag Representative would get programs done to ensure long-term expansion and the Flag Banking Officer would handle the finances. In retrospect, I could not help but notice some possible ulterior motives – Flag Representatives were also excellent spies, so nothing was hidden from the watchful eyes of Hubbard (and subsequently, international management), and the actual primary purpose of the Flag Banking Officer was to make sure that International Management got its fee for managing the orgs, no matter what financial state the org was in. The Flag Banking Officer had to be set up as the only signatory on the bank account where all the income of the org was deposited. All cash payments were to be turned over to this person on a daily basis. Then each week he paid International Management, and then turned over the rest of the money to the org (he even had the right to with-hold part of it, if the gross income exceeded the dollar value of services fully delivered). Even then, the org executives could only propose how to spend the expense sum thus allocated, and the Flag Banking Officer still had the final say.

Due to the shortage of personnel, we could not part with veteran Sea Org members to fill these positions. Instead, we chose two new recruits. The future Flag Representative of Budapest Org was a military college student, who had only recently been introduced to Scientology. Before joining the Sea Org he was working for a supermarket chain as a shelf-stacker and then as a cashier at a fast food restaurant. And let's just say that good manners were not one of his strong points. The Flag Banking Officer was working as a Dianetics auditor, a well-intentioned, nice if somewhat naive young woman with no background or education in finances whatsoever. Tamás, the Executive Director, was not exactly happy to see his powers limited, especially his financial control. He almost had a stroke when he found out that the newly appointed Flag Bank-ing Officer bought a super cleaning machine from the first vacuum cleaner salesman who came along, for a discounted of price of only 1,500 USD. After the initial conflicts and turf war died down, they began to reluctantly work together, keeping the end goal of Scientology in mind.

I tried to expand the training center after that. I had my eyes on one of the teachers in a language school that had ties to Scientology. Her name was An-drea and I had noticed her when she did Course Supervisor training. I thought that the Sea Org could use another Course Supervisor and I could have an-other shot at having a proper girlfriend. I recruited her for the Sea Org and felt that the attraction was mutual. We started to date after she completed her basic training, but I didn't have much opportunity to develop our relationship, as (unsurprisingly) a new campaign was launched by International Manage-ment. This time a *What is Scientology?* exhibit was created, with the intention of traveling all over the Europe (to each city where there was an org) to show "real Scientology" to the people of the world. OTL was required to send a few people to be part of the crew, and Andrea was one of them.

As a note: Walter gave us strict orders to send good-looking people only, as it was supposedly a multi-million dollar exhibit, financed by the International Association of Scientologists. When we proposed one of our not-so-attractive crew members, he rejected her with a resounding "no," proclaiming that "she was the ugliest person he had ever seen in his entire life."

THE Y2K PROJECT AND BATTLEFIELD EARTH

As 1 January 2000 approached, the Church became increasingly affected by the doom hysteria surrounding the so-called Y2K bug. Preparing for an armageddon fit well with the siege mentality of Scientology, so it soon became official -- we received orders from International Management to prepare for the worst, i.e. the global collapse of public utilities and IT infrastructure. We were required to buy or otherwise obtain a generator, a truckload of canned food, barrels of water and a few chests of candles in order to survive the first few weeks and the expected sustained blackout.

We also had to attend martial arts training, in case orderly civilization collapsed completely. A Scientologist ex-police officer helped us master the basics of self-defense and taught us a few jiu-jitsu moves.

We gathered before midnight, anxiously waiting with candles ready, to see what happened. The world did not end, everything returned to normal and we soon forgot about the whole thing.

A few days later, we had to watch the church's international 2000 New Years Event that had been held in Los Angeles, video'd and sent out to all Scientology orgs and missions to view. David Miscavige, the head of Scientology was the main speaker and he had exciting news! *Battlefield Earth*, an L. Ron Hubbard science-fiction novel, had been turned into a feature film and would be released in movie theaters in May, 2000. Miscavige talked about the movie for at least 30 minutes, calling it a masterpiece and even proclaimed it was destined to surpass the *Star Trek* and *Star Wars* franchises in popularity. He added that it would mean a tremendous shift in the general opinion about Scientology, as the success of the movie would make Hubbard (and consequently Scientology) extremely popular.

In May, upper management was surprisingly silent about the film and we were cautiously advised not to watch it. According to the few remaining non-Scientology acquaintances I had, the movie bombed at the box office and it was absolutely and ridiculously terrible. Miscavige never ever mentioned the film in subsequent events – it was as if it had never been made.

I found out several years later that it won 9 Razzie Awards and was widely considered one of the worst films ever made.

EXTERNAL ATTACKS

My old nemesis, OSA, started to come after me again. After two relatively harmless Hungarian OSA Directors (the first Walter called a total wimp in an informal meeting), a very aggressive and ruthless example of a tough Sea Org officer was installed as the new Commanding Officer of OSA Hungary. His name was Lajos Fritzlauf. He had previously been the head of OSA in Russia, but for some undisclosed reason, he had to leave Moscow in a hurry. I immediately became a target due to my history with OSA, and Lajos also began demanding additional training and auditing services for his OSA staff members. His other obsession was food – he was a trained chef and if he did not like the quality or quantity of the food served, he made a huge scene in the galley. It seemed his favorite pastime was terrorizing the cooks and purchasers, and he frequently complained to Miklós and his deputy for internal matters about the food and offered up lengthy and mostly unwanted advice.

Officially, he had been sent to Hungary because of the mounting legal and financial threats against Scientology in our country. The Hungarian Tax and Financial Control Administration launched simultaneous tax inspections against the major corporations of the Church in Hungary, and judging from the messy state of our accounting, we faced huge fines. The Hungarian Labor Inspectorate also visited the missions and fined most of them due to violations of labor laws. On top of it, the new Hungarian government issued a decree which mandated all registered Churches pay taxes (as if being paid minimum wage) for all ecclesiastical employees. This alone threatened to bankrupt the org and the OTL. We had 90 staff members, the org had 120, and our income was not even remotely enough to pay these taxes.

Lajos began tackling these issues with his usual brutal and direct methods. He hired a tax expert (a former division head of the tax office) and a constitutional lawyer, so he could play the religion card against the Labor Inspectorate in court. Regarding the newly required payroll taxes he was adamant that we should just make more money and simply pay it.

In order to fully protect the religious recognition of Scientology in Hungary, he conducted some corporate reorganization. The umbrella corporation called "Church of Scientology Hungary," which had the right to establish new (and tax exempt) Scientology organizations in Hungary, was emptied. It ended up with no staff members and the three mandatory board members were simply volunteers. It was stripped of all functions except a) incorporating new Church organizations and b) accepting the 1% income tax contribution sum and forwarding it to the org and the OTL. The underlying reason was simple – if the "mother Church" does not do anything, it cannot be attacked and the religious recognition of Scientology would never be endangered.

The state of our accounting also needed urgent handling. First, it was not uncommon that master copies of invoices were missing. Also, in the early days, invoices were issued by virtually any staff member, and knowing no better they wrote the actual truth on them – they were issued for "royalty payments," "training" etc. Tax inspectors treated them as taxable for-profit activities, which were not covered by the tax exempt status (tax exemption only applied to payments for "traditional" Church services, like marriages, funerals etc and direct donations).

After lengthy consultation with tax experts, a simple rule was introduced. All invoices were to be issued for donations (this was the key word the tax inspectors had to see) only – like "donation for auditing services," "donation for communication training" etc. Royalty payments and management fees paid by lower level Church organization were also to be invoiced as donations.

However, the problem of past errors remained. Lajos resorted to the only option he had – the application of delaying tactics. Incredibly, he managed to stall the completion of the investigation for four (!) years, and the statue of limitations expired on most of the questionable accounting. According to Lajos, at the very end of the whole affair, in 2005, he went to the central headquarters of the Hungarian Tax and Financial Control Administration, dressed in full ministerial garb and made a big scene, complete with yelling at the division head responsible for the investigation. They subsequently agreed to a grand total of 250 USD in fines.

The constitutional lawyer, Dr. István Szikinger, advised us to appeal in court against the resolutions issued by the Labor Inspectorate. Lajos and his deputy purchased ministerial garb (though they were not actual ministers, even by internal Scientology standards), and appeared in these court sessions and hearings as a form of moral pressure. Lajos even invented a title for himself – "Lead Minister" – though he was neither a leader nor a minister of the Church.

In the filings of the Church, the orders of the Labor Inspectorate were portrayed as an attack on religious freedom, steering the cases into the area of constitutional law. It worked – the Church won all of the cases, and all resolutions of the Labor Inspectorate were annulled.

Meanwhile, expansion of the org has mandated another move – OTL had to find new premises so the org could expand to the 2nd floor. A suitable location was found by 2001 and finally all organizational units of OTL were in the same location, including my division, the training org.

There was one big issue remaining – the unpaid payroll taxes and social security contributions. Lajos and Miklós had a series of lengthy and heated debates over this. Miklós looked at a host of alternative solutions (including moving the OTL to Slovakia), but apparently, there was no solution that was safe and defensible. The European OSA office also sent a private investigator to help us out. He only talked to Lajos, so I did not know what he did exactly. However, Lajos held a briefing after the investigator left and shared some details. He claimed that Viktor Orbán, the Prime Minister of Hungary, was a puppet of the psychiatrists and a psychiatric patient himself, treated in an Austrian hospital. He then added that the whole new law about the payment of taxes for Church workers was devised to bankrupt Scientology.

Lacking any other solution, the OTL was forced to register all 80 Sea Org members as ecclesiastical employees retroactively, which meant that we immediately owed around 40,000 USD to the tax office. Before the papers were filed, Miklós had all the money withdrawn from all of our bank accounts and the cash was put in a safe. A week or so later the European OSA office opened a bank account for us in England and a sizeable portion of the money was secretly transferred there.

OTL, by having a significant tax debt, crashed one of the main statistics of OSA, which made Lajos look bad. Both the Hungarian and European OSA kept demanding a solution, but we had no plan. Fortunately, this time I was not enlisted to bring in extra dough, as I was busy executing another super urgent International Management program: the very latest idea to resolve the lack of massive international expansion.

The new bright idea was to have all orgs send 9 people for advanced administrative training to study the entirety of Hubbard's management technology. They would then return to their orgs and start a new phase of expansion, which would clear the planet in no time. The deadline was as usual, RIGHT NOW, and all orgs were supposed to send suitable candidates immediately – meaning experienced and talented staff members qualified to become executives. It was no easy task, as all existing staff members were pretty much cemented into their current positions, so they had to be fully replaced. It took me and two very talented recruiters several months to get all nine candidates from Budapest Org onto their training. Much to my surprise, I found out that Budapest Org was the *first* organization in the world to complete the target (which made me wonder about the activity level and success of the other orgs on the planet). Also, by that time I was money-motivated enough to smell the opportunity to make some extra cash. We worked it out with Miklós to have all the trainees come to OTL's training org to do their courses and we would get the cost of the courses donated by rich Scientologists. 5,000 USD was established as the price of fully training one staff member, so 45,000 USD was the overall target. I grabbed the rich man list and also asked the biggest WISE management consulting company to help collect the money for the standard 10% commission. By the time all the trainees arrived, I had collected all the money, and as a side benefit, the weekly wage in OTL (including mine) jumped from 5 USD to 20 USD. It was a strict rule in the Sea Org that the salary sum was divided equally – everyone from the Commanding Officer down to the Receptionist was paid the same amount.

The doubts I had about Scientology and the Church resurfaced again during all this fundraising. At one point I resorted to a rather peculiar method to close the sale. I had identified the person as a prime target for donations as he had difficulty saying no. He was generous by nature, but his financial resources were limited. So I told him that if he donated for this campaign, then OTL would not contact him for any more Scientology-related donations in the calendar year. It worked, and he was actually grateful for letting him off the hook for a while. I realized a few minutes later that this approach, in principle, was similar to mobster protection rackets. It made me wonder for a while about the real purpose of the Church, but once again I cast my doubts aside and got on with doing my job.

As the number of VIP (which was a euphemism in the Church for wealthy) public Scientologists in the training org grew, I became rather skilled at parting these whales from their hard-earned cash. One day, Miklós called me into his office and told me that he really needed my help to get this "mess" with the tax office resolved (he meant the social security contribution and payroll tax bill). I told him about an incident that had happened a few days ago. A leading WISE consultant told me that one of the richest Hungarian Scientologists had asked him for advice regarding the handling of past tax evasion. He confessed during his auditing that his books were cooked and he evaded paying a hefty sum to the Hungarian tax office. He now had to handle it, and was trying to find a way to get this money into the coffers of the state without implicating himself. The attorneys he consulted usually just had a good laugh about the situation – one of them jokingly advised him to purchase revenue stamps for the amount of unpaid tax and then burn them in his courtyard.

I told Miklós that this was a situation that could be exploited if we played it properly. Miklós became enthused and ordered me to see this guy in his mansion and to bring the WISE Consultant with me to help. We were to convince him that the Church was in mortal danger and the "suppressives" wanted to destroy it financially – but if he gave his "black money" to us, we would pay our back taxes, and it would be a win-win scenario. His money would find its way to the state, his conscience would rest easy and the Church would be saved. It was Wednesday, so Miklós added, half-jokingly, that we should get the money (it was around 40,000 USD at that time) before Thursday 14:00 and should not bother returning without it.

We visited him in the evening and he took the idea surprisingly well. The WISE Consultant was also a sales expert, so we convinced him of the brilliance of this solution without much trouble. Then we proceeded to the harder part:

we would need a first installment of 40,000 USD. He nodded, went to his study and came back with 40,000 USD in cash in a plastic shopping bag. I could hardly believe my eyes. I had not thought I could pull this off that easily. The guy was in a good mood – he added that he would calculate how much money he owed to us and we would talk about it later. He told me that under no circumstances should we put his name on the invoice or on any document associated with this sum.

Miklós was overjoyed when I arrived to the OTL with the bag of cash. A few days later we got a call from our donor – he finished calculating how much black money he had and came up with a grand total of 120,000 USD. So he still sort of owed us 80,000 USD. Understandably, Miklós was rather reluctant to hand over all this money to the government, so he told Lajos in no uncertain terms that OTL would only register a few employees and he had to find a solution to employ the rest. The legal counsel of the Church (who was ironically a constitutional lawyer and allegedly a human rights expert) came up with a way to resolve the situation. OTL should register its most important executives as ecclesiastical employees (the top executives and the signatories on the various accounts, around 7 people, including me) plus we added 2 of the staff members who were in bad shape (so their medical costs were paid by the government – one was a Treasury staff member who had a chronic illness requiring lengthy treatment and our cook had ulcers, probably due to the terrorizing behavior of Lajos).

The rest of the crew (around 70-80) became "volunteers." The lawyers drafted a declaration that every one of them had to sign, stating that they agreed to do voluntary work for the OTL for a nominal weekly fee of 1000 HUF (around 4.50 USD).

When this was settled, my private life also started to look better. My beloved Andrea returned from the European "*What is Scientology?*" Exhibit Tour. We got married shortly thereafter at the end of March, 2001 (and are still living together happily). Due to my somewhat special status (the moneymaking guy was afforded privileges in the Sea Org) I was allowed to move in with Andrea in her flat, which was added to the list of Sea Org berthing and all its expenses were paid by the Church.

In the summer of 2001, I was fired on two missions. Both were related to money or making more money. The Sea Org needed my special expertise. The first was to conduct a surprise inspection in the mission of my hometown, Pécs, where my Scientology career has begun. I was supposed to look around and write a detailed report about what was going on there. The most important part of the mission was to check their accounting to find out whether they were withholding tithes (meaning the 10% royalty payments). I went down and did some interviews, looked through some documents and soon found out that by applying creative accounting techniques, they had hidden some of their income and thus failed to pay around 3,200 USD in tithes. It was considered to be Ron's money, so I ordered them to pay the full amount in 48 hours or face severe justice actions. The approach worked and they paid the OTL. Mission accomplished.

Naturally, it was a strange feeling to meet old acquaintances in this way. Scientology organizations generally have a high turnover rate, so half of the staff was unknown to me, but I did see a few of my old comrades. The time spent in the Sea Org and the training I had completed made me tough enough not to fraternize with them and to represent the interests of top management properly.

Dedicated, committed and relentless. That's what's was expected of all Sea Org members, and I did my best to live up to these standards.

After that Lajos, of all people, wanted me for a "special OSA mission." I was not happy about it, and I still did not forgive OSA for the ordeal they put me through in 1998. And I especially hated its obnoxious Hungarian commanding officer with a passion. But it was my duty to accept such assignments, so I reluctantly agreed.

The "special OSA mission" was... yes, fundraising again. OSA International decided to launch its 2001 "Marathon for Human Rights" in Budapest. This event was organized to increase the profile and acceptance of Scientology in society. It was a pure PR stunt to position the Church as an advocate of human rights. The runners participating in the lengthy marathon paid visits to city officials, got signatures on various proclamations supporting the *United Nations Universal Declaration of Human Rights* and when they arrived in Brussels, the destination of these series of events, they presented PR packages containing photos of the Marathon, copies of the signed proclamations, a conservative-looking book about the life of Hubbard and brochures about the Church and its related organizations etc. to EU officials.

Lajos drew up a budget of 12,000 USD for the opening event, and my job was simple – get the money (which was the only reason OSA wanted me for the project). He also had a "bright idea" to generate more funds – he planned to invest 3,000 USD into producing special commemorative T-shirts for Scientologists to buy, and we would use the profits to make the event more classy and memorable. (Naturally, it did not work out. OSA staff sold a few shirts, but 95% were unsold and consequently we wore them for years and gave a lot away to OSA volunteers as a cheap gift.)

The OSA PR person organized a rather eclectic show for the start of the Marathon. It was a strange mix, featuring an opera singer performing *Hazám,*

hazám (Homeland, homeland) from the famous Hungarian opera *Bánk bán*, followed by a jazz band, a pop singer and a boy band. I did not understand the concept or what kind of audience was being targeted. I wondered silently about the turnout such a program would attract. Additionally, two "celebrities" were shoehorned into the agenda. A kung-fu master called Sifu Robert Lyons (I had never heard of him previously) and István Nemere, a well-known Hungarian sci-fi author. They both had short speeches to deliver. Nemere was invited to be a VIP speaker by one of his publishers, a Scientologist (he founded his publishing company by borrowing a huge sum from another Scientologist, and it was supposed to be some sort of cultural mission. He paid Nemere to write an anti-psychiatry book called *The Ratman*, so he could use his name in the fight against the "evil psychs." The company folded a few years later.)

In addition to getting the funding handled, I also had to make sure that all active Scientologists attended the event and arrange for 30,000 fliers to be printed and distributed to get as many wogs to attend as possible. I got my assistant to handle the call-in of Scientologists and the fliers and started to reg[24] the money. I managed to get the whole sum together while my deputy mobilized about 80% of the active Scientologists in Hungary (around 1,000 showed up). The total attendance was close to 1,200, so the event attracted 200 non-Scientologists.

Unfortunately, I had to spend a sizeable amount of time with Lajos in lengthy and totally unnecessary coordination meetings. Shrouded in secrecy and thick cigarette smoke, these get-togethers mostly consisted of tall tales from the apparently very colorful life of the chain smoker Lajos. His storytelling style (and the veracity of his tales) was eerily reminiscent of a certain L. Ron Hubbard. I recall these legendary exploits of his:

Tale #1: He was a taxi driver during the Taxi Blockade[25] in 1990. He was there when the Minister of Interior, Balázs Horváth appeared at a window of the Parliament (and almost fell out). According to Lajos, one of his fellow taxi drivers aimed a fully loaded Uzi submachine gun at the minister, but Lajos noticed it in time and wrestled it away from him, thereby preventing a possible bloodbath.

Tale #2: his cab was a Polski Fiat 126p which he had pimped so its maximum speed was 130 km/h (81 mph) instead of the 105 km/h (65 mph) facto-

---

[24] to reg(ister): collect money for Scientology purposes (services or projects). Derived from Registrar (salesperson) and registration (sales).

[25] Taxi Blockade: on 25 October 1990, after the Hungarian government increased the price of gasoline by 65 percent, striking taxi and truck drivers barricaded roads, bridges, borders and public transport for three days until a compromise was reached.

ry specification. He was once stopped by the police for speeding, but they did not fine him when he let them drive his super-pimped ride.

Tale #3: According to him, he personally knew János Kádár, the leader of Communist Hungary and had even acted as his translator once. Apparently, Lajos's father worked in a high position in one of the holiday resorts of the Communist Party at Lake Balaton, and that's how he met Kádár.

Tale #4: He explained he was a very lucky person, his luck reaching supernatural proportions. He had attended college in the former Czechoslovakia and when he happened into a bar, he threw a coin into the nearest slot machine and hit the jackpot immediately.

Tale #5: While working as the legal director of the OSA office in Moscow (his official post title was "Assistant Legal Aide OSA CIS"), he managed to gain religious recognition for Scientology in Kyrgyzstan. According to Lajos, it was a very important target for Church management at that time, as it was the first recognition in a Muslim-majority country. Therefore Lajos went off the grid to avoid interference from his seniors – turned off his phone and did not answer his e-mails until he got the official documents in hand (It made no sense why this was necessary).

When I had successfully completed the project, Miklós told me that his deputy had to go to Paris for an important mission, and I would have to act as his temporary replacement for a month. I had the feeling I would end up with that job sooner or later.

THE WAKE-UP CALL

The news of the 9/11 terrorist attacks shook the world. Church leader David Miscavige was quick to react releasing a bulletin virtually overnight entitled "Wake-Up Call – The Urgency of Planetary Clearing." In this open letter to all Scientologists, he unsurprisingly blamed the "psychs" for the attacks – according to him, the right hand man of Osama bin Laden, Ayman al-Zawahiri was a psychiatrist and hijackers were hypnotized by psychiatrists employing mind-altering substances. At the time, I believed that. After all, it was coming straight from Miscavige, and his word was proof enough.

Miscavige also explained that this terrorist attack had clearly shown that the decline of civilization on Earth had reached a critical point and Scientology was, of course, the only thing capable of saving it from complete destruction. He gave two tasks to each Scientologist – first, do courses and get auditing to go up the Bridge as fast as possible and second, contribute to the expansion of the Church (preferably by joining staff or the Sea Org).

142

That issue also started a personality cult of Miscavige in the Church. At subsequent Church events, the period between the publication of his issue and the current event (and the soaring, highest ever statistics always shown at such events) was referred to as "since Wake-Up Call" suggesting that the words and personal charisma of Miscavige had reinvigorated the Church in the wake of the catastrophe.

A small devilish thought crept into my mind when reading the issue for the first time – it had an underlying tone of "for you, it is a disaster, but for us, it is an opportunity" but I suppressed it as a good and obedient Sea Org member.

The next scheduled international Scientology event after 9/11 was the anniversary event of the International Association of Scientologists, held at Saint Hill, England, at the beginning of October. This was the first opportunity for Church management to react to the new situation and to provide direction for the followers.

The local showing of the event video was set for 25 October. After the event at Saint Hill was over, we were sent instructions in a package. We were very excited to see how Scientology as a movement would react and what this new situation would mean to us. So we opened the pack and read the instructions.

Well...

In short, it contained the following: the plan to salvage the world from plunging into chaos and oblivion was to train EVERY Scientologist on all the basics of Scientology covered by the *Scientology Handbook* (a large format 950-page illustrated tome, compiled from the works of L. Ron Hubbard) and then appoint them as Volunteer Ministers. The event also gave a glorified report on the activities of Scientology Volunteer Ministers in and around Ground Zero to support this plan.

To accomplish this goal, all Scientologists were expected to do the following before 31 December 2001: a) complete the Scientology Volunteer Minister Course (which was basically a full study of the aforementioned handbook) and b) sign up as a Volunteer Minister and be ready for any disaster or catastrophe.

Meanwhile, the Translation Unit has completed the Hungarian version of the *Scientology Handbook* (most of it had been done earlier), and we had to sell this new release to ALL attendees.

We were also instructed NOT to explain any of this to the public Scientologists, they were to attend the event and hear it from Miscavige firsthand. He would explain what this book was and why they would have to buy it right then and there.

Additionally, a new sales method was introduced, which was to be executed only as laid out in the directions:

Step #1: staff members were organized into groups of three – one salesperson and two clerks. They would be equipped with copies the *Scientology Handbook*, placed in shopping bags, plus invoice pads and credit card debit forms. They were lined up outside the event hall/room, waiting for the audience to come out after the showing of the video.

Step #2: The group would approach the first Scientologist and the salesperson would hand over the shopping bag with the book in it, and at the same time, address the person with these words only: "Here is your *Scientology Handbook*. Cash, check or credit card?" If the person did not pick one of the three payment options, but started to talk, argue or ask questions the group moved on to the next target. As there were around 50 of these sales commando teams, chances were that anyone not buying the book at first would encounter 5-10 more of the same gangs before reaching the exit. Eventually they would buy. If someone did indicate which payment option he or she preferred, one of the clerks would handle the paperwork while the salesperson and other clerk moved on to another target.

The book was priced at 90 USD, which was around half the Hungarian monthly minimum wage.

Miklós called an emergency meeting for all Sea Org executives to work out exactly how we were going to implement this. He added that Walter gave him a quota of 800 books sold (basically the projected attendance of the event, assuming everyone bought a copy) and no one would be allowed to secure on the night of the event until this quota was met.

The New Era Representative stated the sales patter would not work, as checks were not used in Hungary at all and only a handful of people had credit cards. He suggested we change it to "Cash or cash?," as they would have to buy the book anyway. He was quickly jeered down, then we decided that it would be "Cash or org account?," as many people had unused payments on their org accounts.

Even to me, a seasoned Sea Org veteran, this sounded like a sure way to alienate people. If I were a public, I would not want to experience this sort of sales tactic. But it was an order and we had to comply.

Miklós set up daily drilling to get all Sea Org members doing this smoothly. He called a special staff meeting, explained the plan to everyone, then organized us into groups of three and we started to drill. It was role-playing – one half of the crew pretended to be the unsuspecting run-of-the-mill Scientology "public" on their way out of the event hall, and the other half were the sales commandos swarming them with the shopping bags.

Part of me was happy for the opportunity because Sea Org members got 5% commission on each book sold. The pocket money called "Sea Org allowance" we got each week was around 5 USD at that time, so I was eager to make some extra cash. I was already dreaming of meaty hamburger at a fast food restaurant. My blissful thoughts were interrupted by the booming voice of Miklós, who announced that nobody was allowed to sleep on Saturday until the sales quota was met.

The next day Miklós called an executive meeting again, as he had two new ideas – first, we were supposed to call everyone who had confirmed his or her attendance and tell them that they should bring 90 USD in cash to the event, as a publication of historical importance would be released. Naturally, we were not to tell anyone what it was.

He also initiated a donation drive. Imre, President of WISE was on fund-raising detail and I had to assist him. We did our usual routine – the rich men lists were pulled out from the drawers and Imre and I started to call, convincing them to buy packs of 25 books as donations to libraries and organizations with links to Scientology.

The pressure was unusually high on us to fully prepare for the event. We had to drill the sales pattern three times a day. Things got so intense that I could not sleep well, and I even had a strange dream one day – I was chasing people on the street with books in paper bags.

The day of the event finally came. As expected, around 800 Scientologists showed up. Shortly before the showing of the international event video was over, all staff members were deployed in a half-circle formation, blocking all exists – 150 people in groups of three. When the 3-hour video concluded, the attendees started to head for the exits. We launched the initial assault. The staff members, hungry for the book commissions and the proper food they hoped to buy, started to bombard the stunned public with the "cash or org account?" question. The new approach clearly had impact as they quickly adapted new survival strategies to avoid being fleeced at every event. Later, I encountered the following tricks:

-   leaving the event hall 10-15 minutes before the video was over, as usually the staff members were still preparing at that time and they could leave without much hassle;
-   running straight to the restroom as soon as the event was over, waiting there for half an hour until the initial wave subsided, then trying to sneak away;
-   cutting through the battle lines with a cell phone almost glued to the ear, talking or pretending to talk loudly to someone;
-   forming small groups inside the room where the video was shown, talking for a long time until the situation cooled down a bit.

While we were chasing the "public" to make the sales quota, Miklós and a few ethics officers patrolled the area, making sure that every staff member was pushing the book and nobody hid behind a column, for example. I got a separate room with Imre and we pushed people for large donations. We had to meet the quota of 800 books sold or else.

We sold around 250 books to individuals by 8:00 PM and got 200 more donated by WISE members. Only a handful of Scientologists were left, so we retreated to the base to regroup. Miklós told us that we should not even consider giving up on the quota, and we had to get cracking, grab those cell phones and start calling people to buy the book right now.

Naturally this did not go over well, but no one dared voice his or her considerations. We began calling the Scientologists directly as well as putting the pressure on mission holders and field group leaders to help with the effort. I worked with Imre to push more donations. We got 50 more books sold by 11:00 PM, but we were running out of people we could reach at such a late hour. Miklós still insisted on us staying and not going to sleep until the quota was met. However, people started to disappear and one executive after another went home silently. Around midnight Miklós saw that there was not much point in sitting there half asleep, so he also went to bed (he left his cell phone on so he could lie that he was still there working in case someone called from the Copenhagen base). He was indeed called in the middle of the night by Walter (the control was much tighter in Copenhagen, they were in fact not allowed to go bed and spent the entire night trying to reach their quota). The next morning (it did not matter that it was Sunday) we had to continue calling and selling, as we had not met our quota.

That's how life in the Sea Org went when there was an event, and almost every one included a new book or service for sale and the commando drill went into action.

CHAPTER EIGHT

The Right Hand Man

MOUNTING TASKS AND DOUBTS

In December 2001, the internal organization structure of the OTL was changed (see Chapter 4 for the organizational chart of OTL). Up to that point, the Commanding Officer had two deputies – the D/CO Internal supervised the first four divisions (personnel, promotion/translations, treasury, base crew), while the D/CO Operations was responsible for the other three (operations, training org, external relations/PR area control). In the new setup, the D/CO Internal became a new position, now responsible for supervising all divisions of the OTL as the lone deputy of the Commanding Officer. The idea was to unburden the CO so he would not have to be involved in the day-to-day running of the Sea Org unit. Now he could focus on the general expansion of Scientology, coordinating all Scientology-related organizations.

A new position was created to cover the former job of the D/CO Internal (the supervision of the first four divisions), and it was called Supercargo. The D/CO Operations was no longer a direct deputy of the CO, so the post title was renamed Chief Officer.

Miklós had to put someone on the new Supercargo position, and he picked me. As a result, my unofficial money-making function was now officially my job. I also became a member of the Executive Council and I had to participate in coordination meetings with the local representatives of the various Scientology front groups and corporations. Meanwhile my wife, Andrea, was promoted to be the head of Division 1 (called Hubbard Communications Office, so she was called the HCO Chief).

When I took over this position, it immediately became clear that my most important job was raking in the cash, naturally. Additionally, I had to handle our creditors, as we usually could not or did not want to pay them. Our expenses (renting office and berthing spaces for 100 people and feeding them) regularly exceeded our income and as I did not possess the OT powers the Church so eagerly promised its followers, more often than not I had to resort to "handling" them instead of paying them. Usually we paid the most troublesome bills (e.g. if the public service company threatened to cut power) and the rest were paid in the order of their assessed threat level (and how loudly they were pounding on the desk or the door). Additionally, our offices were owned by the landlord of the org, so we had to pay him on time to avoid trouble for them because of us. If we were unable to pay due to cash flow issues, I had to call the owner and sweet-talk him into accepting a delay.

In addition to these financial issues, which was already a full-time job for at least one person, I had to deal with all the personnel-related problems, the occasional translation "evolutions" which usually turned into a full-blown psychotic chaos, the accounting disputes regarding promotional costs, the stream of unsolicited "expert advice" from Lajos regarding meals and food quality, issues with and complaints about the berthing spaces and so on. This period was the most stressful in my entire life so far. I worked late every night, 6-7 hours of sleep was rare. Sometimes I had to work through the night just to keep up with the demands of my duties and all the paperwork. I was still dedicated to the cause though, so I fought through every barrier and the fatigue. I considered was my part in clearing the planet and creating a new civilization. But this dedication slowly eroded in the light of my experiences, and by the end of 2002, I had serious reservations about the upper level management of the Church.

This had developed gradually. By having a firsthand view of our finances, it was very obvious that we were paying a disproportionate amount to continental and international management organizations, while constantly being given new projects to complete, for which no funding was ever provided. The most infuriating was the huge amount of quality translations (Hubbard's books, lectures and other writings and he was very prolific) we had to produce for free, and no one in Europe or Los Angeles was interested in how we solved the problem of getting it done. They "wanted the product," as Hubbard instructed them to do and they accepted no excuses. In the end, the only solution was to get Scientologists to donate: for the IT equipment, software and dictionaries required for such work. In theory, this was forbidden (we were only allowed to collect donations for projects or organizations directly run or supervised by International Management), but I simply had no choice if I wanted to comply with the stream of orders we received. I remember one time when Miklós was ordered to report to Copenhagen for some sort of special briefing, and his deputy, Peter became the temporary CO. In his weekly report, Peter proudly stated that he managed to raise funds for a software application used for translations. Walter was not happy about it – he wrote in his reply that we should knock off this sort of thing immediately, as OTL was not supposed to be "some kind of beggar outfit." Then he called Peter. He told him that actually he did not mind if we solved the problem like this, but he was required to write this on telex lines, as it would be recorded and international management would find out about it eventually.

We were in agreement with Miklós that the current financial setup was not sustainable. I took the time and worked out a proposal for a new financial system, reviewed each element of it with Miklós, and sent it for approval to the continental and international finance directors of the Church. I did not get any answer and finally learned about its fate at the end of the year – but more about that later.

In this period, I also came across three confidential issues, which intensified my lingering doubts. The first was an executive directive, signed by Guillaume Lesèvre, the Executive Director International. It was a summary of Sea Org policies for missions, called "Strategy on Missions." I could not really understand the last point of it – it stated that should a Mission Holder complain about RTC or use Scientology materials without permission, then the Church was to crush him or her using copyright and trademark law and put him/her in jail (and this was an actual, written instruction). The second was the transcript of the 1982 US Mission Holders' Conference in San Francisco. The Sea Org executives who addressed the attendees had openly declared that they were going to take a lot of money from the mission holders, threatening them with expulsion from the Church if they did not comply. Two actual quotes from the document[26]: "right now there is so much criminality floating through the mission network" and [regarding paying 5% of their income for a central dissemination fund] "if I hear one person in this room who is not coughing up 5% as a minimum, you've got an investigation coming your way because you got other crimes in your mission." The third concerned "putting in ethics" on top management and "criminals" who supposedly had infiltrated it. Hubbard advised busting these "crims" and "crushing them like a bulldozer," adding that the noisy screams of the "crims" would be suppressed "by the roar of the engine of the bulldozer" (note: these are not actual quotes, as this issue was never leaked, but the wording was something very similar).

This new (and radical) viewpoint got me thinking about what kind of action would be justifiable as "I did what I had to do to help the expansion of Scientology." According to Hubbard's reasoning, what was considered to be *ethical* would not necessarily be *moral*; or as he put it, acts were considered ethical when they caused the greatest good on the greatest number of dynamics (areas or spheres of life). In light of the above, I realized that Scientology supposedly had such an important and lofty purpose that acts viewed by the

---

[26] subsequently issued as Sea Org Executive Directive 2104 INT, 7 November 1982, THE FLOW UP THE BRIDGE – THE US MISSION HOLDERS CONFERENCE, SAN FRANCISCO 1982.

wog world as criminal might be "ethical deeds" in the eyes of the church. The doubts I first had in Munich resurfaced again.

My belief was still strong in the technology itself, but I began increasingly to distrust upper level Church management, even more than I had in Munich. There was one phenomenon that was particularly disturbing – loyal staff members, who had served the Church for long years, suddenly turned into wretched and evil suppressive persons. Similarities to the Communist propaganda machine were striking; e.g. when certain outstanding fighters of the labor movement were suddenly exposed as imperialist spies serving the Western powers from the beginning, and consequently were erased from official records and archived photos.

I could not understand this. Sometimes we received executive directives or conditions orders from various Scientology organizations around the world, declaring certain Scientologists (and sometimes even Sea Org members) suppressive persons. Surprisingly, most of them were relatively high-level members (Clears or OTs) and veteran staff members. These written directives even gave detailed descriptions of the "crimes" committed by these suppressives, sometimes giving out very intimate details of their private lives. I could not help but wonder whether I would meet the same fate one day.

Due to the nature of the internal system of rules in the Church, many times I was forced to choose between two non-optimum solutions. A classic example: a large sum of money arrives on Thursday, but 10 minutes after 14:00. Theoretically, we could not touch it until next Thursday, but let's say the landlord was annoyed due constantly late payments and threatened to evict us unless I paid him in 24 hours. Then I had to either a) reset the internal clock of the computer to enter the invoice, so it would count as income for the previous week, b) spend the money without authorization by the Financial Planning Committee or c) let the landlord evict us. According to Church policy, all three options are considered actionable crimes or misdemeanors ("entering false data into a computer," "financial irregularity," "committing a problem" or "putting Scientology at risk," respectively). Also, we were sometimes ordered to send one of our veteran (spent at least 1 or 2 years in the SO) Sea Org members to fill a specific position at the European base within 24 hours of receipt of the order. If I followed the order and sent the person without finding and properly training a replacement I committed a crime called "dismantling a working installation." If I did not send the person, then I was guilty of sabotaging the plans of international management.

It gradually dawned on me during these stressful months that it would be easy to compile a list of such crimes for any veteran Sea Org member which would justify him or her being declared a suppressive person. This was rather unnerving, as I was deeply convinced that being in the Sea Org and in Scientology was the only sensible thing to do in the current situation of the planet. I thought that my life would lose its meaning if I were deprived of that. I did not want to get my wife into trouble, so I did not speak to her about my thoughts. I concluded that the only way to avoid being declared was to learn more about others who had suffered this fate, so I could avoid making the same mistakes. As I did not want to worry other Sea Org members by asking them about these negative matters, and risk being reported for spreading "entheta" (bad news, negative topics that portray Scientology or its founder unfavorably), I decided to do some research on the Internet.

It was very complicated to access the Internet as a Sea Org member. We had to use a standalone, dedicated computer for accessing online content, which could not be connected to the internal network. Also, content filtering software was installed on the computer and if someone wanted to access the Internet regularly, he had to request it in writing from OSA International. I submitted a request, and to my surprise, it was approved. I received a user name and a password and I was able to access the Internet through the filter. It turned out that all Scientology staff members were only allowed to access the Internet through a server located in OSA International; i.e. every webpage I visited and everything I downloaded was logged in a file and stored. I was once warned when I downloaded a few free applications for "jamming the comm lines of OSA." The content filter blocked all websites and portals which contained confidential upper-level Scientology materials or were critical of Scientology. Additionally, there was a list of words and expressions referring to materials "forbidden" for Scientologists, and if a set amount of these words appeared on a webpage, it was blocked. Finally, all sexual and pornographic content was also blocked.

When tinkering with the filter (I did not want OSA to know that I was looking up stories of ex-Sea Org members), I discovered the list of words used to determine whether access to a site should be blocked or not. I contained names like Bent Corydon, Arnie Lerma, Steve Hassan, which I presumed were the enemies or critics of Scientology, a familiar name (David Mayo) and a host of nicknames which were obviously used to make jokes about David Miscavige (Napoleon/Miscavige, poodle, dwarf) or Hubbard (charlatan, fraud). Also, the names of the top Scientology executives were on the list as well as the sites of certain newspapers, for example the *St. Petersburg Times*.

After looking through the files, I found an easy way to turn the filter on and off and I wrote a small program to accomplish that. Even after gaining this secret access, I was very careful not to read any confidential (OT) materials, I was merely looking for similar experiences or doubts. The stories of ex-SO members that I found on the Internet just made things worse. Apparently, others had experienced similar problems to mine and sooner or later it ended in them leaving the Sea Org and sometimes Scientology altogether. I also found some "horror stories" where former Sea Org member recounted similar or more harrowing experiences than my adventures in Copenhagen.

Now I understood why OSA was so desperate to control Internet access for staff members. It was considered a crime to use it without the filter and e-metered staff security checks often contained questions about reading anti-Scientology materials on the Internet. As I read these stories, I realized the reason for this preoccupation. The truth in them had an effect on Scientologists, including me (especially the "war stories" of ex-Sea Org members affected me, as I had similar experiences of my own). I became scared and I did not want to risk my eternity, so I refrained from reading further. The sheer volume of tasks I had and my extended schedule kept me occupied enough so that I did not have the time or energy to think things through.

PRODUCE, PRODUCE, PRODUCE

I had enough on my plate to forget about these doubts. We recruited 20 new people into the Sea Org in that year, and we had 5 Israeli nationals who had to do their basic training in Hungary, as they would have required visas to enter Denmark. We also tried to recruit a Hungarian Scientologist celebrity (a singer/TV presenter) who had achieved the state of Clear. He was not completely against the idea of joining the Sea Org and this resulted in us spending hours and hours trying to convince him to join. Finally, a recruitment tour sent by international management won the race, albeit in a tricky way. They somehow managed to convince the Scientologist girlfriend of the celebrity to join the Sea Org, and he followed her. It was quite a sight to behold as this famous person ran around the OTL, cleaned the floors and eating the bad food like the rest of us. He did not spend much time at the OTL though, he was soon sent to Clearwater to train and work. As I (secretly) expected, he did not last long – he had a realization that his life was about being a TV personality and having fans, so after a lengthy exit procedure he quit the Sea Org.

Things were uncharacteristically calm and quiet in the translations unit. We were tasked with translating the administrative technology of Hubbard as well as basic auditor training materials. Apparently, there was some confusion "uplines" about what materials should be translated, as the priority list of translations was changed three times that year. It also had a great side effect – no new materials were released, so we finally had some peace and quiet.

Our translations director (a very atypical Sea Org member, as he was mild-mannered and calm almost all the time) had a theory about the ever changing list of priorities. According to him, the following (vicious) cycle was going on: the international translations director issued a priority list. David Miscavige comes upon and cancels it immediately, as it does not align to strategic planning and announces that he will issue a new and proper one. As Miscavige is super busy, he never gets around to writing it, so the translations director issues another new list, as "waiting for orders" is frowned upon in the Sea Org. Miscavige cancels the new list etc. That's how I learned an unofficial maxim about the Sea Org – the only things that were certain in the Sea Org had happened at least two weeks ago and were already forgotten about by everyone. This applied to other areas as well, not only translations – actually, the Church behaved like a large corporation that was completely micromanaged by its CEO.

Personality-wise, I was not so lucky with my Dissemination Chief, the head of the division responsible for promotion and marketing. He was the nightmare of all top executives – the talented, but uncontrollable mid-level manager. He was extremely intelligent and resourceful and his work output was legendary, but he had his own methods of controlling his bosses to make sure things went his way. He mastered every means to back his seniors into a corner, thus forcing them to do as he wanted. Mostly, he wanted the money various Scientology organizations owed us for producing their promotional materials, as his division got 10% of all funds billed. This 10% was to be used to purchase new printing and IT equipment, typesetting and image editing software etc. If the money was not actively collected, he resorted to various ways to make the life of his seniors a nightmare.

One of his tricks was to stay late into the night on Wednesday "to get his stats up" and then disappear Thursday morning, allegedly to some external printshop and arrive back around 13:30 (half an hour before the weekly statistics were closed). I had a "cowbell" (a word Miklós used for cell phones) given to him, but he usually, and conveniently, left that on his desk. I was a nervous wreck on these occasions, as I had no way of knowing whether he had in fact gotten his stats up or not. Miklós was not interested in problems. He wanted a solution AND an accurate report RIGHT THEN AND THERE.

Most of the problems of the Dissemination Division stemmed from lack of proper foresight and planning for events. Local events (seminars, small training courses, briefings etc.) organized by the various Scientology organizations and front groups frequently required something printed (usually one of Hubbard's writings). These events were organized in the usual Sea Org style – meaning it required brilliant last-minute solution to make up for the almost complete lack of prior planning. Ironically, the local WISE office was the worst offender in that regard – the ones who were supposed to teach the best organizational technology on earth. This then resulted in the Dissemination Division only having 1 or 2 days to produce all the materials for these events, including all typesetting, printing etc. That meant no sleep for that period. But our Dissemination Chief always paid them back – he deliberately slowed things down to make sure they were only completed minutes before the event started, failed to report to the ones who ordered the materials about the status or simply announced that they would not be ready on time. That was his way of trying to get them to plan these events properly and leave enough time for everything to be printed.

I was also responsible for making sure all 100 crew members were properly fed. Our so called "galley" was located in a rented flat, and it did not have any permits required to operate a facility providing daily food for one hundred people. This illegal kitchen was also one of the main points of contention between the OTL and the OSA office. Lajos as I have mentioned was a bit of a gourmet. But the money allocated to food, being a low priority item, was nowhere near enough to produce anything of real nutritional value. So, one day he pulled a nasty trick – he made a dramatic entrance into the executive council meeting and (with a lot of theatrics) announced that he was shutting down the galley as its mere existence was a legal threat to the Church.

Part of the problem was the quality of personnel. The "Base Crew" division had the lowest priority possible when allocating personnel, so usually the people posted there were found unqualified or unsuitable for any other area. Trained cooks were not exactly attracted by the Sea Org lifestyle, not even the Scientologist chefs. Our first cook was formerly a switchyard worker, followed by a floor tiler and then a painter. All of them had to learn the intricacies of cooking from zero.

When Lajos finally stormed out, I suddenly had an idea. A WISE consultant had recently mentioned to me that one of the biggest Hungarian food courier companies was implementing parts of the admin tech and the CEO had a good opinion about Hubbard and Scientology in general. I called the consultant to talk to that CEO about helping us out in our time of need. I complained a bit to him about the suppressive National Public Health and Medical Officer Service of Hungary and we had to shut down the kitchen and how we could no longer serve warm meals to Sea Org members working tirelessly to save the planet. Amazingly, the consultant managed to convince the CEO to help and the first shipment arrived the next day. It turned out they sent their leftovers and unclaimed orders to various charities, and we had now replaced all those other charities as the recipient of their goodwill.

154

This did not go over well at the company, so in a week we made a deal with them to get a special 50% discount on all of their prices and became regular customers. In the next few weeks, my popularity reached unprecedented levels. Crew members, who had hardly seen meat could now order proper food from a menu. I even received written commendations from the most grateful ones. Lajos was the only one who was unhappy. He behaved like a child whose ball had been taken away. He could no longer terrorize kitchen staff and he had no reason to hold court and give lengthy lectures about operating a large kitchen and his epic purchasing deals. So he began to undermine the new setup. He was constantly complaining about the quality of the food provided (which was completely unfounded, as it was a massive improvement over the cheap, unhealthy meals we served before) to any executive he encountered. Then he started nagging Miklós to cancel this set up, as "OTL couldn't afford it" (which was a lie as it was not much more expensive) and it was "not standard" as Hubbard dictated all Sea Org units to have their own "galleys" manned by Sea Org members. According to his theory, I was too lazy to work on the real solution (establishing a "standard, on-policy galley" with all the necessary equipment, acquiring all the required official permits and authorizations, recruiting and posting a trained cook, training purchasers to find and/or get very good deals etc.). He also argued that food deprivation was a traditional disciplinary method in the Sea Org (Hubbard did write that crew members who failed to perform adequately were assigned to eat cold rice & beans every day for a set period) and food could no longer be used to keep people in line with the current setup.

In order to calm Lajos down, we implemented a rewards and penalties system. Only people who were considered upstat were allowed to order from the food courier company, the rest were served the old-style self-prepared terrible food again. This caused great outrage – I was physically assaulted by the Chief Officer when I put him on the "bad food only" list for being downstat.

The undermining efforts of Lajos were ultimately successful, as Miklós finally decided to ditch the food courier and fully revert to the old ways. Lajos was happy to resume his favorite pastime – hounding the kitchen staff and giving lengthy and unsolicited expert advice.

He regularly interfered with food purchasing. There were three foods that he considered mortal enemies. First on his list was the so-called machine-made egg barley[27] – he only allowed handmade egg barley be bought. The other two were hot dog sausages and the local plain variety of mortadella called "pariser."

---

[27] egg barley: is a Hungarian specialty. It is a very simple food; made of wheat flour, water and whole eggs, which are formed into barley-sized "grains" either by hand or cutting.

I remember one time he saw an unfortunate crew member bring in hot dogs to serve and Lajos immediately started screaming at him "you have written orders from Miklós that you cannot buy hot dogs!"

There was another issue that regularly caused conflict on the base. The good and caring souls working in the kitchen sometimes got the idea to help out the lowest ranking Sea Org members by giving them better food, while the high-ranking ones were served something of lower quality. This practice was called the "Romero Policy" after an actual incident. Once we had bought a lot of ice cream bars for the crew to celebrate some minor achievement. The kitchen staff gave the best ones (the brand name of the ice cream was "Romero," hence the name) to the EPF'ers[28], and the rest went to the regular Sea Org crew and executives. Of course, this violated the internal rewards and penalties policy. So, if any instance of the Romero Policy was detected in the OTL, I got into trouble for it.

In addition to his Super Galley Crusade, Lajos was always glad to remind me that security of the premises was a function of one of the divisions I supervised. The office we rented was not in a particularly good neighborhood and not all windows had protective bars – so it was absolutely no surprise when one of our E-meters was stolen when someone accidently left a window open.

Lajos threw a tantrum when he learned about this. He yelled at the Security Chief for almost half an hour, and proceeded to share his dramatic visions with Miklós – proclaiming careless Sea Org members were as criminal as the street children who presumably stole the e-meter. His main problem was that confidential documents could have been stolen as well, potentially causing a lot of trouble and embarrassment for the Church.

So, I had to get grates installed on all windows and purchase surveillance equipment. There was no money for this of course, so I had to "obtain" everything. Fortunately, one of the WISE members owned a security equipment wholesaling business. Off I went to "reg" a few outdoor surveillance cameras and the necessary cables and accessories as a donation.

After this issue died down, Lajos resumed the holy war on bad food and cooking. As the next step, he turned to Walter. In an emotional telex appeal, he pleaded for him to intervene and take effective action to resolve food issues, as "OSA staff members were too hungry to work effectively and cannot concentrate properly on their duties." Walter sent the order down in his usual no-nonsense style – Miklós was to make sure there was proper food, report compliance with photographic evidence of good, nutritious meals prepared for

---

[28] members of the Estates Project Force, which was the name of basic training (i.e. boot camp) of the Sea Org

the crew and "had to sign it with his own blood that it was actually happening." Miklós was not too happy about having to deal with this as well, but he worked with me. We allocated a bit more money for food, added a new person to the galley and managed to get food quality improved.

It did not last long, however. We simply did not have adequate income to sustain a higher allocation for food and we had to transfer someone from the galley to another position which had higher priority. So in 2 months the food was back to the bearable-terrible range. Lajos went into attack mode and had one of his juniors write a lengthy "knowledge report" about me and the galley crew, loaded with his usual accusations. He sent it to Walter and his deputies.

It was one of the best days of my life when we received Walter's reply. He was furious that he was being repeatedly harassed about such a trivial issue and by OSA of all the Scientology entities. So he took the time to properly retaliate. He paid a visit to the Commanding Officer of OSA Europe and got permission to get Lajos and the unfortunate OSA staff member who written the report hauled in and put on the E-meter for some questioning. According to Hubbard, harsh and carping criticism was a result of harmful acts of commission or omission committed against the target of the critical remarks. So, this logic dictated that Lajos must have done something bad to be so critical. He was questioned by one of our auditors and confessed to some minor work-related infractions. As a result, he had to report to Copenhagen for further "handling."

After this incident, Lajos became much more civilized regarding the whole subject of crew food, and did not harass the galley crew as often as earlier. And when he was in a better mood, he even helped them find and/or cut better deals. But on his bad days he was back to his old self with all the yelling and theatrics – and he didn't care if any "wog" visitors or public Scientologists heard him screaming and using a lot of expletives.

FINANCES RELOADED

No matter what other duties I had, most of my time was still spent handling our finances. The first priority was to handle some embarrassing phone bills. One of the recent translations campaigns had been one of the most basic books of Scientology (*Scientology: Fundamentals of Thought*). I was under watch in Copenhagen at that time so I fortunately missed it. No funding was provided, so the work had to be done by Slovakian, Croatian, Romanian etc. volunteer Scientologists. As a result, a lot of international phone calls were made. At the time they had "solved" the problem by ordering new phone lines, with Sea Org translators as the nominal subscribers. These phones were then used day and night until the phone company disconnected them for non-payment.

The net result was 5,000 USD plus interests in unpaid bills. Though it was not directly owed by OTL, it was included as part of our bills summary (rather than let the Sea Org members get into legal trouble). This then had a negative effect on the "cash/bills ratio" statistic, which was one of the statistics of the Commanding Officer. Miklós wanted a solution. He sent me to negotiate with the phone company to beat down the debt as much as possible and then arrange to pay in installments. He said that Imre might be able to help as there was a similar problem shortly after OTL was founded, and Imre handled it at that time. Imre told me who to contact and I went to see her and her assistant.

The negotiations were successful. I knew how I was supposed to handle "wogs" as a good Scientologist – I told them an acceptable truth. I gave them part of the story, explaining that some of the subscribers were no longer in the country so they had no chance of collecting anything from them. I made it look like that we were doing them a favor by taking responsibility for the unpaid bills by offering to pay a portion of them in installments. They wanted better terms, but they did not really have much choice so a compromise was reached. They forfeited all interest, gave a 20% discount on the bills and agreed to monthly installments to pay off the balance.

My next job was to establish a new income source. If a Scientologist went to a higher-level organization abroad for services and the OTL had actively assisted in getting the person there and had proof, then we received a 5% commission. It was potentially a lot of money for us, as these upper-level services were expensive, sometimes tens of thousands of dollars. As a first step, we opened an office for the representatives of these orgs and provided translators for them. Then I had to establish communication lines with the disbursement directors of these orgs so they would forward us any owed commissions. Their willingness to pay was similar to ours, so sometimes it took considerable effort to get our cut.

As this was much needed income, Miklós wanted these funds right away and preferably before Thursday 14:00. More often than not it was sent to us by Western Union. The business rolled along even during the holiday session. I remember my Christmas lunch on 25 December, 2002. I was sitting at the table with my family when Miklós texted me a reminder about my weekly income collection duties. I excused myself and went out to call the disbursement director in Copenhagen, so I could convince her to run to the nearest Western Union office and send our commission.

As I alluded to in the previous paragraph, cooperation among Scientology organizations was not always smooth, to put it mildly. There was one particular incident which made OTL Hungary somewhat infamous in the world of Scientology. In 2002, Flag Service Organization sent two people to Budapest to recruit new personnel for them. The prospect of working in the US was attractive for a lot of Hungarians, so they had a lot of sign-ups. To prevent their new recruits from having second thoughts, they started them on their Sea Org basic training in the OTL, while they obtained US religious worker visas for them. Visas were not that easy to get and in the end, most of their recruits were stuck in Hungary. We provided food and accommodations and so billed these services to the Clearwater organization, but they did not pay. Apparently, Flag considered themselves a senior organization, and felt we should help them in any way we could.

After three months of non-payment Miklós and I decided to stop giving them any food and evict them if the bills weren't paid. I informed their chief recruiter and alerted our security chief to prepare for this action. The security chief was a young, enthusiastic and a slightly overzealous guy. He decided to do it the Sea Org way – showing initiative and not waiting for further orders. He evicted all of their staff that evening. It was November and it was pretty chilly outside, so they were mightily upset.

I was not particularly interested when I found out about his drastic action. I shared the same opinion as Miklós on the matter – we had to put up with the ire of our creditors and suppliers because of their refusal to pay, and they were shielded from the real-world consequences of such situations. I felt it was time to have them experience the real world.

Flag Service Organization came up with the money soon thereafter, but their recruiters also wrote a lengthy report about me, Miklós and the security chief and sent copies to every imaginable senior executive in international management (or in European Sea Org slang, "it was sent to God and his mother"). Naturally, I was the main culprit (they were somewhat fearful of provoking the smart and vindictive Miklós) and they concluded that I was, in fact, a suppressive person, hell-bent on destroying the OTL and the Sea Org. Miklós showed me a Hubbard writing to ease my concerns, where the "old man" related his experiences as the executive director of Saint Hill, the first large organization in the history of Scientology. He mentioned that most of the knowledge reports were written on product-oriented executives who were getting the staff to work. In the end, the incident did not have any major consequences.

As I mentioned earlier, another income source was the collection of debts "owed" by former Sea Org members called "freeloader debts." The so-called freeloaders were among the most hated people by Sea Org members as they were considered traitors, even more despised than wogs. It was almost like a religious duty to constantly harass and pressure them until they came up with the dough. If they were minors, then I had to go after their parents who were usually Scientologists.

In addition to being the primary target of the director of income, they were also frequently the butt of nasty jokes. For example, one of the ex-Sea Org members was kicked out because he ran off with a girl and made out for a day before coming back. After he was dismissed, he founded a small enterprise and wanted to pay his bill from its revenues. When I told Miklós he smiled wryly and asked me, "And what would be the name of that company? Rabbit Llc?"

However, the most insulting jokes were reserved for ex-Sea Org members who had children after leaving the SO. They were the "baby boomers" – in the Sea Org, they were supposed to boom the small and failing orgs they were sent to with their newborns, but in our view they had deserted us and now they were "booming their babies."

Interestingly, Scientologist parents were sometimes harder to convince about paying the bills incurred by their children than their wog counterparts. For example, one Scientologist mother refused to pay the bill incurred by her daughter. She was 16 years old, spent just half a year in the Sea Org, but still managed to incur 4,000 USD of debt. Her mother claimed that paying the bill would create an out-exchange situation and according to one of the policies of Ron, that might make a criminal out of her daughter. She was referring to this quote from a policy letter dated 4 April 1972:

"A lot of this exchange imbalance comes from child psychology where the child is not contributing anything and is not permitted to contribute.

"It is this which first overwhelms him with feelings of obligation to his parents and then bursts out as total revolt in his teens.

"Children who are permitted to contribute (not as a cute thing to do but actually) make non-contributing children of the same age look like raving maniacs! It is the cruel sadism of modern times to destroy the next generation this way."

. . .

"So if a person is brought up this life with the exchange all awry, the Est O[29] has his hands full sometimes!

"He is dealing with trained-in criminality!" – *L. Ron Hubbard*

Probably she just did not want to pay, but if she said that, she would have been in trouble, so she resorted to this tactic. It was not easy to deal with someone quoting LRH to support their argument. I did a little digging, asked a few people about her in the local mission and found out that the family had

---

[29] short for Establishment Officer, an executive responsible for hiring, training and correcting staff members

recently taken a vacation abroad, including the girl. So I called her back to ask her about out-exchange and how rewarding her traitor of a daughter with an expensive vacation fit into the picture. She reluctantly paid a small down payment. I was satisfied as even though the full amount wasn't collected, I had at least made their lives a bit miserable which seemed appropriate punishment for what their daughter had done.

In addition to all this hunting for money, I had to finally comply with an outstanding order to implement the so-called Finance System. It was contained in a software application produced by INCOMM, the in-house software developer of the Church. This program tracked every cent and implemented Hubbard's complex financial system in full. It was also designed to essentially prevent any "off-policy"[30] financial operation or transaction, forcing the user to strictly adhere to Church regulations. It also meant an additional 1-2 hours of work each day to enter all data in addition to huge piles of paper documents for internal use. Copies of its database had to be sent to Copenhagen and international management on a regular basis, so they could monitor all of our finances. Note: treasury personnel were also subject to regular metered checks and any small irregularity had serious consequences. Probably the areas connected to money were under the strictest control in the Sea Org.

A "Continental Finance Director" was also posted in the OTL to implement and supervise the new financial setup. She was the financial decision-maker for OTL and all the related entities (including WISE and ABLE, which were independent and secular organizations on paper). Miklós urged me to befriend her as a strategic move, so I could manipulate her if needed.

COMMITTEE SESSIONS, MEETINGS AND OTHER DELICACIES

Unsurprisingly, Miscavige's vision of a perfect Sea Org management organization also included various committees, tacked onto the existing setup, which was already overcomplicated and unwieldy.

As the Supercargo OTL, I had to attend the following (committee) meetings:

Product Conference: every day with the heads of the four divisions supervised by me. Subject: what was done that day, setting targets for the next day and review of the daily production statistics.

Executive Council Product Conference: every day with Miklós, his deputy, me and the Chief Officer, with the same agenda.

---

[30] contrary to or not in alignment with any of Hubbard's administrative policies

Management Coordination Committee: once a week, usually Friday morning. Attendees: the four OTL Executive Council members and the Commanding Officers/Executive Directors of the various entities (ABLE, WISE, OSA etc). It was supposedly a forum for coordinating the weekly "battle plans"[31], but more about the actual subjects later.

Base Coordination Committee: once a week (or daily before large events). Attended by roughly the same executives as the Management Coordination Committee, it was used to coordinate efforts and activities related to events.

Executive Council: once a week with Miklós, his deputy, me and the Chief Officer. Agenda: coordination of weekly plans, setting weekly production quotas, approving financial planning.

Perimeter Council: attended by all executives as well as OSA, the security chief and the director of personnel enhancement. It was a forum to coordinate any serious issues with staff considered a threat to the Sea Org base – crew members "blowing" (leaving in an unauthorized manner) or having mental breakdowns, serious ethics offenses, security breaches etc.

Staff meeting: every Friday night, attended by the entire crew. Chaired by the Commanding Officer, it was used to recap the achievement of the last week (or the lack of them) and to brief the crew about the production targets for this week.

The meetings of the various coordination committees were more often than not derailed from the original agenda – fizzling out in usually unresolved disputes about the correct interpretation of what LRH wrote or Lajos, who considered himself to be an expert at everything, took over to share his sage advice with all present. Sometimes the meetings degenerated into lengthy name, blame and shame sessions, with accusations flying around how the lack of action on someone else's part made it completely impossible to do one's own job.

Fortunately there were a few topics which helped to lighten the usual boring or tense mood. One of them was event call-in to get people to the local showing of the videos of international Church events. This was universally hated by every executive of the OTL, as we considered this to be the job of the Division 6 of Budapest Org, but we were under strict orders to make sure the attendance quotas were met.

Though these were organized by the Church, the so-called secular Scientology organizations (WISE and ABLE) were also supposed to mobilize their field and get them to attend these events. I remember one time when the Executive Director of ABLE tried to shirk this task by stating that there were

---

[31] all daily, weekly and weekly production plans were called "battle plans," in alignment with the (somewhat faux) naval tradition of the Sea Org

no people in the ABLE area that could be considered "Scientologists," as they were licensing the secular version of the philosophy. Miklós, not easily fazed by lame excuses, replied with a terse "you should invite all the Hubbardists then and make sure they attend."

Though it sounds trivial, organizing the food for Sea Org members working at the events was a separate and important job. We had no funds to hire a catering company, and if left to their own devices, the Base Crew usually botched it. On one nightmarish occasion I forgot to properly organize this and the resulting mess was remembered for a long time. They prepared bean soup with onions (a LOT of onions) and brought it to the event hall in a large cauldron, leaving us with the flatulent consequences for our conversations with the public. The second dish was a sandwich. They were thrown into a black garbage bag, as they had no proper containers and one of the kitchen hands in his food-stained and smelly overalls carried it through the elegant crowd of Scientologists to one of the small rooms in the back of the event hall.

Sometimes Lajos was actually entertaining during these dreadful meetings, when he launched himself into conspiracy theory nut mode, rambling about an international cabal of Illuminati hell-bent on taking over the world. His primary sources were the books of János Drábik, a self-appointed expert, most notably, "Usury Civilization" and "Interest Capitalism." According to Lajos, the information in those books was a "90% match" to "OSA intelligence data" and was in alignment with LRH's views as he had announced them to Scientologists in one of his most famous lectures:

"Our enemies on this planet are less than twelve men. They are members of the Bank of England and other higher financial circles. They own and control newspaper chains, and they are, oddly enough, directors in all the mental health groups in the world which have sprung up. Now these chaps are very interesting fellows: They have fantastically corrupt backgrounds; illegitimate children; government graft; a very unsavory lot. And they apparently, sometime in the rather distant past, had determined on a course of action. Being in control of most of the gold supplies of the planet, they entered upon a program of bringing every government to bankruptcy and under their thumb, so that no government would be able to act politically without their permission." – L. Ron Hubbard, Ron's Journal 67, dated 2 September 1967.

Product conferences were another matter, though. The mood was usually quite stern and serious. The targets that were set at the beginning of the week were unrealistic in the first place, so generally only partial accomplishments were recorded. The weekly battle plans submitted by the division heads and Exec Council member had to reflect the urgency of planetary clearing. Miklós used these battle plans to write his own, adding a host of new targets and increasing quotas. That combined battle plan was sent to Walter for approval, and he only approved it if it contained bold targets and impressive production quotas or in the internal language of the Sea Org, they were in alignment with the concept of "thinking big." "Small think" was considered treasonous.

Under these circumstances, humor was the only tool to lighten the mood. To this day I recall two memorable incidents. At the end of 2002, three-story bunks were installed in the flats used for staff berthing to keep up with the increasing number of crew members. When they were assembled, it turned out that the director of maintenance had forgotten to include ladders in his blueprints. Miklós went ballistic when he discovered this at the product conference, and asked the head of the Base Crew division: "Who do you think works here? Gummi Bears? Or Sergei Bubka impersonators?"

The second incident was about a target on the weekly battle plan of the Base Crew division: "collect all LRH writings about the proper use and maintenance of cars and stick to the policies contained in them." I asked the director of maintenance what was done. He thought for a while, then said, "The writings were collected, now the only thing lacking is the sticking to them part."

"OUR ORG PEOPLE WILL BE VICTORIOUS"

This was our permanent slogan in 2002, inspired by a catchphrase (originally "Our hard-working people will be victorious!") from the 1980 French comedy *Les Sous-doués* (English title: *The Under-Gifted*), which enjoyed cult status in Hungary. Suddenly, the expansion of Budapest Org became top priority. At the beginning of 2002, Walter told Miklós that International Management wanted Budapest Org to win the LRH Birthday Game. It was mainly for PR reasons – apparently they wanted to demonstrate to the orgs in the US and Europe, which had been founded decades ago, that you only need dedication and enthusiasm to achieve significant expansion.

There were 156 orgs around the world, and in January 2002, Budapest Org was in 7th place in the overall rankings. The race ended on 13th March, so we had 2 and half months to climb to the top. Miklós sat down with Tamás Nagy, the Executive Director of the org, to work out the details. There were 24 main statistics that were part of the game. The org got 1 point for each statistic that was in Normal condition (i.e. it increased slightly) and 3 points per each statistic in Affluence condition (i.e. which increased markedly). Miklós was a seasoned veteran of the controlled management of Scientology statistics, so he knew how much each had to go up weekly to maximize the point haul.

For example, gross income and course completions had to be carefully timed so the statistic would go up each week just a bit. Nevertheless, there were some physical limitations (e.g. the course room or auditor capacity), so we used some tricks. The auditors were talked into auditing 8-10 hours per day and were promised a two-week leave after the game was over. The course completion statistic was handled by selling a lot of small courses to Scientologists using the birthday game gimmick. The course room was opened for the night, so people could be called in to study more and complete additional courses if the weekly statistic needed it. A lot of advance payments were regged to artificially push the gross income up by pushing the patriotism button (Hungary had to win the game!).

In the end, we were successful and Budapest Org managed to win the game. But we could not sit on our laurels for long. Apparently, International Management was excited Budapest Org was doing so well and they ordered Walter to get Budapest Org to achieve "Saint Hill size." Here is what that meant:

Apparently, Hubbard had an exact plan for clearing the planet and securing the ultimate victory of Scientology. (Note: I have never seen this plan in writing, only heard about it countless times from various people in Church management). According to that plan, it was enough to simply issue the next two unreleased OT levels, namely OT IX and OT X. If 10,000 Scientologists were to complete these two levels, there would be a massive shift in the collective mind of humanity. One of the effects would be a huge increase of interest in Scientology and masses of people would come into the Church, demanding training and auditing. The "inflow" would be so enormous that the current organizational structure would not be able to handle it and would collapse.

So, according to Church management, Hubbard instructed them to get all the 150-something orgs to achieve the size of Old Saint Hill – which was the first Scientology organization, personally run by Hubbard in the '60s. When this target was achieved, management would then make OT IX and X available and in a few years, Scientology would take over the planet.

In retrospect, this plan was probably publicized as a kind of dangling carrot to keep the staff members working and Scientologists paying. We will probably never know if Hubbard sincerely believed in this or it was just a part of a cosmic con game.

In any case, International Management simply had to present at least 2-3 Saint Hill orgs per year to maintain the illusion of taking significant steps forward. This was usually enough to convince the average Scientologist that real progress was being made and the goal could realistically be achieved in a few decades. Thus they would continue to happily donate for supporting the "upstat" Church and the whole system could continue to operate.

This illusion was the most important commodity of the Church. The ultimate reward for staying loyal to the Church was the creation of an utopian civilization and the opportunity to become a powerful and influential figure in that civilization as one of the early believers of the vision.

The definition of what actually constitutes "Saint Hill size" was not as clear though. For some reason, Hubbard never defined the exact requirements, so current Church management reviewed the statistics of the original Saint Hill org to determine the level of production needed. In 2002, it was 1000 "well done auditing hours" and 40 major course completions per week, 200 students had to be on course per week and the org had to have 20 trained auditors on post.

The biggest issue we faced was the lack of auditors. Despite the use of the much hyped "Golden Age of Tech" methods and materials, the total number of trained auditors in Hungary was around 30 and six of them were on staff. The rest did not really want to join.

Walter got the order to fix the auditor problem. He came to Budapest just before the next scheduled international Church event video showing. He shared his plan with us – he would hold a cracking pep talk about how much Hungarian people loved freedom, mentioning the major historical examples. Walter was surprisingly well acquainted with our history. He even read *Eclipse of the Crescent Moon* by Géza Gárdonyi and referred to it and the characters of the novel to Miklós in his written communications. His other favorite point of reference was the Revolution of 1848. After his speech, Sea Org members would swoop down on the audience, doing sell recruitment on the most promising suspects.

However, the event did not go as planned. Walter got overly enthusiastic during his speech and started to recruit people from the stage and passionately urged people to step up and join staff right then and there. He was very loud, yelling in his microphone and looked and sounded like a general in a World War II movie, as he was tall, muscular and had a strong Austrian accent. Most of the Sea Org crew (including me) stood around with a stunned look on our faces and only after 15-20 minutes did we begin helping Walter by urging people to go up on stage and join him.

The initial shock had worn off by then and the attendees started to slip away and head for the exits. This made our initial plan unworkable as we could no longer swarm the "public" so the whole thing ended in few recruitment interviews.

Walter was surprisingly calm and withdrawn during the after event meeting. He looked a bit sad even. He exercised some self-criticism and said that he should not have started to recruit people from the stage, as it was not prepared properly. He then added that after he came off stage, a wog reporter approached him and accused him of brainwashing people. He was not happy about it, but to my surprise, he let it go.

I could not understand this sudden change in his behavior, which was in such stark contrast to what I observed in Copenhagen. He was in Budapest for two days and was nice to everyone all the time, told quite a few jokes and even admitted to his mistakes. I concluded that probably the intense pressure he was under in Copenhagen made him behave like a violent dictator when he was there.

We did make some minor progress, but we remained far from having the 20 auditors needed for Saint Hill size. We still needed 14 more and had no idea how to get them.

International management was not happy with our lack of progress, so they sent one of their universal troubleshooters, a veteran Sea Org officer named Fred Harris, on a mission to get this done. Upon arriving, he introduced himself as a member of the IMPR (International Management Public Relations) division and told us in no uncertain terms that we had three weeks to turn Budapest into a Saint Hill size org because it was going to be featured in one of the upcoming international Church events in June. Awkward silence followed his announcement, as we believed there were simply not enough trained auditors available and willing to join staff to get the complement filled.

Mr. Harris certainly did not waste a minute in accomplishing his apparently impossible mission. First, he set the date of the event to celebrate the achievement of Saint Hill Size, so there was no way back. He told us that the clock was ticking and we better get rolling. We were going to meet the target even if it meant not sleeping for three weeks. He then sat down with Miklós and made a list of every possible prospect and idea, no matter how far-fetched, for the remaining 14 auditor seats. To my astonishment, he pulled off a miracle and made the target. I was not directly involved in the headhunt, but I heard from Miklós how he did it.

He used three methods: First of all, Budapest already had some auditors in training at the Copenhagen Advanced Organization. Mr. Harris called Walter and told him that he had to push through the most promising ones and get them graduated. And he did not care how, but he needed them back in three weeks. He also got some auditors by having them transferred or loaned from missions for some financial compensation (in theory, this was against policy). Finally, he signed up the rest by promising them special privileges (extra pay, more holidays and day-offs etc.), which was also against Church policy. He made sure though that these "off-policy" deals could not be tracked back to him and there was no paper trail. He and Miklós were basically camped at the org, virtually day and night and carefully micromanaged every aspect of the delivery of service, so the quota of 1000 auditing hours and 40 course completions was reached two weeks in a row.

We also had to prepare for the event. Mr. Harris was still busy with getting the last auditor signings finalized, so he just told us that we had to put on a majestic show, so it would be a memorable enough occasion for such a grand announcement. As it turned out he had completely different ideas (and standards) than the people in the org who normally organized the local events. Two days before the event, when the ink was dry on the contract of the last auditor, he shared his ideas with us. He wanted a laser show, a procession of hussars, a gypsy band and folk dancers performing as a bare minimum. During his speech, we were supposed to show slides to illustrate the points he made or to prove the claims he uttered. The executives of the org and the 20 auditors were to come up to the stage at one point, everyone in tuxedos or formal evening gowns.

When we first heard this we hoped he was joking. Unfortunately, he was not. The org staff reluctantly began to make arrangements to accommodate his wishes, but the key organizers were sure that half of these things would not happen as the org had neither the time nor the money to arrange them.

The event was scheduled to start on Sunday afternoon. Mr. Harris showed up Saturday at noon to check on the progress. I knew that we were in serious trouble, as the executive director Tamás Nagy had simply cancelled most of the extra show elements due to financial concerns.

Mr. Harris was having none of it and ordered the OTL to literally get the show on the read and find the money. He also added that he would need a lectern with a large Scientology cross and we had to install a bust of LRH on the stage, and put a large Ron picture on the curtain behind him, otherwise he simply would not go on stage and we would be in the worst kind of trouble as Sea Org members.

Miklós sent me to the finance director to beg for a couple thousand bucks for the event. Imre got a gypsy band and one of the OTL crew members managed to program a laser show during the night. Miklós fortunately convinced Mr. Harris to give up on the hussars, and one of the Sea Org translators was an accomplished folk dancer, so he was able to put on a small show.

I was told to get the remaining props together. I managed to locate a suitable lectern with a big Scientology cross in a remote city and had it transported to Budapest. The only problem was the LRH bust. There was not a single one

168

in the entire country. In the end, I called the Executive Director of the org in Vienna and after a lengthy conversation, he finally agreed to loan it to us.

The last thing we had to handle was the tuxedos. For some reason, Tamás Nagy hated tuxedos with a passion. He defiantly announced a few hours before the event that he would not don a tuxedo no matter what – even if he was declared as a Suppressive Person for his refusal. He then added that he would not pay a dime for renting tuxedos for the auditors either. Miklós had a talk with him and after 30 minutes of the proven mixture of threats and flattery, Tamás gave up and agreed to wear a tuxedo. Meanwhile, I joined forces with one of the org executives and convinced the owner of a tuxedo rental shop to come in and open to accommodate us.

Walter was also ordered by Mr. Harris to come down and make sure that there would be no problems with the execution of the event. No staff member had much sleep in the frantic last two days, including Walter, but the event went down relatively smoothly. Walter was in a foul mood though for some reason. When a public Scientologists accidentally stepped on his shoes, he turned to the culprit, looked him in the eye and said, "fuck you." Luckily, that person did not speak any English.

A month or two later the big announcement was made during the annual Maiden Voyage Anniversary Event, aboard the church's luxury cruise liner called *Freewinds*. I am sure that Church fundraisers had a field day after that as apparently there was huge expansion going on in Hungary, which was indeed well on its way to becoming the first Clear country.

Reality, though, confirmed our secret fears. The balloon burst after Mr. Harris left. The level of production dropped and most of the newly recruited auditors left staff, one after the other, since the org was not willing or able to fulfill the promises given to them in their special, unwritten employment contracts. I suspect that the majority of the so-called Saint Hill size orgs suffered the same fate – statistics were pushed up in a completely unsustainable way before the international announcement and after that the whole org crashed back to its previous activity level.

After the target of making a Saint Hill size org was theoretically accomplished, we moved on to our next task: we were supposed turn the mission in Pécs (my hometown) into a proper Scientology org. The project, after half a year of trying, failed miserably. We were ordered onto another priority and the Pécs project was never completed.

At the end of the year, we received a sort of reply to my request and recommendations for a new financial setup. The official response was the personal appearance of one of Walter's deputies, the Deputy CO for Ethics & Image of the European Sea Org base. She conducted an ethics investigation in OTL including e-metered interviews to locate the source of critical thoughts about continental and international management. As it turned out, my submission was considered critical of them, as it contained the cancellation of a certain type of management fee (which we paid for but received nothing, as that type of Scientology management organization had no representatives in Hungary). As I was never afraid to speak my mind about upper level management to my fellow executives, they were all too happy to throw me under the bus. So I became the primary suspect and target, again. I suspected that Miklós also played a part in this – the new finance system was originally his idea, but he sought to avoid trouble, so he probably put it all on me. In the end, I was ordered to go to Copenhagen for "handling," while the other OTL executives were let off the hook with a warning.

I was prepared for the worst – another 24-hour watch, kitchen and cleaning detail, screaming sessions, security checks. To my extreme surprise, I received completely fair and proper treatment. No yelling, I was free to go wherever I wanted and I was not even required to do menial jobs as punishment. I had to see a few people from OSA and the ethics section and they mostly tried to give me plausible reasons for the things I read on the Internet earlier and had heard from my fellow inmates (Robert Dale and Ralph Pieters-Kwiers). I was told that Robert and Ralph had been declared SPs. I was convinced to some degree by their reasoning, but not all my doubts had vanished.

During one of the conversations, I mentioned that I read something about Walter on the Internet. This news somehow reached Walter, who then paid me a visit. I was terrified that I would get the yelling treatment, but fortunately he was having a good day. He came in with a big smile and asked what I read on the Internet about him. I told him briefly that the write-up was authored by an ex-Sea Org member, who had worked in the Translation Unit. It contained a detailed description of Walter's somewhat eccentric behavior as an executive – which I had also experience firsthand – and also an analysis of the constant changes in translation methodologies used by the Church. Walter had a good laugh, remarked, "So I am famous now." and then left.

Chaired by the Supercargo of the Copenhagen Sea Org base, an Executive Court of Ethics was held. The chairman was surprisingly friendly and gave a very reasonable verdict. He ordered me to complete a study of various LRH writings and I had to make up for the minor irregularities I had committed. He told me that he completely understood my situation and he also regularly faced tough choices (he essentially had the same post and functions), so he did not feel I deserved any harsh punishment. I was then sent back to Hungary.

Upon arriving, Miklós called me into his office and told me that I would be stripped of all my functions, special rights and titles. I did not know what to make of it. It seemed though that he still felt personally threatened by results of the recent investigation. I think he must have been implicated in some of the irregularities and criticisms, so he wanted to demonstrate his utmost loyalty and tried to pin everything on somebody else in self-defense.

According to the relevant LRH policies, only a properly convened Committee of Evidence had the right to demote me, but Miklós used another LRH policy to trump that, namely a policy letter dated 31 October 1966, called ACTIONS, EXECUTIVE, FOR HANDLING DISASTROUS OCCURRENCES. According to the procedure outlined in that policy, he was able to reverse the sequence if there was a disaster – and he thought there was. So he removed me from my position by issuing an urgent directive and then requested a Committee of Evidence to review the matter. All in all, he had the right to do that and the policy was open to that sort of interpretation. I did not put up much of a fight. I did not want to risk another nightmarish handling like the one I had in 1998, so I accepted my fate. The authoritative system of the Sea Org had made me accustomed to obeying orders without asking questions.

This incident illustrates one of the many controversial aspects of Scientology. In theory, I had a lot of rights and protection from haphazard or unjust actions. In actual fact, there were always certain completely legal and official ways and methods to circumvent and nullify those rights.

In the new setup, I was basically demoted to executive assistant until my so-called handlings were completed. Miklós added a lot of materials to the study program I received in Copenhagen, so it looked like it would last a few months. After a few days, I began to enjoy it. I no longer had to deal with all those pesky personnel, financial, feeding and translations-related insanities. My stress level dropped to the very lowest mark. I was able to consistently sleep 7-8 hours a day, study the required 12.5 hours per week and had much more of my own time. I even bought lottery tickets every week and to my absolute surprise, I won 2,500 USD (which was a huge sum for me). I bought a personal laptop, so I could resume my previous favorite pastime, playing video games after 23:00 each day and Saturday mornings.

Andrea, my wife, was no longer my junior, which had a rather positive effect on our relationship. It became as harmonious as it was possible given the external circumstances.

Needless to say, a lot of my fellow shipmates were rather irritated by this turn of events. When I was shipped off to Copenhagen a few weeks earlier, Miklós made sure that everyone in the OTL knew that I was that incorrigible jerk who had forced the hand of the European base to send an investigator. Now the out-ethics saboteur was back, enjoying life on a lower post and he looks fresh and cheerful every morning, and even wins a lot of money, owns a laptop, lives in his wife's posh apartment and has time to spend on his own interests despite being a total scumbag.

The situation was quite reminiscent of the old, not-so-politically-correct joke about Hungarians:

St. Peter visits hell one day. He is showed around by Lucifer. They stop at a large cauldron. People are cooking in the hot water. Armed guards are beating back the ones who try to escape.
  - *Who are these?*
  - *These are the Russians.*
At next cauldron St. Peter sees a sign: "Climbing out Verboten!"
There are no guards posted.
  - *Who are these ones?*
  - *The Germans.*
They finally arrive to a cauldron but there are no signs or guards.
  - *How come there are no signs or guards?*
  - *Well, these are the Hungarians. If anyone tries to climb out, the others will pull him or her back instantly.*

I completed my study assignment by the end of February, 2003 and Miklós sent a telex to Walter about me and my next step. In two weeks, we got a written reply. The International Justice Chief (the top justice official in the Church) found no grounds to convene a Committee of Evidence, as I had not committed any serious crime. Miklós was ordered to cancel the urgent directive and reinstate me to my former position as Supercargo.

My relationship with Miklós remained strained, though. He still felt that he got into trouble because of me and did not appreciate that the whole matter was ultimately not resolved to his liking. I was resentful towards him for so quickly throwing me under the bus and making no real effort to protect me, despite his assurances to the contrary.

After the success of the Budapest Saint Hill size program and the failure of the org making efforts in Pécs, Miklós felt that we needed a new major expansion target. He knew it had to be an exciting purpose which could be used to enthuse the Scientologists and keep them donating.

At around that time, the international finance office of the Church sent two Hungarian Sea Org veterans (Susan and Csaba Ködmön, a married couple) to take over the supervision of the finances of Budapest Org. Susan became the Flag Banking Officer and Csaba was her deputy, primarily responsible for sales & marketing of the materials (books, e-meters, AV properties etc.) sold by the org. They had been working in the US and Canada previously. They had joined the Sea Org back in the early '90s, when there was no base in Hungary.

Shortly after they arrived, they began a local fundraising project to purchase a new building for the org and organized a few events to get donations flowing for this new purpose. They even had a suitable building targeted, located next to the largest farmers' market in Budapest, on the Váci Street.

When I heard about it, I instantly loved the idea. It sounded like the next logical step forward and the building looked great. I told Miklós that we should join forces with the org and that if we invest sufficient resources, we could take the usual 10% commission for all donations our crew members arranged. The purchase of the building required a few million USD, so 10% of any sizeable donation would be a pretty nice sum and according to policy, it could go straight into the staff pay fund.

The original plan was to get together around 400,000 USD (that was the absolute maximum we realistically calculated to be obtainable from Hungarian Scientologists) and then we would ask for a loan from international Church management to cover the rest of the purchase price. Apparently, there was such an option – it was called a BIC (Building Investment Committee) loan. Susan had already put together the request for the loan and they had collected a few thousand dollars already.

After some negotiations (mainly about how and when the 10% was to be paid to the OTL), we reached an agreement and I became joint project manager with Susan.

Chapter Nine

Fundraising for the Building

THE BOYS OF VÁCI STREET

We had three main goals at the outset. First and foremost, we had to make sure that the owner of the building (one of the largest real estate developers in Hungary) would not sell it to someone else. We also had to pry a favorable reply out of International Management to our submission. Finally, we had to get the 400,000 USD from local contributors.

We were able to keep the owners interested for a few months (ironically, they knew who we were and thought the Scientologists must be full of money), but in September, they realized that something was awry and started to look for other potential buyers. According to our inside source, they found an investment company with ties to Russia that was genuinely interested in the building. We quickly held an emergency meeting and found a Scientologist who knew the majority shareholder of the holding company that owned the building. He was one of the richest men in Hungary, so the President WISE told us to be very careful in our dealings as we would not want an enemy like him. Nevertheless, we arranged a meeting with this wealthy businessmen and Imre was sent to try to buy us some more time or at least stop the sale to the Russians. Imre even had a certificate of acknowledgment made for this person, for his "contributions to the economy of Hungary" and presented it when they met. The meeting was inconclusive, as the gentleman was unwilling to interfere with efforts of his CEO to sell the building.

As expected, the building was sold to the investment company. We did not want to give up on the property, so we met the Russian representative of the new owners and asked them if they were willing to sell. They were surprised but they were open to suggestions – though the asking price was now quite a bit higher.

At the end of December, Tamás Nagy, the Executive Director of Budapest Org, received a telex out of the blue from one of the top financial executives of International Church Management, expressing interest in the building and after a few exchanges we were told that two missionaires would arrive shortly to negotiate the purchase and conditions.

Everyone was over the moon, as it seemed our submission had been accepted. A week later we got a new telex, stating that we would not get a dime for the building and we should get the full sum donated by Hungarian Scientologists, as this was now the new international building acquisition strategy – locally financed in full.

We did not really understand what happened but we had no option but to accept it and move on. Unfortunately, our fundraising efforts were not as successful as we had initially hoped. We managed to collect 250,000 USD, but then the momentum began to die down. It seemed we had no real hope of getting the 2-3 million USD necessary to buy a suitable building. This was also evident to the wealthiest Scientologists, so they were rather reluctant to part with their hard-earned money for such an uncertain project.

The most successful way of fundraising turned out to be events. Susan and her husband wrote a play called "Asterix in Pannonia," which was the adaptation of the rivalry between Asterix and Julius Caesar to the situation of Scientology in Hungary, full of cultural references like a typical Tarantino movie. The actors were recruited among the org staff. Even one of the Sea Org members was cast as "Tom Cruise" (to be fair, when he put on his sunglasses he did look like him). The plot was written in a way that it stopped at certain points and required an amount of pledged donations in order to continue. The idea and its execution were surprisingly successful.

Two glossy magazines were also produced to aid the fundraising efforts and to publicize our grand plan. One was sent to people who did at least one so-called major service[32] (there were around 3000 people on that list) and another to everyone who bought at least a book from the org (around 40,000 people). We added two pay-in slips to the magazine – one was blank and the other was for 10 USD.

Naturally, quite a number of these bookbuyers did not like Scientology at all. For example, we received a donation of 0.01 USD from a small city in Hungary, paid by "L. Ron Hubbard." As the bank charged a fee for processing these slips, his (?) donation ended up costing us money, which was probably the intention.

The magazine did not bring in as much money as expected, but nevertheless we reached the 350,000 USD mark by the end of March and we had around 550,000 USD more pledged (though around 50% of that amount was rather dubious). But the momentum was fading. The targeted building was sold and we had not found another suitable one. Also, we basically ran out of ideas on how to make more money and as we had spoken to every wealthy Scientologist already, it seemed that we would not be able to make much more

---

[32] a Scientology course or auditing action which was listed in the main central area of The Bridge to Total Freedom

than 600,000 USD, considerably less than what was required to buy anything decent.

Based on this, the project was increasingly viewed as a failure by European management. Miklós was ordered (again) to get me "handled" and I had to undergo a new round of confessionals. All my "crimes" that I had ever committed in the Sea Org and any and all so-called "irregularities" I had been involved in were taken up. Again. The end result was a new study program, which I completed. My auditor was Charlie Miklán, the husband of Judith Miklán, who was apparently still my worst enemy in the Sea Org. I found out that they were still convinced that I was a Suppressive Person, and tried to get Miklós to initiate harsh internal justice actions against me. In his summary report of my confessional auditing, Charlie distorted a lot of the things I said in the sessions to make me look bad and blew a whole host of small things out of proportion. He also sent a copy of his extremely lengthy report, containing a lot of intimate details about my personal life, to all senior members of European and International Church Management.

The Mikláns had their way after that. Miklós apparently felt that he must do something to protect himself, so he cancelled the fundraising project. He learned his lesson from the previous similar incident, so he did not demote me this time. I had to resume my duties as Supercargo. Our relationship was rather sour at this point. When the Mikláns were not there, we could work together and have civil conversations about the day-to-day matters of the OTL. When they were around, Miklós turned into a different person and yelled at me for even the slightest mistakes.

Nevertheless, I continued to soldier along. I had to become accustomed once again to long hours and extended periods of sleep deprivation. Apparently, there was a new plan to accelerate planetary clearing and it involved the translation of the congresses L. Ron Hubbard held for Scientologists in the '50s and '60s. Of course, once again this required an extreme amount of effort on our part. I still had to deal with the usual financial problems as well, and I was also back to hunting down the freeloaders and getting them to pay their arbitrary debts.

However, I was not as driven as I used to be. I had just about had enough of the fact that whatever I did, it was never good enough. A few people in European management still seemed to hate me for some reason, and now there were people in the OTL who actively tried to have me removed from any position of power. Lajos was still mad at me and suspected me of being a spy. And the Mikláns could not forget my interference with the replacement of Charlie in the West US management organization and still wanted their revenge.

I was not feeling well spiritually. I had dedicated my whole life to Scientology and put everything in that basket. I was increasingly concerned about the speed of planetary clearing, as it seemed that the planet would not become Clear anytime soon. Sometimes, when I was taking the 15-minute walk from the OTL to the org, I took an honest look around and thought about the real situation of Scientology in Hungary. Apparently, the "wog world" could not care less about our efforts to create a new civilization on Earth. The majority of Hungarians had no idea that we even existed; and those who did know something about us, had mostly only heard negative things. At that time, I had been in Scientology for nine years, working day and night to achieve the most holy of purposes. We didn't make much progress as an organization, but we did not move an inch closer to accomplishing our actual end goal during that entire time.

So, after nine years, I still had some doubts about Scientology, which was not a comforting thought (they were not a major concern at that time, but the fact remains that I had them). I wanted some sort of reassurance or confirmation that we were indeed making progress and I wanted to see a workable plan for planetary clearing.

THE BUFFALO PROJECT

In July 2004, Miscavige found the underlying Why for all of our problems. It was now the second time he has done that – the first was the "Golden Age of Tech" in 1996, which according to the promises at the time should have solved the majority of our problems by then. European management sent two people, who showed us a video of a three-hour briefing that Miscavige had given aboard the *Freewinds* to OT VIIIs gathered from around the world.

We also received the transcription of the briefing for translation. Accidentally, Golden Era Productions sent the unedited version of the speech at first, which they hastily corrected by sending an "approved" transcript. My curiosity got the better of me, so I secretly copied both files and compared the two versions in my office. I found out that he had his speech censored. Two sentences were cut from the final version.

The first was a complaint about an org building where "pimps and prostitutes" were around and "people were fornicating" in its vicinity. The second was about Buffalo Org, and he made a remark that "he was sick of only hearing bad news from there." It was not hard to guess why these were removed. His use of the word "pimp" was probably an image-related problem, and he did not want to confirm to staff members that there were indeed certain orgs in

178

the world which were not doing well. I also suspected that the first version we received had already been edited once.

The briefing itself was centered on two new major international campaigns. The first was the "ideal org" campaign. Every org in the world (there were still around 150) was supposed to purchase a large (at least 3000 square meters in size) building in a good location. The money was to be collected from local Scientologists by fundraising. He mentioned that a few locations of strategic importance (Washington D.C., London, Berlin etc.) would be financed centrally, but every other org had to solve this problem on its own. Budapest was not considered important, so we had to gather the full sum locally.

His explanation was simple. First, he told us what we already knew deep down – though Scientology did go through a great deal of expansion since L. Ron Hubbard had founded it, in terms of planetary Clearing, "we barely scratched the surface." His "Ideal Org Program" was created to resolve this – he wanted huge org buildings in each major city in the world, and their effect on society would kickstart the creation of a new civilization and ultimately, a Cleared planet.

The second big announcement was the impending re-release of the fully "on-Source"[33] versions of all the 18 Hubbard books on Dianetics and Scientology (called "Basics" in Scientologese), and the Congresses Hubbard had conducted for Scientologists (which we were already translating). Miscavige wanted all these materials released in one month. (*Note:* the Congresses were published in October, and the Basics were released two years later.)

We were required to watch the briefing three times, so we would not miss anything. A day or two later, the implementation order from Walter arrived – we had to restart fundraising for the building with a bang, and we had to find a building, get the money together and purchase it this year, and it had to be fully renovated and opened by 13th March, 2005. Additionally, we had to get as many dignitaries and celebrities to the grand opening as possible, and we were to convince the Mayor of Budapest to be one of the speakers and say a few good words about Scientology.

We also got instructions on how to proceed with fundraising. The write-up was primarily based on the experiences of a successfully completed building acquisition project in Buffalo. The key point was the recruitment of a head for the project. According to the write-up, it had to be one of the wealthiest local Scientologists (the richest one if possible). We were to convince the targeted person by telling him that taking responsibility for this project was totally in

---

[33] in full adherence with the writings of L. Ron Hubbard (the self-appointed "Source" of Scientology) or written or authorized exclusively by him

his best interests, as this way he could make sure that he would not be the only one making big donations. Also, the more he collected from others, the less he would have to donate himself. There was also an ulterior motive – this prospective fundraising in-charge would have do a lot of convincing about the importance of donating for the purchase of the building, so he would also inadvertently convince himself to give much more than he originally planned.

Somewhat surprisingly, the Church turned to an external source for the "technology" of fundraising. As part of our crash training to be fundraisers, we had to read a book called *"Asking: A 59-Minute Guide to Everything Board Members, Volunteers, and Staff Must Know to Secure the Gift"* by a top American fundraiser named Jerold Panas. According to the write-up, the most important rule in that book was the following: 90% of the donations come from 10% of the donors. So, the idea that we would need a large base of donors for a big project was false – which essentially meant that we were trying to do it the wrong way. Ganging up on the whales was preferred to getting everyone involved and contributing.

These short instructions were accompanied by an order – we were to fire a mission which would collect the money needed (around 2.5 million USD), find a suitable building and purchase it for the Church.

It was not hard to guess who would get the job. I was not too happy about it, though. I knew the financial situation of most of the Hungarian Scientologists pretty well. It was not impossible to collect that much money, but a select few would have to make extraordinary sacrifices in order to make it happen. Additionally, these people were already contacted and "regged" numerous times for the building and had already given a lot of money.

There was one solution, though – mercilessly invading the privacy of the wealthiest people and ruthless and consistent use of high pressure tactics and manipulation techniques. I simply did not feel that I could do this for a prolonged time. There was always a line in fundraising I never had the inner strength to cross – when I felt that pressuring the subject further would cause too much distress or hardship for that individual. I think despite the conditioning I got in Scientology and its utilitarian ethics, I was still too empathetic to completely ignore other's feelings. I knew this "blind spot" would be my downfall, but as a good Sea Org member I had no choice but to accept the mission. I felt it was my duty, and I had to put my personal feelings aside.

As a part of the briefing and preparation process, I have finished reading the book by Jerold Panas. In the previous eight years 100% of the materials I studied for training purposes was either written by Hubbard or directly recommended by him, so it was a strange feeling to read a book from a "wog" author. Hubbard dedicated a separate policy letter to "false data" and the dangers associated with it. He even devised a procedure called "false data stripping" to nullify the effect so-called "false data" (i.e. anything that was not in alignment with Hubbard's writings). So, as a good Scientologist, I tried to steer clear of "wog" textbooks to avoid any contact with all that dangerous false data floating around in society.

The *Asking* book was really good though. Unlike the writings of Hubbard, it was easy to understand, was not full of supposedly funny anecdotes which had nothing to do with the subject matter and it contained rather useful information. As I already had some experience with fundraising, I could relate it to the contents of the book. I was in a bit better mood after reading it, but the goal still looked very distant and very hard to attain. I secretly hoped that Miscavige would present this plan to the general Scientology public in one of the upcoming events and sell them the idea so they would really fork over all their money.

Before the mission officially began I was required to do two smaller tasks. I had to get 15,000 USD raised for the International Association of Scientologists before the upcoming anniversary event (all Sea Org members were assigned to fundraising for a few days and I had to coordinate the whole effort), and I had to take part in the direct sales of a Hubbard sci-fi novel called *"To the Stars"* which had been released in Hungarian for the first time (we had to sell a couple hundred copies to Scientologists). After these were accomplished, I was officially the Budapest Buffalo Project In-Charge.

I followed the instructions and started to interview and push the richest Scientologists to recruit a suitable leader for the project. Our sustained efforts were successful – eventually the three key people in the Scientology field (the CEO of the largest WISE management consulting company and the two wealthiest Scientologists) agreed to form a committee to raise the money.

Cooperation was not always smooth in the beginning, as the enormity of the sum we needed made most of the members a bit tense. For example, one of the big supporters came to visit the org on a Wednesday afternoon (needless to say, this project was also subject to the "Thursday 14:00" rule) and brought 13,000 USD in cash with him. As "no one asked him to donate," he went back to his hometown without giving the money, so I had to drive to his house Thursday morning to pick it up. As Scientologists were afraid to lose the "only path to spiritual freedom," they rarely dared to do anything more drastic; that was about the most extreme level of passive resistance they put up.

Despite these sorts of small hitches, the fundraising machine started to gain momentum. It did not make me much happier though, I was still overstressed due to the enormous target. And to put it mildly, Miklós was not satisfied with the progress and he became increasingly impatient. Our relationship was sour enough to begin with and the lack of the expected huge donations just made it worse. Miscavige had a favorite LRH quote and this was used by Miklós to gauge my effectiveness: *"The consideration that it takes a long time to build something is not true. That itself is an aberration, an effort to discourage destruction by pretending creation takes a long time. It took only a few weeks to build the old Saint Hill org."* – L. Ron Hubbard, Executive Directive #339R-1 dated 10 October 1982. So the expectation was (and what my attitude should have been) that EVERYTHING had to be put there RIGHT NOW so "time" would not infest it, as it was the "primary source of untruth." Therefore, it was a "false datum" that we were supposed to build the org gradually.

Compared to this sort of standard, the project was indeed a colossal failure. Building donations averaged 4,000-5,000 USD a week, which was nowhere near the order of magnitude required to complete the target quickly. I started to slowly collapse spiritually, as a) I was under constant pressure to get in more, more and even more money, b) Miklós was hounding me constantly, uninterested in reality and demanding a solution, c) the targeted amount was unrealistically high to me and d) I felt really bad for letting down the Sea Org and LRH by not being good enough to successfully complete this project. For the first time in my Sea Org career, I just could not take it anymore and started to run away from the problem; e.g. sometimes I took an unauthorized break by announcing that I had an "interview with a prospect" and then took off for a 30-minute aimless walk in the city. It was a sort of a spiritual self-defense; I felt that if I didn't take a break I would lose my mind.

As a kind of escape from the grim situation I started to play video games again. I finally found a good way to spend all those fundraising commissions and I bought a few games for my laptop. My personal favorites at that time were parts 1 and 2 of *Baldur's Gate*, a high fantasy role-playing game. The story revolved around a basic question about human nature – does one overcome his destructive impulses and become a force of good or succumb to them and try to rely on their dark power.

The various "ethics handlings" and "justice cycles" I was subjected to were also focused around this very subject. According to LRH, every human being had hidden evil purposes (varying from person to person) that influenced the way one acted. In his various policy letters about executive qualifications, he made it mandatory for executives to get special auditing to address these hidden evil purposes called "False Purpose Rundown" or "FPRD." I did not really understand the purpose of the occasional snide remark I got from Ethics Officers etc. that I should get these false purposes handled. It was not beneficial to my general mental health to wonder about these malicious intents deeply buried in my mind.

By September, I was in trouble again. Miklós summoned me to his office and told me that he wanted to clear up my status once and for all and somehow make sure that my past history with OSA and my "disaffection with management" would never come back to haunt me again. To accomplish that, he had convened a Committee of Evidence to go through my Sea Org ethics record, review every disciplinary action I had been subjected to and ascertain all the facts regarding me and my behavior. He assured me that it was not meant as punishment – it was a fact-finding action intended to give me a fresh start. There was a catch, though. He asked me to resign from my position (I was officially still the Supercargo of OTL Hungary). I believed him and did as he asked.

Needless to say, I still had to work full time on fundraising until that got sorted out. We also got a new order to translate the inspirational essay *A Message to Garcia* by Elbert Hubbard (note: our Hubbard read the whole thing aloud in one of his lectures, that's why it was considered acceptable). We were then to distribute it to the members of the fundraising committee and everyone else who was working on any project related to the creation of the Ideal Org. The hypocrisy of the Church concerning the use of copyrighted intellectual property was also evident – we did not pay a single cent to the actual holder of the copyright, but in a few months the in-house publishing company of the Church, New Era Publications filed a claim with Budapest Org for the royalties (citing that it was also included in a lecture published by the Church). The booklets were printed and distributed, as ordered.

An unexpected thing happened about a month later, at the end of October, 2004. As a part of the annual anniversary gala of the International Association of Scientology, Tom Cruise received the most prestigious award in Scientology for his dissemination efforts, presented in person by Miscavige. It was specifically created for him and called the "Freedom Medal of Valor."

In his speech, Miscavige even called him "the most dedicated Scientologist he knows." And as if that was not enough, two Sea Org members arrived the next day from the European IAS office to collect money using the Tom Cruise interview that was shown in the event. They were almost drooling over how great Tom was.

Even as a dedicated Sea Org member, I felt his whole story was a gigantic insult to all hard-working Sea Org members. I had been working day and night for the Church for the last seven years, enduring all the extreme production demands, yelling, humiliation in the name of greater good etc. and then Tom Fucking Cruise gets a medal, despite the fact that he was only disseminating over the previous 1 or 2 years. By the way, I never really liked Tom Cruise – he was a kind of a symbol of what was wrong with mainstream US culture. He was not even a Sea Org member, just a public Scientologist, whom we considered loser dilettantes for not taking real responsibility for clearing the planet.

After these series of events related to Tom Cruise and in the name of "thinking big" (to be honest, we simply ran out of ideas to get all that money so we began to try all kinds of far-fetched approaches to solve the problem), we also tried to reactive the recruitment of celebrities and engaged in political lobbying activities. For example, out of desperation, I sought an appointment with the Minister of Youth Affairs and Sports, Ferenc Gyurcsány, who was tipped to be the next Prime Minister. All I managed was to meet his secretary. We also tried to get one of the Scientologist hunting mates of the president of the largest bank in Hungary to arrange a favorable bank loan for purchasing the building, but he successfully evaded all our attempts to get him involved. We also tried to locate a Hungarian celebrity who could play the same role as Tom Cruise played for the Church in the US, but no Scientologist in Hungary was nearly famous enough for that task.

I also had a cheeky idea (and I also felt a bit vengeful for that medal) – why not ask Tom Cruise and John Travolta for donations? I got their addresses and wrote letters to both of them. A few weeks later I received a letter from Celebrity Center International (it turned out that Travolta simply forwarded my letter to CC Int), stating that I should never, ever try to solicit donations from them directly, and I would face serious justice actions if I did such a thing again.

We also received instructions from the European base that as part of the overarching Ideal Org strategy, we were to push Scientologists to get into important positions in society. There was a policy letter, dated 10 June 1960 called *"What We Expect of a Scientologist"* and this order was to be implemented:

"The factories, the marts of trade, the homes, the neighbourhoods, these are the places we want trained Scientologists. In that way alone, we're on the busy, still healthy communication lines of the world.

...

"We are not doctors. We are the world's trouble shooters. When we make a company win, the whole world wins, when we make a neighborhood win, we all win.

"A full time Scientologist makes life better wherever he is. And that is enough pro activity for anyone.

"What do we expect of you? To become the best Scientologist that can be and to get on the comm lines of the world and bring a big win where it counts. We don't expect you to hang up a shingle as a doctor and have a private practice. We'll respect you if you do. But we'll respect you just as much and even more if you get trained as a pro and go out and up in the world of action and of life.

"Hit for the key spots by whatever means, the head of the women's club, the per-sonnel director of a company, the leader of a good orchestra, the president's secretary, the advisor of the trade union – any key spot. Make a good sound living at it, drive a good car, but get your job done, handle and better the people you meet and bring about a better earth." – L. Ron Hubbard.

In October, I also got a new assistant – a newly recruited Sea Org member named Krisztián Harmath was added to the project. His recruitment was considered to be a sort of a coup, as he was a young, successful and relatively wealthy entrepreneur and even brought his own BMW with him. This setup was short-lived though, as Miklós unexpectedly changed our roles, promoting Krisztián to be the head of the project, and I was demoted to his assistant. Miklós also became actively and personally involved in regging building do-nations.

He explained this move by stating that the expected numbers were simply not met and Krisztián had proven in the wog world that he was able to "at-tract" money.

THE PUSKIN STREET BUILDING

We found a new prospective building for the future ideal org. It was a his-toric property that served as the headquarters of several trade unions. As the project assistant I had to compile the submission to get the building approved for purchase. Theoretically, it was a very thorough process to make sure there was nothing wrong with the building. As a part of it, an expert opinion was needed from a licensed architect. As usual, there was zero funding for such an unimportant "organizational" cycle, so I had to ask a Scientologist architect to do it for free. All the paperwork was completed in a week and sent to Los Angeles for approval.

Meanwhile, Krisztián and Miklós were working on the whales. They ad-opted a new approach. They organized mini events, held lengthy briefings and visited every wealthy Scientologist. They were not much more effective than I was, but they were definitely better at getting people involved and enthusiastic.

My next assignment was to work out the legal details of the purchase, and I was supposed to work together with OSA. Fortunately, Lajos did not really want to get involved and delegated the matter to his legal director, so I did not have to put up with his mood swings.

The most important factor was to protect the building from the "suppres-sive" government, so no matter what happened, the Church would not lose the Ideal Org. There were several options, but the safest way seemed to be to have the building purchased by an offshore non-profit corporation controlled by the Church. I had to do full research on this as well as look into alternative solutions (if any).

An external tax expert was also hired by OSA to assist in this matter – and for some unknown reason, they chose the former head of the criminal investigations division of the Hungarian Tax Authority. I paid several visits to him, with the OSA legal director and we talked over every aspect of the transaction. It was evident from his facial expression that he considered us white-collar criminals, and he talked to us like a sleazy lawyer would speak to his mobster client. At that time, I considered the Church to be a very ethical organization, so I was considerably irritated by the choice OSA made in this matter.

A small reorganization followed and I was assigned one more task – to collect the pledged donations that had not paid on time. I did well, collecting around 120,000 USD between Oct 2004 and April 2005.

Meanwhile Miscavige launched his promised re-release of Scientology materials. He was the undisputed expert at selling almost any idea to Scientologists, no matter how ludicrous. And he did not disappoint with his latest campaign. In one of the Autumn events, he pulled a new rabbit out of his hat, dubbing this re-release of materials as the "Golden Age of Knowledge." As the first step of what he promised would be many to come, he published all the so-called "Congresses" on compact disks, complete with transcripts and glossaries. These series of lectures had been delivered by Hubbard in the first two decades of Scientology, when he summoned Scientologists to announce his latest breakthroughs in his so-called research.

According to Miscavige's sales pitch, the lecture series were priced very reasonably. Each Congress was contained in a plastic holder and each lecture was recorded on an individual CD. The complete package of 18 Congresses (6-12 lectures per congress) was sold for 3,000 USD. As a comparison, the average monthly wage in Hungary at that time was 500 USD. All the lectures could have been put on a single mp3 player – but obviously, much more money could be made by publishing them in fancy plastic boxes and putting each lecture on a separate CD.

Miscavige also told to the audience that new state-of-the-art audiovisual manufacturing equipment had been installed at the international headquarters of Scientology in Hemet, California. So, these were produced by Sea Org members. The actual manufacturing costs must have been a fraction of the asking price.

Our part in the grand plan of Miscavige was simple enough – we had to sell the materials in huge quantity. We thought that we knew what kind of pressure to expect to meet the quota and we prepared mentally for some incessant badgering for a few days. We were wrong. Very wrong. The pressure to meet the quota was elevated to a completely new level.

Acting on Walter's orders, Miklós assigned almost every Sea Org member to fulltime sales duty. A huge board was installed in the main corridor, where the names were listed of all public Scientologists who were thought to be able to afford the full package. Various signs were used to mark whether the targeted persons bought the full package, a part of it or bought more than one package. Teams of two were formed and the qualified (internal word for those who could potentially afford the new release) Scientologists were assigned to these teams. I got a remote city in Hungary and a few Scientologists from Budapest. I sold 7 packages with my salesmate. We did this without respite for three weeks and virtually every wealthy Scientologist was contacted, most of them repeatedly. After this was over, I returned to regging donations for the building.

However, I could not really resume my duties on the building project, as Miklós continued to pass me the financial problems he did not want to deal with. This included fundraising for the IAS. At the end of November, Mr. Achim Bendig, the head of the European IAS office (euphemistically called Membership Office) arrived in Hungary. He told Miklós that Hungary had a quota of 100,000 USD, which had to be met by 31 December, as International Management needed more money for "planetary dissemination campaigns." Nobody wanted this as we were targeting the same prospects for building donations and were still a long way away from meeting our target. But we had no choice, as the IAS was considered an International Management level organization and we had to obey.

Miklós delegated this problem to me and appointed me as the assistant to Mr. Bendig as a living, tangible contribution of the OTL to the international goal. I experienced firsthand how much pressure Achim was under – he was called four-five times a day from the central IAS offices on the *Freewinds* by screaming maniacs, demanding huge sums to be collected NOW. I was mainly trying to get lifetime memberships (which was 3,000 USD back then), while Achim was going after the whales.

His favorite way of making money was to hold a "special briefing" for a select few. We invited 5-10 "extraordinarily qualified" Scientologists to these briefings where Achim dished out heavy doses of Scientology conspiracy theories (the planet was controlled by 12 Suppressive Persons; there was a secret plan, hatched by pharmaceutical companies and their lapdogs, the psychiatrists, to drug the whole society and take over the planet; psychiatrists were responsible for the Holocaust, the 9/11 bombings etc.). When his audience was shocked enough by the bleakness of the situation and the dark future

Achim painted, he then explained that there was a solution to make it all go away. Unsurprisingly, this was the donation of huge sums to the IAS for the international campaigns of Scientology which were supposedly eliminating this suppression. The most important was the anti-psychiatry one, renamed each year for sales & marketing purposes using the synonyms for destruction – one year, it was "Psychiatry – Global Eradication" and then next year it was "Global Disintegration" and so on.

At the beginning of January 2005, Miklós got an order to report to Copenhagen at once. He did not tell anyone why he had to go, but rumors floated around. It was no secret that Walter was not happy with the rate of progress on the building. To be more exact, he was really unhappy about the lack of progress. The all-important ideal org project was going nowhere and Budapest Org was also in decline. After a few weeks, Miklós called me from Copenhagen. He told me that the Committee of Evidence for clearing up my ethics history was finally convened and I should travel to Copenhagen for the scheduled hearings. The Deputy Commanding Officer, who was the temporary CO in the absence of Miklós, told me that I was considered to be a downstat ethics particle and OTL would not support down statistics, so I had to pay my travel expenses out of my own pocket. (Unfortunately, he knew I had recently inherited a modest sum.) I could not help but think that he and Miklós were both desperately poor and were annoyed to see me doing well financially, and that might have been a factor in the decision.

The fact-finding Committee of Evidence was not about any evidence and did not bother to establish the facts, but I was used to that. Basically, they collected all reports ever written about me and I then had to explain myself. It was a rather impossible situation, as they reprimanded me any time I tried to shift blame, criticize others or question the integrity of the author of the reports. There were three hearings, each lasted somewhere between half an hour and an hour, and then I was sent back to the OTL.

I was still a dedicated Sea Org member, but I grew a bit cynical about these internal "justice" procedures. I thought this would be delayed somewhere along the line, and then someone on the approval chain would reject it (probably for some administrative omission) and the whole thing would be cancelled and my status would remain uncertain. It had happened that way so many times in the past.

CHAPTER TEN

The End

WELCOME TO THE REVISION TEAM

In March, one of the European base executives arrived to speed up the fundraising efforts. Her name was Monica Aslanis, and her official post title was EU Landlord. Theoretically, she was responsible for acquiring and managing all Church-owned properties. My role in the project was even more restricted, as she mainly worked with Krisztián and Miklós. My career as a so-called New Civilization Builder was soon over, as in April she announced to me that I had been officially removed from the project due to the ongoing Committee of Evidence.

One day Miklós got fed up with slow progress and decided to adopt a very aggressive approach, justified as "eliminating the time factor from the pledged donations." In practice it meant they got into Krisztián's BMW and paid a visit to the richest Scientologist one by one during the evening and night. The message was clear: the money was to be put together NOW and every rich Scientologist must donate the maximum amount he or she could possibly spare. Though the raids were not as successful as they initially hoped, the fundraising gained new momentum. When they finished talking with someone, they brought them along to help convince the next target, with the idea of uniting the rich Scientologist camp. One guy did not respond to the doorbell though. Miklós was his usual confident and commanding self, so he started to bang on the door in the middle of the night and calling on the phone repeatedly. Eventually, they gave up and left, but the next day he paid a visit to the guy at his company and in no uncertain terms told him what he thought about his refusal to respond the previous night.

At that point, I realized that this was the kind of approach that would be required to complete this project in the foreseeable future. The *Asking* book and training materials sent by International Management were based on the situation and the culture of donations in the US. I did some online research on fundraising in America, and it was shocking to see how financing non-profit institutions was a normal part of life. In Hungary, it was not part of the general social culture at all and was rarely done, as most non-profit organizations were subsidized by the government. Undoubtedly this approach, which appealed to the Hungarian bravado, met with greater acceptance among the rich entrepreneurs who literally considered themselves the aristocracy of Scientology.

As a temporary measure, I was transferred back to the translation unit. Hubbard's books on Scientology (the so-called Basics) and the Congresses were being translated and the situation could be summed up in two words: total chaos. The primary problem was the unfinished nature of the English originals. The books were still in the process of being recompiled, reedited and finalized by Miscavige. For example, after receiving a "final version" of one of the books, "definitely the final one" arrived a day later. The translations had to be matched each time to the ever-changing English originals, while keeping up the work on the untranslated parts. Actually, these books had been translated a few years earlier, but new translation methods and policies were implemented and we had to translate every book from scratch again. The initial translations were very close translations of the original versions, even if the sentences sounded foreign to the Hungarian ear. Now we had to make sure that the wording sounded natural in Hungarian while remaining faithful to the concept conveyed by the English original.

The changes were tracked in the documents so I had the opportunity to see for myself what Miscavige changed in the books. In the first briefing about the subject (in August the previous year), he stated that the books would completely match the original Hubbard manuscripts and recordings; additionally, all typographical and grammatical errors and any and all discrepancies would be corrected (according to him, mostly committed by the original typesetters and transcriptionists). Basically, they would become 100% "on-Source" materials.

The most likely reason was completely different though. I learned years later that the books had to be republished as the copyrights of the original works were soon to expire and the materials would have gone into the public domain. As I was working on Book One (a codename for *Dianetics: The Modern Science of Mental Health*, the first book Hubbard published in 1950 on the subject), I could only see the changes made to that book. Two paragraphs were cut (in the first, Hubbard was condemning medical doctors in general and in the second, he was complimenting a psychiatrist) and certain grammatical errors were fixed, mostly by adding a lot of semicolons. So, probably "grammar Nazi edition" or "attorney approved edition" would have been better phrases to describe these books. The Basics were now all hardbound (probably to justify the hefty price tags) and contained full glossaries (which was a welcome addition).

The circumstances were the usual "evolution schedule," working till 2-3 AM until we were falling asleep in front of our computers. Massive doses of cola and green tea were consumed by the crew in efforts to stay awake. In addition to the books themselves, we were also sent a large volume of related marketing materials to translate. A lot of promotional videos were also made and we had to create Hungarian subtitles for them. The wording of these commercials was so ridiculously over the top (reminiscent of the worst infomercials of the '80s and '90s), that I and a few fellow translators laughed out loud when reading the convoluted and overly dramatic wording.

Save for the amusement factor of the copy, I was in a very bad mood. I felt that I was the main reason for the failure of the building project, and my guilt was compounded by my conviction that I had betrayed the entire human race by failing this all-important task. My future appeared murky, uncertain and rather dark. It seemed that I would either spend a few years in a low position (as a translator) or if things turned worse, I would be assigned to the "Rehabilitation Project Force" to battle the evil inside me.

Miklós and Monica tried to convince me that the latter option would be my way out of being constantly in the crosshairs. Miklós even suggested that I should request an assignment to the RPF as European Management would see this in a positive light and it would send the right kind of message about my willingness to "handle myself." After completing the RPF I would have a clean slate and be in the perfect position to have a magnificent career in the Sea Org and play an important role in the expansion of Scientology. I gave it some thought and decided to make the ultimate sacrifice by accepting the harsh conditions of the RPF and forfeiting all material pursuits for the sake of the greater purpose and ultimate victory of Scientology.

I really wanted to believe that the new civilization envisioned by Hubbard was attainable. I did not want to desert my hard-working comrades and I did not want to be singled out as someone who had not helped if Scientology indeed succeeded in clearing the planet. I did not want to lose my wife either (I thought that she would leave me if I left the Sea Org for any reason), and finally, I was so deeply involved with the movement that I could not even imagine any realistic alternative to that life.

I really believed at that time what the Church said about the outside world – the "wog" world was considered to be an insane asylum full of aberrated persons, with the psychiatrists in charge. And they were working hard to make it even worse. I had no wealth, no reserves, no degree, no meaningful education and almost no relationships with anyone outside the Church. I was not on the best terms with my family either, so I felt I didn't have any other viable options.

After I submitted my application to be transferred to the RPF, I had to travel to Copenhagen. Once again I had to pay for that privilege out of my own pocket.

DISCARDED

Upon arriving in Copenhagen, I was told that I was to do menial work, mostly helping in the kitchen, until my request to be sent to the RPF had been reviewed. I was preparing myself mentally for the RPF, so I accepted this. RPF members sometimes worked with my ilk, the fallen Sea Org members. I watched them from the corner of my eye. Their state of mind and general behavior was not a good advertisement for the program. They looked like broken and humiliated members of a POW camp.

I had to keep in touch with the Continental Justice Chief about my next step. He told me that they considered it a good sign that I volunteered for the RPF and he therefore put the Committee of Evidence process on hold and said he would issue the directive regarding my RPF assignment. He told me that it could take a few days until all the paperwork is handled, so I should wait patiently and continue to work in the kitchen. Then he contacted me the next day and told me that he had been instructed to send all my folders to Los Angeles for review, so I would have to wait a bit longer. I resigned myself to my fate and resumed dishwashing, but a few hours later a security guard showed up and escorted me to the security office. A young and somewhat arrogant German guy greeted me and introduced himself as Adrian Bethke, Security Investigations In-Charge. He told me that I had to appear before a Fitness Board as I was found unqualified for the Sea Org. I lost the plot at that point. I had been working in the Sea Org for the last seven and a half years and was familiar with the vast majority of the personnel policies. I had absolutely no idea how on earth I had suddenly become unqualified.

The "Board" consisted of one person. I told him that I could not understand this surprising development, but I still wanted to rehabilitate myself and do my part in clearing the planet. After the interview was over, I gathered all the courage I had and confronted Adrian about the exact nature of my apparent lack of qualifications. He evaded the question and tried to brush me off, but I refused to leave until he gave me an appropriate answer. He finally gave up and told me reluctantly that I was psychotic and therefore I needed to leave the Sea Org. He added that I demonstrated several characteristic mentioned by LRH when he was describing the behavior of psychotic people, and the people who had previously been handling my ethics and justice matters were simply reasonable[34] and had failed to standardly, consistently and ruthlessly

---

[34] in Scientology, this is considered to be a bad thing. In this instance, he implied that these people failed to admit or recognize that I was that bad and explained away my shortcomings instead of dealing with what I really was.

apply LRH policies. He told me that I should not be concerned as I would be given a return program, and once complete I may be eligible for the Sea Org again. He then patted me on the shoulders condescendingly and told me that I was still young and with all I had learned in the Sea Org I shouldn't have a problem making a lot of money and going up the Bridge. I was then told to leave the base immediately and return to Hungary. It seemed I had no choice, so I reluctantly packed my things and went back to Hungary.

Upon arriving at the OTL, I found myself in the office of Miklós in short order. Miklós was genuinely surprised about this development, and he tried to comfort me. He told me that he did not agree with this and would attempt to find out what this was really all about. He then sent me back to the translations unit and told me to prepare myself mentally for the RPF until this was sorted out. I did what he asked.

Three weeks later, a two-man mission arrived from Copenhagen with one of the top financial executives of New Era Publications in charge. She was tasked with finding any and all unpaid royalties by OTL and Budapest org and getting these paid. Additionally, she had to investigate a potentially serious matter – according to reports, around 5,000 USD supposedly belonging to International Management had mysteriously vanished from one of the bank accounts of OTL Hungary.

Two days later she called me into her temporary interrogation room and told me that she knew that I was supervising finance matters for a long time and the data they initially uncovered suggested that I had embezzled the money. She added that if I wanted to avoid being turned over to the police and possible jail time, then I should come clean and immediately put the money I stole on the table.

I had experienced my fair share of accusations in the Sea Org. I had been called a lot of things. I had been yelled at for all kinds of reasons. But this was a first. I told her that though I had played fast and loose with the rules sometimes, though only for the right reasons, I had never ever stolen money from the Church, not even a cent.

She did not believe me and with the all-familiar trademark Sea Org executive icy stare, she told me that this was not over and I would get an e-metered interrogation to uncover all the crimes I was sitting on. She then changed the subject to the matter of unpaid royalties she apparently uncovered.

She told me about the time we had sold the Organizational Executive Course[35] to certain WISE members and they had been given the course ma-

---

[35] a course teaching the entirety of LRH's admin technology. It consists of the study of the so-called OEC Volumes or Green Volumes. OEC Volume 0 contains all the policies and know-how

terials on CD in Hungarian (the printed volumes had not yet been published in Hungarian). She told me that the only reason these WISE members bought the course was the CD itself, so in actual fact, we sold the CD for 5,000 USD and the course was a gift. According to this reasoning and since the CD contained LRH materials, OTL had to pay royalties for selling the CDs plus pay interest as a fine for not reporting and withholding these payments for years. I strongly disagreed with her logic, but she did not really care.

That evening when I arrived home to our flat, I suddenly remembered that I had earlier made some CDs with translated LRH materials for reference. I did not want to get into more trouble, so I decided to destroy them. I cut up every CD with scissors (as Church security policy dictated) and threw them in the garbage.

The next morning when I showed up for work, two OSA staff members were waiting for me at the entrance. I was placed under 24 hour watch (again) as I was still the major suspect for embezzling Church funds. I was assigned to the kitchen (which was in a separate building). I also had to move out of my own flat and into one of the other Sea Org flats so they could monitor me at night as well.

They then forced my wife to turn over the key to our apartment. OSA staff searched the premises. The public relations officer of OTL (a retired police officer, who worked as a detective for decades) accompanied them. They even searched the garbage bins of the apartment block (which was most probably illegal). They found the destroyed CDs, which caused a huge panic in the OSA office. Lajos was now convinced that I was a secret service agent and I had just destroyed the evidence of that. For security reasons, Lajos then confiscated my laptop, mobile phone and all data storages devices I owned.

To make matters worse, the finance missionaire was still trying to pin the embezzlement on me. She ordered the local OSA office to get the itemized monthly statements for my personal bank account for the last two years. A day later, three OSA staff members escorted me to the nearest branch of my bank. I was told that this was my chance to prove my innocence, and if I refused to comply with this request, I would be declared a suppressive person on the spot, every Scientologist would have to disconnect from me and I would be reported to the police. As I had nothing to hide, I obtained the statements while they waited outside.

---

about being a staff member in general, and each division (from 1 to 7) on the organizing board of Scientology has a volume dedicated to it, containing all LRH writings about the operation, rules and know-how of that division.

Later that day, I was escorted to Lajos' office, where he, Miklós and the finance missionaire were waiting for me, looking very stern and seething with anger. As soon as I sat down, they started yelling at me simultaneously, waving my account statements in may face, calling me a fucking criminal, embezzler and an SP, and they claimed to have found evidence that I had embezzled the missing 5,000 USD.

A year before I had inherited around 12,000 USD. At that time, I converted this into a time deposit, but then withdrew it, donated a total of 4,000 USD to various Church projects and put 8,000 USD into a new time deposit. On the account statements, it looked like 12,000 USD appeared on my account as a result of an internal transaction and a week later 8,000 USD disappeared due to another internal transaction. Unaware of the delicacies of non-LRH wog accounting, they thought they had me.

I tried to remain calm in spite of all the harsh accusations and screaming, and I told them what actually happened. They did not believe me (to be fair, Miklós sort of did, as he knew me well enough to know that I would never resort to stealing money from the Church) and sent me back to the illegally operated kitchen to peel potatoes.

Around 10 PM, I was escorted to the main building again. Miklós and the finance missionaire told me that they calculated the backlog royalties OTL owed to New Era Publications for the Organizational Executive Course CDs and the *Message to Garcia* booklets. Miklós said that I should pay these out of my pocket on behalf of the OTL. They also found one expense in the building project accounting, a purchase of a desktop PC for 600 USD, which I was told I had to pay back (the same accounting contained 300 USD Armani shirts for Miklós so he could look good when regging the whales). The final sum was around 8,000 USD, which not coincidentally matched the balance of my bank account.

Miklós added that by paying this sum, I could avoid being SP declared and might have a chance of being assigned to the RPF. He reminded me that the gates to eternity were shut forever to SPs. I was so overwhelmed at this point by the utter collapse of my life that I started to doubt my own innocence. I waved the white flag and agreed to whatever they wanted. Needless to say, I had to turn over the money right away, so I was escorted to the nearest ATM, withdrew 8,000 USD in cash and gave it to the finance missionaire.

A host of e-metered interrogations followed over the next several days, otherwise I worked in the kitchen as an assistant to the cook. As I was still under watch and OTL had no security personnel, about half the crew was rotated in 4-hour shifts to watch over me. They were mostly sympathetic with my plight, so at least I had good company.

The interrogations ultimately proved to be a complete waste of time. I had run out of things to confess to. However, OSA still considered me a threat and were trying to work out a way to protect the Church from me. One day, three OSA staff members showed up in the kitchen and brought me to the law offices of Schiffer and Partners, who represented the Church at that time. In the presence of two attorneys, Vilmos, the legal director of OSA Hungary, gave me a lengthy declaration to sign. The whole procedure was videotaped by the ex-police officer Zoltán Tumpek, the public relations director of OTL.

The document listed every imaginable improper or even questionable thing I had ever admitted about handling Church finances (naturally, anything that incriminated the Church was carefully left out) I also had to take full responsibility for the copyright violations committed by OTL while excusing everyone else involved. I was required to sign this and it was countersigned by the Church. I was never given a copy. I did one thing however, to avoid any further fleecing. I asked the OSA guy to add a clause to the document that the Church had no further financial demands from me and considered all matters fully settled and handled by my admission and the subsequent payment of 8,000 USD.

I thought it could not get worse at this point. But it did. A few days later an "ethics mission" arrived to the OTL.

THE VERY END

The advertised purpose of the three-man ethics mission was to "clean up the out-ethics OTL" and then get a 10-man translations unit formed on a right-now basis, or "slam dunked" as they put it, to cope with the massive amount of translations David Miscavige wanted done.

According to them, the main ethics problem of OTL was the lack of real expansion and meaningful production. In their words, we were lazy and ineffective and only Miscavige & RTC were really busy and actually working. They chose to interpret LRH policies in a way that attributed the lack of real progress to crimes committed by the staff members responsible for the area.

So, the hunt for hidden crimes began. Everyone who was even remotely considered to be an executive was subjected to lengthy e-metered interrogations, delving deeply into their private lives. They wanted the juicy details and were very interested in any sexual misconduct, infidelity, perversions, homosexual tendencies or acts etc. The interrogated Sea Org members were also told in no uncertain terms that they were required to tell what they knew about others – covering up for someone else meant that you got the same punish-

196

ment as the actual culprit. The dirty laundry they managed to gather was then collated and another round of interrogations was conducted in light of what had now been revealed.

They did not even bother to speak with me as I had already hit rock bottom in their eyes (OSA particle, probable psychotic and embezzler, under 24 hour watch etc) – they simply banned me from the main building. I could only enter the kitchen and the apartment which was the male berthing. I was not allowed to call my parents without a security guard present who had to listen in to the call.

Interestingly, they found the person who actually embezzled the 5,000 USD. But this did not help me much, as the unpaid royalties they attributed to me was reason enough to keep me under surveillance. According to their reasoning I was guilty of stealing Ron's money.

Meanwhile, my wife got into trouble. The missionaires put her under pressure for being the wife of the biggest SP in Hungary. They told her that she must have something to hide, too, as she did not divorce me when she found out that I was such a lowlife scumbag. Theoretically, she had been responsible for recruiting 8 new Scientologists to the Sea Org in two weeks, to be posted in the translations unit. Of course, this was an impossible order and unsurprisingly, she failed, recruiting only 2 people. So she too was also assigned to menial labor. They told her that she would be forced to do something that she considered "too gruesome" (that was the phrase they repeated) so she would "wake the fuck up, stop dramatizing and come into present time and start producing." They required her to clean the toilets in front of everyone as a "too gruesome" assignment. She was also required to admit to the "crimes" she had supposedly committed.

They also tried to "salvage" her. By this they meant they believed she was under my influence, a real badass SP and so she would have to be convinced to dump me. A "Separation Order" was issued – Andrea was ordered in writing not to contact me in any way, shape or form. She was then forced to move out of her own apartment and into female berthing. The missionaires then moved themselves into our apartment.

Andrea's schedule was organized so she had no real chance to see me (she defied them though and met me a few times). She was pressured every day to divorce me as I was a "low toned suppressive person," who was destroying her life. They shared with her everything bad I had ever confessed in every interrogation and auditing session.

I feared the worst. My wife was the last remaining positive element of my screwed up life, and it seemed that I would lose her, too. Despite all I had been through, I still believed in Scientology and decided to leave this matter to the organization too. I spent all the money I had left at that time on Hubbard's lectures on human evaluation and asked one of my watchers to give them to her. I thought that she could decide then where I was situated on the Tone Scale (aka Hubbard Chart of Human Evaluation) and whether I was a suppressive person or not (to be honest, by then I had started to believe that I was indeed a suppressive person).

In an attempt to save his skin, Miklós tried to pin every possible fishy matter on me. I was informed from time to time what new accusations had been leveled against me. I panicked after a few days and thought that if I didn't do something I would soon be kicked out the Sea Org. Desperate, I wrote a petition to the European representative of RTC, requesting an RPF assignment. A few days later I got a phone call from the Senior Investigations & Reports Director Europe. She told me that she was handling the matter and I should contact her and only her if I had something to say. She also informed me that the previous Committee of Evidence had been delayed somewhere along the chain of command, so whatever they had decided was no longer valid. She convened a new one (again!) to resolve the situation and she told me that I would have to travel to Copenhagen (again!) for the hearing.

Nothing much happened until mid-June, when I was told that it was time to go to Copenhagen. I had to borrow money to cover my travel expenses, as I had nothing left and OTL refused to pay (again!). I was banned from entering any Sea Org facility, so I had to rent a hotel room. This Committee of Evidence was even more ridiculous than the previous one. The whole hearing lasted 15 minutes, and for some reason the only matter they examined was the situation of the unpaid royalties for the OEC Course on CD. They asked me whether I wanted to handle it or not. I still wanted to remain a Scientologist, so I said yes. By now it was pretty obvious that I would be kicked out of the Sea Org.

After I arrived home, my suspicion was confirmed. I was told by OSA to move out of the Sea Org berthing, back to my apartment (which had been vacated by the missionaires). They said they would contact me if there was any development but I was not allowed to enter any Scientology organization until my status was clarified. I also had to get a Leaving Staff Security Check, basically another e-metered interrogation. I had to come in for these sessions whenever the auditor had time. The auditing room was set up in one of the Church warehouses so I would not meet any Sea Org member or defile the base with my presence. This lasted until 19 July 2005.

Despite all the bans, verbal threats and ethics orders, my wife and I managed to meet every night in secret. When I had been in Copenhagen, she was assigned to the kitchen. She was only allowed to do menial jobs and a Committee of Evidence was convened to punish her for her "reasonableness" (i.e. not divorcing me). Fortunately, she was not under watch, so she was able to sneak out after 11 PM to a nearby meeting place where she gave me some food for the next day (as I had absolutely no money left). We still loved each other very much. I felt guilty about it, though – I did not want to make my situation worse by trying to convince her to leave the Sea Org for me. According to Scientology's internal code of discipline, this would have been a "high crime." Despite the odds, I still secretly harbored a small hope that some high-level executive would see the matter for what it was and rectify the gross injustice by allowing me to redeem myself.

On 19 July 2005, Lajos called me and told me to come in immediately as the resolution of the Committee of Evidence was approved by the International Justice Chief. He was in a good mood and told me that I was probably the luckiest person on the planet as I somehow managed to avoid being SP declared. He even gave me back my laptop, but kept the hard drive "for security reasons." He then gave me the directive to read (I was not allowed to keep it though).

It contained the following:

1. Immediate dismissal from the Sea Org as I was found to be unqualified;
2. I was declared to be a common criminal for copyright violations, or "PTS Type B" in Scientology – until this label was lifted, I was not allowed to do any course or receive auditing;
3. I had to do 1500 hours of amends for the benefit of the Church of Scientology;
4. I had to receive a "False Purpose Rundown" (an auditing action for handling evil purposes) for the area of finances and copyrights;
5. my Sea Org Ethics Specialist certificate was revoked, as well as all advanced administrative training certificates I had received;
6. and I had to pay for all the courses I received as a Sea Org member – the total bill was around 9,000 USD.

The fate of my wife was still not sorted and I was still not allowed to speak to her. The ethics officer of OTL wanted to throw me out of my apartment (as it was owned by Andrea), stating that my wife would stay and divorce me anyway. I had nothing to lose at that point, so I point-blank refused to move.

The worst month of my life ensued. I felt utterly destroyed. My big dream of spearheading the creation of a new civilization was crushed. I spent 10 years working for the Church, giving up on all my ambitions and career options. I spent all the money I ever had on Scientology. And the end result was practically nothing. It looked impossible to continue on the Bridge to Total Freedom, and I even had to fight and work for the right to achieve the level of a wog person who never even heard of Scientology. They needed 1,500 more hours of work and 9,000 USD just to be even, and my wife and the apartment was probably gone, too. All I could show in the real world was a high school education, a good command of the English language and a mysterious 10-year gap in my life where I was apparently off to save the world. I knew almost nobody who was not a Scientologist. I had been virtually living in a bubble and knew little about the so-called wog world.

I was in total apathy. For a few days I did nothing. I slept at night and walked around aimlessly during the day. In a spiritual sense, I felt that I was dead. I failed to achieve the purpose of my life, so there seemed to be no sense in continuing to live. I even contemplated suicide at that time, but I did not want to make the life of my relatives even worse. I had a lot of time to think though. I started to think about the concept of a "cleared planet" and what it actually meant. Finally, I came to the conclusion that I did not want to live in a world that was controlled by the Sea Org and the Church. For all intents and purposes, it would have been an Orwellian nightmare. I stopped thinking further at this point, but the doubts I always had became even more pronounced.

I felt that the whole procedure was unjust. I gave it one more chance – I asked European Church management to review the whole matter. I received an answer a month later. It basically said that I should be glad that I got off the hook so easily, and if a review was done, a much more severe punishment would probably be leveled. I got the point and accepted the fact that I was probably a despicable person who still had to work for the right to advance spiritually.

Meanwhile, my wife decided to stay with me and leave the Sea Org. She was not allowed to talk to me during her fight to be allowed to leave, so one day she just appeared on the doorstep. She told me that she had been pressured constantly for the last two months to divorce me and remain in the Sea Org. She was adamant that she wanted to leave, so the standard leaving procedure was started. She had to get a Security Check, but she had a "special case problem," which meant that she was to wait for a few months until an auditor became available to deliver the action required to resolve that problem.

She then wrote a request to Miklós, asking him for permission to leave without receiving that auditing action. Miklós simply ignored the request, so he would not be responsible for the potential problem either option could have generated. So Andrea decided to escape – she waited in the morning until everyone left for the main building, packed her things and ran.

I was overjoyed, as her decision restored meaning to my life. Despite all we had been through, we still wanted to continue in Scientology as "public" – our purpose still was the achievement of total spiritual freedom.

AFTERMATH

After spending the summer recuperating and slowly regaining the will to do something constructive with my life, I started to re-establish myself in the world. Ignoring or circumventing the request of the Church to avoid Scientologists altogether, I started to talk to some of the people I met through Scientology and managed to get some paying jobs. The small enterprise I founded was also involved in online trading, which I had always wanted to do. OTL did not forget me, or at least its Treasury Division did not – they wanted the 9,000 USD freeloader bill paid. I borrowed that money from a Scientologist acquaintance and paid the OTL. But I was unable to solve the hefty bill of my wife: she "owed" 25,000 USD to the Sea Org, mostly to the Flag Service Organization in Clearwater, as she had done some courses there. As good Scientologists, we finally gave in to the demands, and took out a Swiss franc-based mortgage on our apartment to pay her bill. We also used that loan to finance the auditor training of my wife (the E-meter alone was around 4,000 USD plus each auditor training course was at least 1,000 USD), as Andrea wanted to become a field auditor.

I managed to get the PTS Type B declare revoked and I started on the required 1500 hours of amends. I volunteered to help the Marathon for a Drug-free Hungary and I did translations for the Church and its various satellite organizations.

Naturally, I could not avoid being pressured for donations. I was probably considered to be an easy target, as I was an ex-SO member with a somewhat guilty conscience, trying to work his way back into the good graces of the Church. For example, in September 2005, the International Association of Scientologists wanted me to become a Lifetime Member (as a Sea Org member, I was automatically a Lifetime Member but that was cancelled when I was offloaded). I gave 2,500 USD to the IAS earlier from my inheritance, so I had to give 500 USD more to become a Lifetime Member – again. I soon got my new membership card.

As I was now a Scientologist businessman, so I had to join WISE as well, with the cheapest annual membership costing 350 USD.

But things were not the same regarding Scientology. I could never really get over the fact that I was kicked out of the Sea Org. I still believed it was a gross injustice. Deep down in my heart, I knew that something was wrong the Church and Hubbard's technology also had its fair share of issues. However, I did not dare to admit this even to myself. It was very hard to face the fact that I had been such a sucker and had fallen for a sleazy con game like the Church of Scientology.

I was under such extreme control in the Sea Org, but now I had ample opportunity to look at Scientology from the outside. It was embarrassingly apparent that nothing of real importance or magnitude happened or got done in the Church. The people involved in the movement were very busy and enthusiastic, but they had virtually zero impact on the world, except for the occasional meltdown in the media. I continued to attend Scientology events, but the news of "unprecedented" expansion got old fast for me as a public Scientologist. It just made me suspect even more that something was wrong, as theoretically the Church was expanding at lightning speed, but you could not see any independent evidence of it.

As I was dependent on my Scientology connections for my business (and livelihood), I never really entertained the idea of leaving Scientology altogether. I lived my life, did my job and tried to become a successful and good Scientologist. I could not really live up to the expectations of the Church. I made enough money to cover the necessities and pay the monthly mortgage payments, but I could not afford to give sizeable donations (which they relentlessly wanted and asked for, even for the Ideal Org project).

A year later, I found out that Miklós had left the Sea Org. He still remained active in the Ideal Org project as a public Scientologist. Apparently, he even did some soul-searching as he called me and apologized for not backing me and letting European management completely ignore my accomplishments and unjustly fire me.

To be honest, I did not really believe him and I did not think it was a sincere and heartfelt gesture. And I had too many horrific, soul-crushing experiences associated with my dismissal to be able to accept his apology anyway. I did meet him a few times, but it was rather weird to talk to him and it reminded of my sorrowful past. So I avoided any further contact after a while.

By the summer of 2007, my doubts concerning the Church became stronger and I started to look up Scientology on the Internet to find out some answers to the nagging questions that were never properly answered by the Church. I was increasingly annoyed by the unlimited greed of the Church. I was also at the end of the ridiculous 1500-hour amends, and I had come to feel that I was contributing a great deal to the Church while getting next to nothing in exchange.

Nevertheless, I was still not ready to face the truth. I convinced myself that the end goal was valuable enough to make all sacrifices worthwhile.

At around the same time, the package of the 18 books Hubbard wrote on Scientology and the accompanying lecture series were finally released in a brand new, thoroughly edited version (as explained earlier). All Scientologists absolutely HAD to buy the entire package for a whopping total "package price" of 3,000 USD. The pressure really ramped up to the level of complete insanity – even I was called almost every day by Sea Org members from all around the world. I heard from other Scientologists that they got calls on weekends and during the week after 10 PM. As an ex-Sea Org member, I was quite immune to such insane pressuring, but it was too much for me even.

Finally, I gave in to a "special offer," made by one of the Ethics Officers at the Flag Service Org. I was able to buy the entire set for 1800 USD, and I was told that an "ethics particle" would cover the rest of the purchase as amends for some sort of crime he had committed. I reluctantly agreed and paid for the package, maxing out my credit card in the process. Needless to say, it took 2 months and numerous e-mails and phone calls to get the materials actually shipped to me.

I started to read the books, hoping that they would give me new-found confidence and stability to kickstart my second, hopefully more successful stint in Scientology. I could not really concentrate on the words of LRH as much as I had done earlier – the spiritual traumas I suffered kept coming to mind. It seemed that I had no choice but to enroll on a course to study them in a proper Scientology course room, to keep these incidents from interfering with the study of the materials.

In order to do that, I had to formally complete the ethics program, i.e. to prove that I had indeed completed 1500 hours of amends for the Church. I put together a submission, including an itemized list of all the volunteer work I had done for the Church, and sent it to the Continental Justice Chief.

He called me two weeks later (a few days before Christmas). He repri-manded me from deviating from my original plans for the amends (he was right in that regard). I told him that the situation had changed, but it did not matter as I done the required amount of hours anyway. I reiterated my desire to progress on the Bridge and study the Basics. He said he could not approve the request in its current form, but he had an idea for a fast amends project which could make up for my shortcomings.

He then gave the receiver to a "high-ranking executive," who explained the plan. I was supposed buy 10 complete Basics packages for around 25,000 USD and then resell these packages to Scientologists for the full 3000 USD price each. If I paid the money right there, then they would consider the 1500 hours of amends done. I told them that I had no money and I would like to concentrate on studying the Basics and going up the Bridge. This mysterious executive then became aggressive, and told me in a threatening manner that I had two options – the easy way and the hard way. I either paid the money and the whole thing would be over or I didn't, in which case I would then have to do the 1500 hours of amends again.

This was the last straw. I had enough of the insatiable greed of Scientology. My only regret at this point was that it took so long – 10 years of hard work as a virtual slave and throwing 50,000 USD out the window. All the bitterness that had accumulated over these long years came out in a big burst of anger – I screamed at the guy for using Mafia tactics and I told him I would not pay a fucking cent. My conscience was clear, I added, I did everything they asked and if they did not like the type of amends I did, they should get back to me in writing. I then hung up on him.

When I put down receiver, I knew it was over and there was no way back. *I was no longer a member of the Church.* I could not care less about their weird rules, their lust for money and planetary clearing for that matter.

I experienced a tremendous relief. I was free of the constant guilt that I was not disseminating Scientology and had not done enough to help the Church achieve its aims. After that I spent my free time browsing anti-Scientology pages on the Internet. I learned much more about the Church and Hubbard in two months than during the entire 10-year period I spent in the Sea Org. I was really frustrated and angry when I discovered the truth.

Nevertheless, I still thought that Scientology as a philosophy had valuable elements, which were worth salvaging from the corrupt and sinister Church of Scientology. I wanted reforms to take place, so for that reason, I started a blog called *Scientology objectively* (later on, I changed to it *Scientology: Objectively and subjectively)*. The original idea was to start a dialogue with the general public, to get recognition for the valuable elements of the "tech" and to separate the philosophy from the Church in the minds of the people.

It turned out that neither the Church nor the general public wanted this. I sent an e-mail to all Scientologists under an alias, trying to find out how many people wanted or would back reforms and I included some rather sordid facts about David Miscavige. The responses were a mixture of sad and hilarious. Only three (!) people were interested in any reform, while a few more expressed some sort of agreement with my position, but most of the responses were threats or calling me an SP for even suggesting the need for reforms or telling me that my e-mail was forwarded to OSA and I should not write them again.

I also tried to convince Miklós to help in this project, but he refused and insisted that 100% standard admin tech should be used only, fully adhering to the instructions of LRH. I favored a different approach, so we could not come to an agreement.

Probably just to remind me of the good old times, Miklós ratted me out to OSA and told them that I was the source of the e-mail. Apparently, Lajos did not have the courage to confront such a massive SP, so he sent me a message through one of my Scientologist business associates that if I wanted to handle it then I should contact him. In my reply, I made clear to Lajos that I did not want to continue as a reformist, as the vast majority of Church members clearly did not want any changes. I had no intention of going in for an "interview" as I did not want to listen to the usual rant about me being the biggest SP in the world "but a large donation could change all that."

I continued blogging and I met a lot of people who had been harmed by the Church and its toxic disconnection policy. This made me revise my stance about the true value of Scientology and the tech and after a while, I gave up on this philosophy altogether. Meanwhile, I changed my business profile so I do not depend on Scientologists and started a completely new life.

There was one last thing I felt I had to do. I thought that I should contribute to making the real nature of the Church of Scientology well known to everyone. That's why this book was written.

Thank you for reading it.

Glossary of Scientology-related Terms

(Note: words used in the definitions which have special meaning in Scientology are in *italics* and are separately defined in this glossary.)

aberration: used in Scientology to denote any form of departure or deviation from rational thought or behaviour.

ABLE: Association for Better Living and Education – a theoretically secular management entity responsible for the social betterment activities of Scientology, with four subsidiaries under its umbrella. Narconon – drug prevention and rehabilitation; Criminon – crime prevention, rehabilitation of criminals; Way to Happiness Foundation – handling the moral decline in society; and Applied Scholastics – providing tools for educators and educational institutions.

Advanced Org(anization): upper level Scientology organizations, which deliver the *OT* levels I, II, III, IV and V as well as various advanced Scientology training courses. There are Advanced Organizations in Copenhagen, Denmark; *St. Hill*, England; Los Angeles and Sydney, Australia.

auditing: in Scientology, it is a general term denoting any and all personal therapy sessions, delivered by a practitioner of Scientology (called an auditor, a term derived from the Latin *audire* to listen). There are many types of auditing, ranging from finding and relieving the effects of past painful incidents to so-called Confessionals, where the patient is supposed to disclose his wrongdoings in detail.

battle plan: all daily, weekly and weekly production plans were called "battle plans," in alignment with the (somewhat faux) naval tradition of the Sea Org.

Birthday Game: a competition in which all Scientology organizations around the world participate. It is basically a year-long production contest, starting and ending on Hubbard's birthday (13th of March) each year. It was launched by the man himself in 1983. The production and performance of Scientology organizations is measured on a weekly basis (which ends and begins at 14:00 every Thursday). Points are awarded for rising statistics (1 for small, 3 for large increases). The calculation is based on the degree of expansion happening locally. All continental Sea Org bases have a person responsible for calculating the weekly points and sending the standings to each org. In addition to that, they are also responsible for getting the org staff members enthusiastic about the game and to produce more.

Bridge to Total Freedom, The or simply "The Bridge": a chart that contains the exact sequence of Scientology services that must be completed to achieve "total spiritual freedom," the advertised end product of Scientology.

case: the totality of issues, psychological problems, *aberrations* etc. plaguing someone.

Case Supervisor: the person responsible for supervising all auditors and auditing actions (see also *case* in this glossary).

Clear: a state of spiritual awareness in Scientology, described as being completely rational and having no personal *aberrations*. It is theoretically achieved by erasing one's *reactive mind* through auditing.

Committee of Evidence: a kind of a Scientology trial by jury, which is supposed to be impartial, establish all the facts and come up with a ruling.

Continental Liaison Office (CLO): a management organization responsible for the management and expansion of all Scientology organizations and groups on its continent. The CLO for Europe is located in Copenhagen, Denmark.

DB: an abbreviation for *degraded being*.

degraded beings: spiritual beings who were under suppression for a lengthy period and were wrecked by it in this or in an earlier lifetime, and are unable function normally. They always felt an internal compulsion to disobey any orders given and were unrepentant "alterers" – incapable of doing exactly what was asked of them and if they were to pass information along, they would surely alter it. Additionally, they had an inherent hatred of "big beings" like L. Ron Hubbard (and presumably, the better Scientologists).

downstat: Having downward trending production statistics and/or performing badly.

E-meter: short for Electropsychometer, an instrument used in *auditing*. It measures electrical resistance and skin conductivity. According to Scientology, "the static field" around one's body is reflective of one's mental state, and therefore such a device can be used to detect or locate areas of spiritual distress and to ascertain whether or not someone has been relieved of the effects of such past traumatic moments during an auditing session.

EstO: short for **Establishment Officer**, an executive responsible for hiring, training and correcting staff members.

Field Staff Member: a *public* Scientologist who sends people for Scientology services to Scientology organizations and receives 10–15% commission for his or her work.

Finance Network: a separate network inside the Church, responsible for monitoring finances and collecting the management and licensing fees for top-level Church organizations.

Fitness Board: Every *Sea Org* base has such a board for reviewing eligibility for *Sea Org* membership, theoretically operating according to the relevant policies of Hubbard. *Sea Org* members are required to appear before this board after completing their basic training, or any time circumstances warranted it. The committee usually consisted of three members, chaired by the head of the qualifications (quality control) division.

FSM: an abbreviation of Field Staff Member.

Flag: a short name for the *Flag Service Organization.*

Flag Service Organization: located in Clearwater, Florida, it is one of the top Scientology service organizations, responsible for delivering *OT* levels VI and VII as well as other special training and auditing services.

flap: serious issue or problem

HCO Executive Secretary: the executive over Divisions 1 (personnel, communications, ethics & justice matters) and 2 (sales and marketing of books, lectures and courses to existing public). "HCO" stands for "Hubbard Communications Office," the name of Division 1 in Scientology Churches.

little brown church in the vale, the: a reference to an L. Ron Hubbard writing of 23 March 1985, where he condemns the kind of image where a Scientology Church is portrayed as a place "where people can get together, sing and are not too unhappy."

major service: a Scientology course or auditing action listed in the main central area of The Bridge to Total Freedom.

mission: 1. the most basic type of Scientology Church organizations, responsible for delivering introductory courses and sending people to services to the nearby *org;* **2.** also called *Sea Org* mission; a team of *Sea Org* members sent to complete a special task or resolve an emergency situation.

missionaire: member of a Sea Org *mission.*

New Era Publications: the European publishing corporation of the Church located in Copenhagen, Denmark.

off-policy: contrary to or not in alignment with any of Hubbard's administrative policies.

Office of Special Affairs: the legal, intelligence and PR arm of the Church. It is a separate network inside Scientology. Its functions included monitoring the enemies of Scientology as well as suspicious members of the Church. They work with the attorneys and sometimes employ Private Investigators for certain operations. They also supervise the Citizens' Commission on Human Rights, an anti-psychiatry organization founded by the Church.

on-source: in full adherence with the written and spoken words of L. Ron Hubbard, the self-appointed "Source" of Scientology.

Operating Thetan: enhanced states of spiritual awareness, which are theoretically attainable after one achieves the state of *Clear.*

Operation & Transport Liaison (OTL): a management unit in Scientology, responsible for managing a certain part of a continent. In essence, it was a small *CLO.*

Operation Snow White: a project during the 1970s to purge unfavorable records about Scientology and its founder L. Ron Hubbard. This project included infiltration and thefts from 136 government agencies, foreign embassies and consulates, as well as private organizations critical of Scientology, in more than 30 countries. This program included the single largest infiltration of the United States government in history.

org: short for organization, a local Scientology Church where services up to the level of *Clear* on the *Bridge* are delivered.

Organization Executive Course: a course teaching the entirety of LRH's admin technology. It consists of the study of the so-called OEC Volumes or Green Volumes. OEC Volume 0 contains all the policies and know-how about being a staff member in general, and each division (from 1 to 7) on the organizing board of Scientology has a volume dedicated to it, containing all LRH writings about the operation, rules and know-how of that division.

OSA: an abbreviation of *Office of Special Affairs.*

OT: an abbreviation of *Operating Thetan.*

OTL: an abbreviation of *Operation and Transport Liaison.*

overt/withhold writeup: an enforced confession of all harmful acts of commission or omission, to be submitted in writing to the officer ordering it; it has a specific format, containing the time, place, form and event of each act committed.

particle: in Scientology, everything is considered a "particle" that travels on communication lines (including people).

Potential Trouble Source: someone currently or formerly connected to a *Suppressive Person*, and this association still affects him or her in some way.

preclear: someone who has started to receive Scientology *auditing*, but has not achieved the state of *Clear* yet.

PTS: an abbreviation of *Potential Trouble Source.*

public: someone who is not a staff member, just a regular member of the Church of Scientology, a "parishioner." It is used as a singular noun in Scientology.

reactive mind: a Scientology term for the subconscious mind. According to L. Ron Hubbard, it is a collection of moments of pain and unconsciousness as well as various other mental mechanisms and is the sole source of nonoptimum behaviour.

reg(ister): collect money for Scientology purposes (services or projects). Derived from Registrar (salesperson) and registration (sales).

RTC: short for **Religious Technology Center**; in theory, this corporation is the protector of Scientology trademarks and copyrights, and has no management duties or rights. In actual fact, it is the top organization in the Scientology hierarchy; its Chairman/CEO is David Miscavige, the *de facto* leader of the Church.

Saint Hill (St Hill): L. Ron Hubbard's home in the 1960's. Located near East Grinstead about 50 miles south of London, the estate was home to the international headquarters of Scientology when Hubbard lived there from 1959 to 1967. Today it is an *Advanced Org*.

Sea Organization: the elite of Scientology staff. It is theoretically the religious order of the Church. Sea Org membership is mandatory for filling any upper-level management position or holding a position in all higher level Scientology organizations. It was founded by L. Ron Hubbard in 1967 and originally operated aboard a small fleet of ships in the Mediterranean (hence the name).

second dynamic: Hubbard claimed that the command "Survive!" was the lowest common denominator of all existence, and the primary purpose of all life forms.

He divided this urge into 8 subdivisions (self, sex&family, group, mankind, all life, the physical universe, spiritual beings, and God or Infinity). The second dynamic covers all sexual activity and anything related to raising children and having a family.

Security Check: metered interrogation not protected by priest-penitent privilege; everything the suspect says is actionable.

SMI: Scientology Missions International – a Scientology management entity responsible for the management of *missions*

SP: an abbreviation of *Suppressive Person*.

Suppressive Person: an evil, antisocial person. Also used to denote people who are critical of Scientology or considered to be enemies of the movement.

tech or **technology**: the term used in Scientology to describe the application of Hubbard's methods.

theta: as an adjective, it means something aesthetic, causing good feelings or spiritual joy; cute and charming in case of a person. As a noun, it means "life force" in Scientology.

thetan: a Scientology word for a spiritual being. According to Scientology, every human being is a thetan, inhabiting a body, which he or she controls with the mind.

upstat: having upward trending production statistics and/or performing well.

whole track: also referred to as time track, and refers to the duration of the entire physical universe.

WISE: World Institute of Scientology Enterprises – a theoretically secular membership organization for Scientologist business people which also licenses Hubbard's administrative methodology for a fee.

CPSIA information can be obtained
at www.ICGtesting.com
Printed in the USA
LVOW13s1346300117

522605LV00018BA/605/P